SPORT PSYCHOLOGY: THE BASICS
Optimising Human Performance

SPORT PSYCHOLOGY: THE BASICS

Optimising Human Performance

RHONDA COHEN

BLOOMSBURY

LONDON · NEW DELHI · NEW YORK · SYDNEY

Bloomsbury Sport
An imprint of Bloomsbury Publishing Plc

50 Bedford Square　　　　　　1385 Broadway
London　　　　　　　　　　　New York
WC1B 3DP　　　　　　　　　　NY 10018
UK　　　　　　　　　　　　　USA

www.bloomsbury.com

BLOOMSBURY and the Diana logo are trademarks of Bloomsbury Publishing Plc

First published 2016

British Library Cataloguing-in-Publication Data
A catalogue record for this book is available from the British Library.

Library of Congress Cataloguing-in-Publication data has been applied for.
ISBN: PB: 978-1-4081-7209-4
ePDF: 978-1-4081-8217-8
ePub: 978-1-4081-8218-5

2 4 6 8 10 9 7 5 3 1

Typeset in Minion by Deanta Global Publishing Services, Chennai, India
Printed and bound in Great Britain by CPI Group (UK) Ltd, Croydon CR0 4YY

To find out more about our authors and books visit www.bloomsbury.com.
Here you will find extracts, author interviews, details of forthcoming
events and the option to sign up for our newsletters.

CONTENTS

Part 3: Setting Skills and Using Techniques

Part 4: Stress, Health and Injury

12 Injury Interventions

How can I use the various techniques in PST to overcome a sporting injury?

What do you need socially and emotionally to overcome a sporting injury?

Reflective Practice: Judging Response to Injury

13 Exercise Psychology

What are the psychological benefits of exercise?

Why do people exercise?

Reflective Practice: Changing Exercise Behaviour in the
Transtheoretical Model

Part 5: Unique and Individual Aspects

14 Talent Identification

How can you measure future talent?

Do you need a structured system to identify talent?

What are the models of talent?

What do experts have that novices don't have?

Reflective Practice: Tap into Talent

15 Extreme Sport

What motivates you to undertake extreme sport?

Measurements for sensation seeking

Reflective Practice: Do you Seek Adventure and Thrills?

16 Reaction Time

Why are quick reaction times needed in sport?

What key factors affect your reaction time and how do they impact
on your sporting performance?

How can you improve reaction time?

Reflective Practice: Improving Reaction Time

17 Gender Differences

Why do we have separate sports for men and women?

What are the psychological differences between females and males in sport?

Is sport homophobic?

Reflective Practice: Observing Gender Differences

Part 6: Into the Future

INTRODUCTION

'Know yourself and you will win all battles.'

Lao Tzu (Chinese philosopher)

The purpose of this book is to draw you nearer to sport psychology from a theoretical and applicable perspective. It is written in a way that you can learn to develop these techniques as an athlete, student or coach. When you can feel that you are capable of doing amazing things in life, then you begin to bridge this gap no matter how big or small. The aim of this book is to help you draw on sport psychological techniques so that you can realise your ideal self.

You have two selves according to Carl Rogers, (1954). The present self is the person you are right now. The ideal self is the person you would like to be. It is your goals and your dreams. These two selves may be one and the same. This gives us a high sense of self-worth. However, most people feel there is a gap between the two selves. It is this gap that prevents you from operating at your maximum level of efficiency. If you want to change the way you think or behave, then you must start by examining the differences in where you are now and where you want to be and then begin to work on it systematically. You also need to believe that you can change.

The structure of the book is designed to help you, as an athlete, coach or student, to understand how to achieve optimal performance through developing an integrated programme of mental skills. Work through the book and build your confidence, develop your focus and if you are injured then push through recovery. Use the positive feelings and connections that make you special and provide you with an enthusiasm and passion for life.

It is amazing how, in sport, we train our bodies yet often neglect to train our minds. This book examines a wide variety of topics all designed to give you the mental edge through information, theory and insight. It will equip you with practical strategies to enhance your performance and to add to your enjoyment of your sport. A structured approach to developing sport psychology skills is similar to a good training routine. Each chapter features quotes, which you use for instant inspiration. There are also specific objectives at the start of each chapter to help you develop a mental map for the topic, which you can refer back to at any time. Towards the end of each chapter there are questions that will prompt you to explore the 'what' and 'how' of the topic under discussion and a number of practice exercises to carry out to enhance your knowledge. A list of further reading is included at the end of each chapter and an exhaustive list of books, journals and other sources is included at the end of the book.

The reflective practice of psychology in sport is an exciting journey in helping you to understand yourself better. It is up to you to motivate yourself and become proficient with these psychological sport skills. Remember that psychological skills can improve your sport and can positively impact on your life.

I hope you enjoy the book.
Dr Rhonda Cohen

ACKNOWLEDGEMENTS

I wish to thank my family for all their support, the encouragement from my daughters, Rachel and Sarah, and the inspiration from my husband, Anthony. My cousins, Susan and Barry, were wonderful in reading and proofing this book, as were my editors, Kirsty and Vicki. A big thanks to my mentors who have been there for me throughout my career: Jan, Madeline and Delly.

PART 1
ASSESSING SKILLS

Heptathlete Jackie Joyner–Kersee

1 SPORT PSYCHOLOGY AND ASSESSING SKILLS

'The battles that count aren't the ones for gold medals. The struggles within yourself – the invisible battles inside all of us – that's where it's at.'
Jesse Owens (Multiple gold medallist at the 1936 Olympics)

Objectives

1. What sport psychology can do for you
2. The importance of self-belief and the mind–body relationship
3. The use of sport psychology should be adapted to meet individual needs

Sport psychology is for everyone who loves a challenge and wants to fulfil their potential in sport or fitness. The main thrust of sport psychology is to help you perform better and more consistently by learning or improving mental strategies. It relies on various techniques, which can impact on everything from enhancing performance to recovering from injury.

There are a variety of reasons why you should use sport psychology. Firstly, it can help you to identify your strengths and weaknesses while providing you with appropriate techniques for a positive mindset. This identification can enable you to get the best out of yourself and in addition prevent injury. You can better integrate physical practice with mental preparation and handle competitive pressure. Sport psychology can help you to build life-skills at any age and develop a strong healthy mind to use both inside and outside of sport.

WHAT DO YOU NEED IN ORDER TO BE SUCCESSFUL IN USING SPORT PSYCHOLOGY?

In order to be successful in using sport psychology, you need to have, or be willing to develop, a sense of self-belief. You need to understand that you can manage your own geneptic predisposition, that there is a connection between your mind and your body, and that you can learn from feedback. Bear in mind that there may be differences depending on your particular sport.

It is important to have self-belief. You need to believe that it is possible to change and improve your performance. If you see yourself as a robot or a pre-programmed computer, then there is little chance of ever doing anything different; whereas, if you believe that life is full of new opportunities and experiences just waiting to happen, then you are open to trying something new and thinking in a novel way. Experience does have an effect on how you consider these options. You are what you think. You can see yourself in various ways. You have chosen to see yourself in a particular way so your thoughts and beliefs will determine your experience of life. Your thoughts, in essence, are self-perpetuating or self-fulfilling. By being aware, trying new ways, adapting a new template for life that suits you will give you a different outcome.

An understanding of your genetic programme is part of the process of developing your performance. You are a product of the genes you were born with and that can't be changed. However, you can learn strategies to help you manage your innate personality. For example, you may be naturally more anxious than other competitors. It is essential to understand that sport psychology works by providing you with coping mechanisms; however, you need to recognize that your own genetic predispositions impact on your current thoughts and behaviour.

> *You are always the expert in how you see the world, so it is important **you** understand how **you** interpret information and how **you** feel about those insights. The skill of self-reflection and awareness is invaluable in gaining insights into what challenges **you** face and how **you** respond.*

The mind–body relationship is established and accepted as an important element in human behaviour. For example, lifting heavy weights is harder when you perceive the weights are heavy in your mind, just as running the last leg of a race is even more exhausting when you believe that your energy fuel gauge is on zero. This is a collaboration of mind and body; two separate entities united. This can be illustrated by the following activity. Place your arm out straight and clear your mind. With your other hand (or borrow someone else's) push it down. This should be relatively easy. Now, try changing your mindset. Prepare yourself mentally by concentrating and visualizing your arm as a concrete rod. Your muscles will tense, and the stronger the thought, the more taut your arm will become. Push your arm down with your other hand; whether it is easier or more difficult to move is based on the mind–body relationship. Your body relies on you as an expert to facilitate the integration of your mind with your body. Take two players with the same physical ability competing side by side and alter the mindset of one of them. Why will one of them win? Physical training alone is not enough to excel in sport.

Understanding sport psychology also relies on the fact that different sports have different tapestries. This means that the psychological requirements in football are not necessarily the same as in golf or BASE jumping. Therefore, understanding the needs of your sport is important. This is where a good coach or trainer can provide key insights.

Learning is a key to change in sport psychology. Neuro-Linguistic Programming (NLP) teaches you that 'failure is one type of feedback'. You learn from everything you do, whether the outcome is successful or not. You should not be afraid to take a risk and try out new strategies to improve. Whether you are an elite or talented athlete in the recovery stage of an injury, a recreational player who wishes to improve, a coach, a student, a (trainee) psychologist or a parent working with any one of these groups, sport psychology empowers you with the idea to believe that you can learn to achieve more.

It is one thing to think about or want to change; it is another thing to go ahead and actually do it. When you commit to your sport, you commit to the psychology of your sport.

ARE THERE DIFFERENT WAYS TO USE SPORT PSYCHOLOGY?

Sport psychology should be adapted to suit different learning styles and the setting in which it is practised. For instance, sport psychology training often focuses on the idea that you can create visions or pictures in your mind that affect how you see and feel. This is something we do well in childhood and many of us can still draw the pictures in our minds of special books that we read, TV programmes that we watched or games that we played as kids. Visual interventions can work well with the young and those who are visual learners. If you struggle with this concept and learning visually doesn't come naturally, then I recommend that you first try to develop the skill by practising the reflective exercises at the end of this chapter (see page 6). If, however, visualization doesn't fit in with your learning style, there are other techniques to use. Perhaps you prefer to learn through words. If so, then work harder on exercises that require you to track your thoughts and perceptions. Positive statements make you believe that you can do anything and brighten your outlook, though you need to set objectives along the way. If you are more of an auditory learner then listen to recordings or apps on your phone. Guide yourself through, hearing how to improve your focus.

Sport psychology can work in different settings. It can be used inside or outside of competition and in- or off-season. A good routine follows a loop or circle: pre-season, the week before the game, the day before, the day of, during the game, after the game (feedback) and back again. Sessions between a player and a sport psychologist can be conducted online when athletes are travelling to different competitions or venues. Electronic messaging enables an athlete, parent or coach to keep in contact with their sport psychologist from anywhere in the world and often the sender gets an immediate answer to a problem. You can arrange one-to-one meetings where strengths and weaknesses can be identified and worked on. It can even be used on the field or pitch.

In conclusion, sport psychology depends on believing that you can change and learn from the experiences and exercises you try out. Like a new food, a new way of thinking may be an acquired taste. Sport psychology tools are dynamic, rather than static. Learning to be the master of your own destiny therefore requires regular practice. The more committed you are, the more chance you have of improving your performance and achieving your goals.

A sport psychology strategy can help you develop your future success. Read the chapters in this book in any order, or pick out any question from the contents that you would like to know more about. This book is designed to help change your mindset, improve what may not be working for you and enhance what is already working. So dive in!

Questions to consider

1. How could sport psychology be important to your development?
2. Are there any mental skills in your sport in particular that need to be taken into consideration?

REFLECTIVE PRACTICE: PERFORMANCE PROFILING; EXAMINING CONNECTIONS

PERFORMANCE PROFILING

Performance Profiling (Butler, 2000) is a good way to start to see what skills you have and what skills you need to work on. This is a visual paper exercise for examining the skills required for performance. I have included this as a linear exercise where the skills roughly correspond to chapters in the book. Rate yourself on each of these skills.

The exercise starts with an assessment of your mental skills. Remember, for this or any of the exercises in this book to be effective, you have to be honest. Begin by listing the mental skill set required for your sport (e.g. confidence, focus, ability to play under pressure, visualisation and so on). Skill 1 is confidence. How do you rate yourself in confidence when you play your sport? Use a 1–5 scale, with 1 representing the lowest and 5 the highest level of confidence. Feel free to rate yourself using fractions, such as 3¼. Other skills to assess might be motivation, concentration, awareness, determination and vision, once again depending on your sport.

The process of doing this empowers you to identify your mental strengths and weaknesses. It helps the coach understand how you are thinking and helps you feel included in the process. Once completed it can also help a coach to develop an individually tailored training programme, the progress of which can be regularly monitored using the self evaluation sheet below.

Skill Profiling Check – Optimizing Human Performance	
Skill 1 Confidence	0 1 2 3 4 5
Skill 2 Focus	0 1 2 3 4 5
Skill 3 Visualization	0 1 2 3 4 5
Skill 4 Resilience (mental toughness package)	0 1 2 3 4 5
Skill 5 Goal setting	0 1 2 3 4 5
Skill 6 Being in the zone (balance the challenge with the right amount of skill)	0 1 2 3 4 5
Skill 7 Ability to handle stress	0 1 2 3 4 5
Skill 8 Anxiety – understand and work with anxiety levels	0 1 2 3 4 5
Skill 9 Able to stay injury free (work on fitness levels)	0 1 2 3 4 5
Skill 10 Be in the moment	0 1 2 3 4 5
Skill 11 Take a risk	0 1 2 3 4 5
Skill 12 Discipline (maintain practice and skills)	0 1 2 3 4 5

Performance profiling can also be used with a team as a whole. For example, the players can each complete a chart based on the general state of the team – including factors such as team spirit, confidence, work rate, attacking and defending qualities and so on. This gives the coach valuable information with which to understand how the players perceive the team's current form.

In terms of this book, a completed performance profile will enable you to work on your strengths, to see if there is any way to improve on your already developed skills, as well as identifying the areas on which you really need to concentrate. It will also help guide you to the sections of this book that discuss your own personal matters of concern.

EXAMINING CONNECTIONS

How you see yourself in relation to those around you can affect your performance. Personal constructs are how you see the world around you. You need to examine how you use labels or phrases to describe those you interact with and then examine the importance of these relationships. One way to start is thinking of the people who are important to you as an athlete and person (Kelley, 1945).

Choose five people who are central to your sport and with whom you interact regularly. Place one name in each of the circles below:

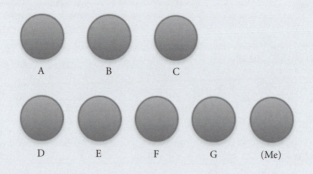

For example, here are five people or groups that I have chosen that are central to me as an athlete: (A) my coach, (B) my trainer, (C) a specific athlete in my team, (D) my whole team, (E) my husband. You can also use places or events: (F) indoor competitions, (G) a specific upcoming competition.

Personal constructs can then be elicited by using groups of three people at a time.

You examine the similarities or differences between people A through C. Is there some way in which you see two of these people as alike/similar and therefore different from the third?

A and B	C
Are motivating	Is very draining and de-motivating
Are supportive	Never helps and is unsupportive of my training

The way you cope in general comes from a collection of all these relationships. If there is negativity among this circle of support, you may find that this creates distress, and in turn a dysfunctional attitude towards achievement. I can't overstate the importance of good support and mentoring. I have been privileged in my life to have had some excellent mentors who have really helped me along the way.

This process is then repeated using other combinations of people, e.g. C and D are ? and E is ?

Questions to consider

1. What have you learned by examining your personal constructs?

2. How do these relationships affect you in your sport? Can you improve or change these relationships so that there is a more positive impact?

Further Reading

Butler, R. (ed.) (2000). *Sports Psychology in Performance.* London: Arnold.

Gucciardi, D. F. and Gordon, S. (2009). 'Revisiting the Performance Profile Technique: Theoretical underpinnings and application'. *The Sport Psychologist,* 2009, 23, 93–117.

PART 2
ENHANCING SKILLS

Tennis player Martina Navratilova

2 CONFIDENCE AND SELF-EFFICACY

'To be a great champion you must believe you are the best. If not, pretend you are.'

Muhammad Ali (World Heavyweight Boxing Champion)

Objectives

1. The difference between confidence and self-efficacy
2. Confidence factors: successive performance accomplishment, vicarious learning, verbal persuasion, emotional arousal, fatigue/pain
3. Bandura's versus Vealey's models of self-confidence

Confidence is the belief that you can accomplish something successfully and that you have the resources to do it. It is seen as one of the most important factors in performance. While confidence is an overall concept, self-efficacy is a micro type of confidence. Self-efficacy is a belief that you can manage to carry out actions needed toward the achievement of specific goals. It is a conviction to achieve your objectives, which drives your behaviour.

WHY IS CONFIDENCE SEEN AS ONE OF THE MOST IMPORTANT FACTORS IN PERFORMANCE?

Confidence in your capabilities is related to many psychological factors, such as effort, motivation, persistence, challenges, pressure goal setting, outlook and even risk taking. Confidence is also inversely related to your anxiety levels, so the more anxiety you feel, the less confidence you demonstrate.

How much effort you put into a task is related to your self-efficacy. The higher your self-efficacy, the longer you will maintain your level of performance even when under intense pressure, which could be either real or perceived. Confidence makes you more resilient in facing challenges that are usually increasing in difficulty. In addition, having high self-efficacy along with sustained effort means that you will be more open to problem solving when you meet obstacles or 'fail' at something. You are then more open to thinking of ways of dealing with new challenges. People with high self-efficacy set more challenging goals, which may be attributed to the link between self-efficacy and optimism as well as risk. They also have a more positive outlook and are willing to take more risks in trying to be successful.

Self-efficacy is related to your expectation as to whether you will be able to perform a sport skill or achieve a specific goal and is therefore an indicator of your outlook on future success or accomplishment. Alternatively, with low self-efficacy you feel more comfortable in maintaining your effort rather than in increasing it to achieve new goals. Self-efficacy does vary individually, as it is linked to your behaviour, and its level depends on what you *really* want.

There is, of course, a balance to be achieved. To underestimate your ability means you run the risk of avoidance and mediocrity. Conversely, if you overestimate your ability, you may run the risk of failure, loss or injury. Therefore, you must be appropriately skilled as well as optimally confident. Once again it is important to point out that sports differ in their psychology. In extreme sport, for example, it is essential that self-efficacy is appropriate, as there is a greater risk of injury or death, e.g. 'if you fall, you die' (Slanger and Rudestam, 1997).

> *Confidence is one of the most influential beliefs in sport. In fact, it can be an even better predictor of performance than the actual performance. It is a necessity in being mentally strong.*

In conclusion, confidence – and within this concept, self-efficacy – is one of the most important skills in sport. It affects your choices, your expectations and your future. Self-efficacy can provide you with a belief that can enhance the quality of your sporting success and a confidence for life in general.

Please note that you may find that the term of self-efficacy as a specific trait is often used interchangeably with confidence and self-confidence in research and in sport psychology books. This is because a lot of early research was conducted before a distinction between the words was acknowledged.

HOW CAN YOU IMPROVE YOUR CONFIDENCE?

Bandura's confidence factors

One of the classic theoretical foundations for confidence originates from Bandura (1977). His social cognitive approach illustrates how behavioural, environmental, cognitive and physical factors impact on each other. This section is based on his model.

The belief that you can do something to a certain level of proficiency is predicted by five factors. In order of importance these are: performance accomplishments, vicarious learning, verbal persuasion, emotional arousal and fatigue/pain.

1. Performance accomplishments are about how many times you have 'successfully' achieved or performed this 'skill'. This is the strongest of the five confidence factors. You can measure your performance accomplishments based on how many times you have achieved success in your performance. The premise is that the more experienced you are, the more confident you are in your ability to be successful. As a coach or player you can simulate this situation by arranging practice sessions or friendly matches where you should/will be successful and/or gain important experience. This will prepare you for what you need to do in future competitions and also give you confidence in your ability to be successful.

2. Vicarious experiences involve watching 'others'. This can be watching others play a sport on TV or in the stands, use of virtual reality, imagery or computer games.

3. Verbal persuasion is the encouragement and feedback given by others, or even yourself, to help improve performance. This can be encouragement from a coach, teammates, the crowd and the media or through self-talk.

4. Emotional arousal is the cognitive interpretation of your physiological response, which is how you interpret your success or your next challenge when you haven't yet achieved what you wanted to.

5. Fatigue and pain may be sources of self-efficacy, as you need to gain experience in being mentally and physically exhausted and yet still continue playing to a high standard. You may even be suffering from an injury, have to push through the end of a marathon, be at the end of a three-day competition or the end of a long season. You need to have the confidence to play through pain and fatigue. Some teams score at the end of the game because they are able to muster up all their strength and continue even when mentally and physically exhausted. It is important to have self-confidence even in this situation.

These factors underpin the techniques and strategies used in optimizing confidence in sport. An exercise in self-talk to see how this can be worked on is included below.

Vealey's Model: trait or state?

Vealey (1986, 2001, 2007, 2009) developed a streamlined model of self-confidence, designed to predict behaviour across a wide range of sporting situations. Self-confidence (or self-efficacy) is regarded as: trait – something you are born with; or state – something specific to the situation.

Primarily, there are two constructs. Trait self-confidence is innate, your natural disposition and as such is likely to be relatively stable. You may be born with a confidence trait, which means you are generally confident as a person. You may also be willing to try something new, always believing that you can give it a go. Alternatively, you may have to work with the fact that deep down you are not confident so you need more coping strategies. The key here is to work with your traits and not to worry about them.

State self-confidence varies depending on your situation. In a given situation, you may respond differently in that your confidence level depends on the task or event. The situation may be facilitative (making it easier for you to feel confident) or debilitative (working against you in feeling confident). Perhaps you are confident in practice but not in a competitive situation. What is useful is that you can always work on a way to improve your confidence in those situations in which you doubt yourself.

In summary, you possess a certain level of trait confidence which, when it interacts with a competitive situation, results in your situational or state of confidence in your sport. Your state of self-confidence is one of the most important predictors of behaviour. State is positively correlated with your performance outcome, so the more confident you are, generally the more likely you will be able to be successful in achieving your objectives. Your confidence levels are also related to how you see your success (attributions), and how satisfied you are about your success.

Low confidence is related to low performance. You will find it difficult if you are low in confidence to go out there and 'try to do your best and win the game' unless you have developed compensatory, coping strategies. How you see and feel about a competition can influence the outcome.

There are criticisms of both Bandura's and Vealey's theories. Bandura's model relies on self-reporting of confidence level while Vealey's model does not. Vealey's model suggests usage of standardized and measurable questionnaires of trait as well as state self-confidence. Furthermore, there are some theorists who see confidence as the flip side of, or as the consequence of, high or low anxiety. The anxiety-reductionist theorists debate that anxiety is the result of self-efficacy expectations and behavioural change. However, the relationship is complicated, as it is not clear whether confidence and anxiety are related or independent constructs. It has been demonstrated that individuals with high self-efficacy are not overly concerned by challenges and difficult problems. When self-efficacy is low then it is more likely that these problems are perceived as threats. High self-efficacy individuals will look to put in more effort so that they can be successful, as stated previously. If you try to maintain lower levels of anxiety then you should have higher confidence levels. However, some athletes have very high levels of anxiety prior to a competition and are still very successful. This is an area where there is still a debate, as high anxiety does not always lead to poor performance. Lower anxiety, however, does seem to be better for your health and your state of mind.

Using Bandura's performance accomplishment means setting up smaller, incremental objectives and achievements along the way. This is a typical goal setting tactic, i.e. set something specific, measureable, achievable, according to a time frame etc. These types of objectives can help you to achieve this. Vealey made a distinction between performance objectives and outcome goal orientation, which is quite similar to Nicholls's (1984) task and ego orientation. That is, that you are more likely to feel successful when you set and achieve objectives that are related specifically to your performance or are geared towards achieving certain tasks (i.e. performance goals), like setting a goal to achieve 75% successful rugby kicks. These objectives may be helpful in building confidence, especially in the run-up to a competition. Ego orientation is similar to outcome objectives, which are objectives that state you should be the best you can. The point of this is that research has shown that using goal setting techniques to set specific performance objectives is useful in confidence building, so being ego oriented may have some disadvantages.

Self-efficacy and past experience

How much you believe in yourself and your ability to do something comes from your past successes, achievements, training and from the people around you. There is a direct correlation between your experiences and your self-efficacy, so it is easy to see how any kind of event, for example, an injury or 'fight' with someone in the team, can affect you.

Just because something 'adverse' happens, this shouldn't knock your self-efficacy completely. The strength of having self-efficacy means that you can tap into the many good feelings, images and sense of accomplishment from things you have already experienced. If you start doubting yourself at any time, then you need to reframe your thoughts (see exercise on reframing on page 42) and remember to tap in to these resources.

Questions to consider

1. Why should self-confidence be encouraged in sport?
2. How can performance accomplishments, vicarious learning and emotional arousal be used during and outside of practice?
3. How can you work with trait and state confidence together to get the best performance?

REFLECTIVE PRACTICE: SELF-EFFICACY

SELF-EFFICACY

Let's start by examining your own self-efficacy (confidence), or those of your athlete.
Complete the following sentences:
1. I get my self-efficacy from:
(e.g. the coach, my teammates, my partner...)

My top sources from the list above are:

1.

2.

Your self-efficacy comes from different places and a lot of it is under your control. The trick is to know how you can boost your self-confidence whenever you need it. My self-efficacy improves when I ...

1.

2.

I doubt myself when I ...

1.

2.

Now try saying the following things to yourself:

I am in control of my thoughts and can recognise when I am doubting myself.
There is no such thing as a negative person, only negative thoughts.
I am my own best friend and can accept that I will make mistakes.
I can manage my confidence.

List the reasons why you should be confident. Such as:

1. My strengths are:

2. I have accomplished something before that I am proud of

3. I have these skills:

4. I can improve on these skills

5. My training gives me confidence by:

6. My commitment is:

7. I have people around me who are supportive

8. I can review and improve on this list!

Exercise Evaluation

Having been through the exercises above, ask yourself the following questions:

Confidence is a state of mind – YES or NO?
I can control my confidence – YES or NO?
I can work on controlling my confidence – YES or NO?
I plan to work on developing my confidence – YES or NO?

Your answers will enable you or your coach to assess the progress you have made towards building your confidence/self-efficacy.

Further Reading

Beattie, S., Hardy, L., Savage, J., Woodman, T., and Callow, N. (2011). 'Development and validation of a trait measure of self-confidence'. *Psychology of Sport and Exercise*, 12, 184–91.

Kingston, K., Lane, A. and Thomas, O. (2010). 'A temporal examination of elite performers' sources of sport confidence'. *The Sport Psychologist*, 18, 313–32.

3 IMAGERY

'I like when you see it in your mind.'
Peyton Manning (NFL Quarterback)

Objectives

1. The use of terms such as imagery, visualization and mental imagery
2. Imagery as a multi-sensory experience
3. Imagery needs vividness and controllability
4. Imagery for cognitive and motivational control
5. The use of PETTLEP to guide the imagery technique

The psychological tool of imagery is probably the most widely used technique for enhancing performance in sport psychology, and it is highly recommended by elite athletes, performers and coaches to give you that added advantage. It is endorsed by many famous sports people, such as: Wayne Rooney, Jonny Wilkinson, Jessica Ennis-Hill, Muhammad Ali, Michael Phelps and Andy Murray, who all claim to use visualization before competition (*Daily Telegraph*, 22 January 2014). Sport psychology literature estimates that it is used by 90 per cent of all athletes.

The terms *imagery, visualization* and *mental imagery* are often used to mean the same thing. Imagery represents a personal experience of using your imagination. The pictures in your mind are 'an internal representation that give rise to the experience of perception in the absence of the appropriate sensory input,' (Wraga and Kosslyn, 2002). In other words, mental imagery is the act of intentionally bringing pictures to the forefront of your mind without physically doing the skill. The ability to engage your mind in a multi-sensory experience is a powerful tool. Using your mind's eye, you can visualise, hear and even feel a scene. Like a TV has digital surround sound, imagery is a multiple sensory surround experience. For example, if you imagine yourself on the track about to run a race or by the pool to swim in a competition – you can see yourself at the start (starting line, pool edge), hear the sounds (of the crowd), experience the taste in your mouth (dry feeling), feel your equipment (your feet on the blocks, box), be physically aware of your body's movement (shoulders, back, legs) and even feel the emotions at this time (slightly nervous).

You probably base this on a similar previous experience or maybe something you have seen on TV. It is really amazing how you can capture experiences in your mind and then play them back from your memory, even in the absence of sensory input. The science of this replay enables you to have a mental practice.

WHAT IS NEEDED IN ORDER TO USE IMAGERY EFFECTIVELY?

One research measure used to evaluate the effectiveness of imagery skills is an exercise focused around vividness and control. Imagine a scene within your sport: how clearly can you see it and how well are you able to manipulate the situation, e.g. to stop or start and change direction? If you need a little help in coming up with images, try using similes, such as 'I am running like a jaguar' or 'I am as strong as a lion'. If you can improve the vividness and controllability of the imagery then you can strengthen your use of this technique.

How vividly you see things varies between individuals – some may see things in colour, others in black and white, some with vague details and others with great clarity. The first step in developing good imagery skills is to work on your ability to see images vividly. Begin by imagining yourself in a very familiar place or scene. Try to see as many details as you possibly can. 'Walk' around the image and notice the details. Imagery creates patterns in the brain, so it is important that it is practised repeatedly.

When you experience a vivid memory it affects the brain as well as your bodily functions, such as your heart rate. More recently, due to technological advances, brain imaging has confirmed that there is activity in the brain as a result of imagery: the occipital lobe, where your vision is coordinated, is activated when you imagine what has previously taken place. Another area of your brain, the parietal lobe, is activated when you manipulate items spatially in your mind. As more than one area of your brain is responsible for imagery, you have different imagery capabilities, therefore some people are better at it than others.

Hearing within imagery is another aspect of the sensory experience. To judge how proficient you are at auditory hearing, consider the following questions: How good are you at recalling songs? Can you hear the voice of a parent or the voice of your coach? What about smell? While it is not as necessary in visualization, it may be one of your stronger senses and you may also have established certain associations. Can you imagine the smell of freshly cut grass on the pitch? Can you feel the bat or the ball? Can you taste the chlorine in your mouth from the swimming pool? Can you feel the swing of your golf club or the feeling as you start to move off the blocks? All these are part of your sensory experience.

There is also an emotional aspect to developing imagery skills, which can help you to handle emotional situations. Imagine, for instance, an event where you are winning or extremely successful. Go through the imagery experience of being in touch with all your senses: where were you, who were you with, what were you experiencing and what sounds did you hear? Add in the emotional experiences, for instance, when you finished, was your heart pounding, pulse racing; were you over the moon, were you angry or sad? After you finish this imagery, notice how long the feeling stays with you. What is interesting about the emotional aspect is that even when you cease the imagery, the emotions will remain with you for a while longer. For this reason, if you get nervous in pre-competition either use a rehearsal mode of the upcoming skill, or a relaxation tactic to help you prepare yourself to focus on the activity rather than on your emotions.

There are various questionnaires that assess imagery however, one very popular one is the Movement Imagery Questionnaire-Revised which was designed for healthy athletes needing high levels of skills and coordination. (Hall & Martin 1997; see also review of the MIQ-R which includes the questionnaire-Gregg, Hall and Butler tinyurl.com/gregghallbutler.

The MIQ-RS (Gregg, Hall and Butler, 2012) has been designed for use with those with restricted mobility. It is useful for those working in sport rehabilitation with athletes recovering from sport injury or other medical conditions, it can also be applied for use with various populations such as those with multiple sclerosis and stroke. http://www.ed.sc.edu/personnel/monsma/6d8dbe26d74a051ec258c9ca92729f19.pdf.

The test measures the ability of an athlete to create images both visually and kinaesthetically (physically). Athletes, such as yourself should have insight into your use of images. Another way to measure imagery is through chronometry, which is how long you visualise. To measure this you can record the time or duration of the movement as imaged and physically performed. The difference between the two scores can then be examined. Using an imagery questionnaire in combination with a chronometric test, you can then compare to see how well self report correlates with your ability to maintain an image (e.g. Williams, Guillot, Di Rienzo and Cumming, 2015).

Studies on mental practice show that imagery is beneficial in improving a skill. This works with both open skills (like a rugby tackle) and closed skills (like a basketball throw). Imagery can't, however, replace physical practice, which is the most effective way to improve a skill. The imagery effects are not long lasting, so research recommends that you practise imagery at least once every two weeks.

> The better the controllability and vividness, the more you will benefit. Vividness and control need to be developed in order to successfully use imagery as a technique.

Control and Motivation

Imagery can be used to control your thoughts (cognitive control), or as a motivational tool. Using imagery as a cognitive technique can help manage anxiety associated with stressful situations and help you to practise working in a positive way, e.g. 'I am handling the pressure'.

As a motivational tool, your images can provide you with a glimpse into the future of a potentially winning situation. Motivation is the direction and intensity of your effort. The images you create are directed towards success or failure. Your visualization can encourage your efforts and the perseverance of future achievements. Motivational imagery can boost confidence, e.g. 'I can see myself achieving a personal best again, as I did when I sprinted across the line last year'; 'I can see and feel that I am at the peak of my fitness'; 'I can see myself crossing the finishing line.' Motivational imagery is used more frequently in competition. College and university students as well as youth teams prefer motivational imagery for specific skill training. Incorporating sayings such as 'I can see myself giving 100 per cent' gives you more confidence in your abilities and a greater sense of self-belief in your objectives being worthy. This type of imagery is very prevalent in competition.

> You will benefit by being better at imagery and the more you use your imagery skill the better it will get. The Sport Imagery Questionnaires (SIQ) and SIQ–RS are useful tests which can help you monitor your imagery skills in order to enhance your performance and if needed, to incorporate in a long term recovery from injury strategy.

HOW CAN IMAGERY BE USED IN TRAINING AND IN COMPETITION?

Imagery can be used to rehearse a skill or play prior to a training session or at some point in a competition. It can be helpful in supporting your skills, when you are injured, en route to a game, or in the wings waiting to execute a move or needing to focus. The technique works before the skill (e.g. about to take a free throw) and it doesn't matter if this includes being in either a relaxed or aroused state. It is even useful after the execution of a skill as feedback analysis so that you can see where you went wrong and adjust it for the next time.

The technique does tend to work more effectively with experts as opposed to novices. This is because experts are usually more proficient at controlling mental skills. The more skilled you are or the more experience you have, the more you can remember and recall more positive images of previous performances. Elite athletes are able to use real time or fast motion more efficiently and can even slow the images down (e.g. a golf putt). Novices are less likely to use imagery, as they find it difficult to control images; this is mostly due to lack of experience in the technique, which takes practice and commitment to learn. How well it works depends on how developed your imagery skills are. The more proficient you are at using this tool, the better it becomes as a technique. Novices tend to visualise at a slower pace so that they can learn while deconstructing a movement (e.g. preparing a golf swing). The speed can also depend on the function of the imagery, such as whether it is cognitive or motivational.

> Imagery research often revolves around theories that explain the effects of mental practice:
>
> 1. The neuromuscular approach postulates that mental practice is due to the movement in the peripheral musculature.

2. The cognitive theory examines how information is stored in your memory system.

3. The bio-informational model examines how mental practice is interlaced with the environment, movement and meaning.

4. The functional equivalence theory is based on the premise that you use the same area of the brain for throwing a football or javelin as you do for imagining that you are throwing a football or javelin.

PETTLEP is an applied procedure that comes from the bio-informational and functional equivalence hypotheses in neuroscience. PETTLEP was developed as a seven-point checklist to help you be more effective in using imagery (Holmes and Collins, 2002).

The acronym PETTLEP stands for physical, environmental, task, time, learning, emotion and perspective. You *physically* imagine standing up, wearing the right kit or uniform, in the usual position. You experience the *environment* and the *task* at the appropriate pace or through *timing*. You are *learning* through recall of memories and feeling the *emotions*, which are important in this procedure. You have a *perspective* such as 'I' for the first person or 's/he' or 'they' for the third person. It is a useful way to organise your imagery and has been shown to be quite effective.

Questions to consider

1. How can you improve your visualisation skills in order to enhance the benefit in your sport?

2. Is motivational or instructional imagery more effective in your sport?

REFLECTIVE PRACTICE: DESIGNING AN IMAGERY SCRIPT

The first step in learning to visualize is to practise breathing techniques. Try this exercise: Take a deep breath in and hold it for 2 seconds, then release it slowly for 4 seconds. This is a way of concentrating on your breath so that you centre yourself and focus prior to beginning an imagery script. It is a way to calm down, get the blood flowing nicely and prepare for an action or for a further technique. Practise this or any other breathing techniques that you know. (For more extensive breathing guidelines, see stress management in Chapter 10.)

When you are relaxed you can begin writing your imagery script: Begin with objectives. Do you want to improve one skill, motivate yourself more or control your thoughts?

Decide whether you are going to start with:

- affective – to enhance your mood, up or down
- behavioural skills – for strategy, routine, healing
- cognitive skills – for motivation, improved self-confidence, to manage concentration, to change thinking

Then visualise the physical area surrounding the competition or event: Consider the full sensory experience e.g. the weather, the sights, the sound and the feel of the place. Decide on the direction, e.g. moving forward in the event. Consider the scene you are watching. Write this down (or record it) as a brief story using short sentences or key words.

Imagine your preparation – waiting or warming-up with your usual routine and perhaps other competitors or coaches who you usually speak with. If you feel anxious at all, then practise relaxing.

Use positive affirmation or self-talk – 'I am calm' and 'I am preparing to be ready'. Use trigger words such as *relaxed* and *confident*. If you get stuck, then rewind and keep trying until you successfully get through a difficult bit. Go through your actions on how to play with confidence.

Here is an example:

- You step out on the tennis court and feel the sun …
- You are on the starting line and feeling the typical excitement … on your body, you are a bit nervous, however, you are ready …
- You are in the changing rooms and begin with your usual stretching exercises, you concentrate on your movement and power …
- You are remembering when you played well as a team in your last match
- You and your teammates are a slick machine supporting each other
- You are exhausted and you are thinking that it is the end of the match; however, you are playing beyond that. You and your teammates are determined
- You are ready for the unexpected as you are attentive and confident

Finally, put it all together so it flows, and adjust it until you are satisfied. Write it out properly or record it on a device. You can then read it or listen to it whenever you feel the need.

Further Reading

Hale, B. and Crisfield, P. (2005). *Imagery Training: Guide for Sports Coaches and Performers*. Leeds: Sports Coach UK.

Morris, T., Spittle, M. and Watt, A. (2005). *Imagery in Sport*. Champaign, IL: Human Kinetics.

Several academic articles on various sports available for free online, e.g.

Parnabas, V., Parnabas, J. and Parnabas, M. (2015). 'The level of cognitive anxiety and sport performances among handball players'. *The International Journal of Indian Psychology*, Vol. 2, Special Issue.

4 CONCENTRATION, ATTENTION AND FOCUS

'I just try to concentrate on concentrating.'
> Martina Navratilova (Tennis player, winner of 18
> Grand Slam singles titles)

Objectives

1. Distinguishing between attention, concentration and focus
2. The fallacy of losing concentration
3. The analogy that focus is like a torch
4. Dissociative versus associative strategies
5. Don't think about it
6. The relationship with emotion

Attention requires effort in diverting your energy towards concentrating on what is important and focusing on specific aspects. There are three key words in understanding this topic: attention, concentration and focus. *Attention* is alertness and selectivity of information. It is a mental effort, which is multidimensional and comprises various components. It is deliberate, selective and allows you to multitask. In being deliberate, you choose to *concentrate* on what you consider to be important. For example, in football the team discusses the game plan beforehand and everyone must concentrate on overall strategy. You are then selective in picking out specific cues either to direct or *focus* your attention on or to ignore. Selective attention means being able to direct your energy between what is relevant and what is irrelevant, e.g. in tennis, concentrating on the ball when you are receiving a serve. While you are processing information you are able to coordinate more than one thing at a time (sharing) or multitask and, in case you are wondering, this is not gender specific! Another aspect of attention may be that you are vigilant, meaning that you can maintain attention for a considerable period of time.

Different regions of the brain are activated during this process. While you are looking for something, the frontal dorsal and parietal regions of your brain are engaged, and when you shift unexpectedly to another cue your ventral frontal cortex is active. Neuroscience is helping us to advance knowledge of *attention* in the brain. Interestingly enough, there may also be a difference in the brains of amateurs or novices compared to those who are more experienced. Brain imaging techniques in examining attention as a physiological experience are, however, in their infancy.

CAN YOU REALLY *LOSE* CONCENTRATION?

You never lose concentration – you only redirect it. Most athletes, coaches and sport psychologists are in agreement that being able to concentrate and focus underpins successful performance. Concentration can be learned and improved by attention control. Elite athletes are usually good at redirecting their concentration to what is relevant. While attending to things that are out of your control, your performance declines. Remember, it is not that you lose concentration but rather that you redirect your energies elsewhere to something perhaps less relevant.

What might capture your attention are the internal and external distractions present at any sports event. External distractions are based on the things that are going on around you. In football, this might be teammates, opponents, coaches, spectators or the media. In golf, it might be weather, spectators, other golfers, etc. These cues can be perceived as ominous and might begin to affect your beliefs and thoughts. External distractions start outside but can turn into internal distractions as you start to think or believe that they affect you: 'I messed up that shot, throw, swing … because of the noise/rain/photographers,' and so on.

Internal distractions are your 'in house' experiences, such as your thoughts and feelings, which are often brought about by the pressure of the situation. Internal distractions can result in cognitive interference. These distractions may also come from your bodily experience, such as pain, which can steal your focus and hinder your ability to concentrate. Be aware of what you are concentrating on and know that you can redirect or focus your energy elsewhere, especially when playing in a new environment or at an important event like the Olympics, Paralympics or World Games. This is a major challenge for athletes and coaches.

> *Sport psychology can be used to help you recognise where you are focusing, what you should be focusing on and how you can redirect your energies.*

Focus is like a torch

Attention has often been compared to the spread of a light beam that shines from a lighted source. The torch, searchlight or spotlight analogy also illustrates how attention, like a beam of light, can cause you to make mistakes. Firstly, the beam of light can be too broad, so you could be taking in too much information and not be focused on what is relevant. Conversely, the beam could be too narrow so that you only focus on a single spot.

In sport, we often refer to broad and narrow focus. In addition we often describe the focus as internal or external. Internal is to focus on your thinking and external is to focus on your environment. For example, in motor racing and football, you need a broad and external focus; as a runner, you require broad and internal focus; if you bat in cricket or baseball, you use a narrow and external focus; as a drag racer or weightlifter, you need a narrow and internal focus. Golfers and tennis players use a variety of focus, depending on at which point in a hole or rally they are executing a shot. For example, external broad when considering the hole or waiting to serve, internal broad when recalling previous shots, internal narrow before swinging, external as well as narrow when swinging. Of course, a tennis player will have to change focus more quickly than a golfer.

One of the most famous ways to test attention is the Test of Attentional and Interpersonal Style (TAIS) (Nideffer, 1976). This examines the width and direction or target of your focus. *Narrow external* is needed to bat a ball whereas *narrow internal* is appropriate for an ice-skating spin or a back somersault in trampolining. The TAIS isn't perfect and has been criticised for being a self-reported test, which measures perceived attention skills, and because it neglects to differentiate between skill levels. Concentration is therefore one of the dynamic processes that can distinguish experts from novices as well as those who are successful from unsuccessful.

The torch analogy can be useful as a visual analogy in helping you to identify what is needed in your particular sport and how to adjust your focus if necessary. However, the analogy is limited in offering a solution on how to improve.

Dissociative versus associative

Having a strategy worked out in advance can be more effective than having to create one as you go along. But when planning your strategy, is it better to go with distraction (dissociative strategies) or by concentrating on bodily sensations and other factors critical to your performance (associative strategies)?

Dissociative strategies involve a conscious effort to direct your attention away from irrelevant cues. This works most effectively in sports that are limited in complexity and those that involve intense fatigue and pain. While *dissociative* is being removed from what's going on, *associative* is being right at the centre of it. Runners, for example, find *associative* techniques useful in assessing their position in the race and race times, while they use dissociative techniques to distract them from pain and fatigue. Endurance runners sometimes claim that they run faster when they are dissociative at the start of a race, as they see their effort and exertion as less at that point, and then become associative towards the end.

Being associative is similar to the concept of staying in the present or 'in the moment', but it is also associated with negative self-talk. If you get stuck on thinking about poor performance or missed opportunities earlier on in the race or match, then you are using up vital storage space in your working memory and not concentrating enough on what you are doing at the time.

Being able to control focus and thoughts is one of the most important tools towards effective performance. Research has demonstrated that an essential part of being in a state of flow, being mindful or 'in the zone' is that concentration and focus are total and in the moment. You cannot actually achieve this state by forcing yourself; you just have to *be* there. Therefore, you must develop the skills that allow you to enter this condition of complete focus. Once in this state, you will find that you can attend to the most appropriate cues, even when under pressure.

Elite performance is linked with being immersed in the present. Thoughts that stay in the past or continually consider the future can hinder progress. However, being in the present requires a high level of concentration as well as control. It requires focusing on what are relevant cues and this requires an awareness of what is going on around you. Remaining in the 'here and now' also requires a flexibility to shift focus when necessary, as well as avoiding insignificant distractions.

Don't think about it

Can you force your thoughts? Your mind wanders and you 'redirect' attention because you try to control it. However, sometimes controlling your thoughts can have the reverse effect. Have you ever had the experience of trying *not* to think about the fact that you are awake and can't get to sleep? What happens? You stay awake even longer. Trying not to think about something is as detrimental as continually thinking about it. The more you force yourself not to think about a distracting thought, the more chance you will be preoccupied with it. Not thinking about something makes it harder to maintain clear thoughts and actually causes you to think about what you're trying to avoid thinking about! This is called 'ironic processing'.

In demonstrating this effect to students/players/coaches, I have often gone with a life-coaching example. There is an exercise that requires you 'not to think' about something–a red balloon, for example. You start by using a relaxation technique. You then begin to think about getting ready for a competition. As you come to grips with this, I feed in the idea of not thinking about something, for instance, 'don't think about a red balloon'. Of course, once this idea is planted in your mind it becomes hard to dismiss it. This is what can happen in sport, when as an athlete, you are preparing for the event however, your coach keeps saying, for example, 'don't think about how this is the Olympics and the pinnacle of your career; 'don't think about how this is the final competition to determine whether you become number 1 or not'. The problem with 'don't think' is that you 'do think'.

Carrying forward a 'don't think' thought can also manifest itself in your head as a negative instruction. In tennis, you may tell yourself 'don't double fault' or in ice hockey, tell yourself 'don't keep your legs straight'. It is impossible to skate with straight knees. Two things are wrong with a negative statement as opposed to a positive instruction. First, 'don't bend your arms' takes longer to think than 'keep your arms straight'. Secondly, you are forcing yourself not to think about something, which means you think about it more.

Compare your brain to a computer that uses a 'search' function. When you look for files that do not contain a word, the search is still actively engaged. With your mind, when you suppress a thought or idea, you scan consciously and unconsciously for thoughts or signs of unwanted thoughts like the ones you are suppressing and also search for those thoughts to see if you have been successful in doing this. Forcing yourself not to think about something in sport is activating the 'Find and Avoid' button. A lot of energy can be wasted in this process; it requires a lot of effort to 'search in reverse'.

So what can be done about this? The point is obvious. Concentrate on what you can do. Use self-talk or positive self statements to keep yourself focused on what you need to do. Train yourself to visualise the correct movement. Stay in the moment and go for the job at hand.

The relationship with emotion

Anxiety hinders concentration in various ways. The working memory system is handling your emotions while you are in a state of making a decision. In calming yourself down and managing your emotions you are better able to perform. Anxiety impacts on what you are thinking about as well as the direction and width of your focus, which can result in cognitive narrowing.

Emotions can lead you to worry or to perceive that the competitive situation is personally threatening. Focus is shifted towards becoming self-referential, which means that there is in an excessive monitoring of your own skills. Emotions can interfere by narrowing your thinking and focusing on what is irrelevant. Using the torch analogy, it means you are restricting the beam of light. Internal emotional distractions may result in your thinking that you can't hit a shot or that you won't be able to get the score that you would like. This self-focused attention can take the shape of doubt, indecision and lack of confidence. It can also generate hypervigilance, in which state you can over-analyse your body movements or any real or perceived threat from other competitors. This can compromise your concentration and make you more susceptible to distractions.

On a final note, when you are experiencing anxiety, try to recognise what you are experiencing, rather than thinking that those internal emotional distractions are taking away your focus. Consider using your energy in your current environment. You can focus on one thing or you can multitask by dividing your attention between co-existing things. You do, however, have a limited capacity for this, so it is important that you train and practise in order to do this effectively and quickly. Whether you decide to use single focus or multi-focus, you still need to ensure it is relevant. Remember that internal and external distractions are disruptive only when you perceive the act of attention as being out of your control. You are, in fact, the master of your focus. You can change your focus or divert your attention at any time. Too much energy is wasted when you try not to do something rather than go for the positive of carrying out the required action.

HOW CAN YOU MANAGE THOUGHTS AND WORDS FOR BETTER FOCUS?

Stopping thoughts requires you to dismiss any thought that is not relevant. You can do this by giving yourself a specific order or by using trigger words, such as go, bounce, jump, spin, stop or clear. You could also use one of your affirmations using a word or phrase, such as 'I can control my own focus' or simply 'control'. Alternatively, your cue or trigger could also be a physical action such as turning a tennis racket in your hands or touching a golf club on the ground. Your visual albums can also be used through a systematic use of imagery (see Chapter 3).

Sports vary as to whether you have time to refocus and restart your routine. In some there are other external considerations, such as a starting gun in athletics or the amber/green lights in a racing tree. The important thing is not to over-analyse the situation or let your mind wander. In some sports, such as golf (putting), cricket (bowling), basketball (free throw) or tennis (serving), you have time to stop and refocus. These are breaks (though some are rather short) in which you can think and readjust your game. You might use the exercise – Identify, Control (stop), Shift, which gives your mind and your body space in which to refocus and restart your routine prior to your next shot, throw or serve.

Self-awareness is important in being able to shift focus. This first step of self-awareness requires you to be able to ascertain whether you are focused or not. You need to catch yourself if you start to drift or think distracting thoughts. Having a sense of self-awareness can be beneficial as long as you are not obsessed with it. If you are too aware, then you may find that you are distracted by thinking about what is happening. The second step is to realise whether or not the distraction is important, and to make a decision to ignore it or focus on it. The final step is when you are ready to surround yourself in your performance.

Sometimes you need to park or save thoughts and return to them later. As stated previously, when thoughts are stuck in your mind, even if you are trying hard not to think about them, they can keep on re-emerging and prevent you from optimizing your performance. A negative situation, such as having had a bad day yesterday or a less than satisfactory performance in the last competition, needs to be thought about and then analysed again later so that complete focus can take place. You need to be able to focus on what is relevant for the duration of your current sporting event regardless of whether it is 2 minutes, 2 hours or more in duration.

When you start your performance you need to take on the role of a focused performer. Being at a competition can be an escape from everyday life, so forget the argument you had the day before or the assignment that is due in after the weekend. You can deal with problems or challenges that need your attention later. When you step into the role of a focused athlete, you need to 'park your life outside.' Remember, attention is deliberate and rather than be distracted you can choose what to focus on. Allow yourself the opportunity to play without any cognitive restrictions.

Improving focus can also be achieved by developing anticipatory skills. How good are you at the 'Sherlock Holmes method' of reading cues? Can you recognise patterns of play and anticipate actions, e.g. in the changing body language of tennis players or in the ebb and flow of a football match? With the use of video analysis you can take your time in analysing how your opponent moves and prepare yourself to focus on these cues to help in your performance.

Questions to consider

1. Does it work when you force yourself not to think about something?
2. Do you really lose concentration or are you just distracted?
3. What other analogies for focus and concentration can you think of?

REFLECTIVE PRACTICE: SELF-TALK; BUILDING A ROUTINE; CONCENTRATION GRIDS

SELF-TALK

Self-talk is any self-statement or thought about yourself that is useful in helping you to focus on the present and in keeping your mind from being distracted. If you are a positive thinker, especially in an intense or stressful situation, then you are bound to be more successful in your sport. Affirmations, such as 'that's great', 'keep doing your best', 'move quickly' and 'breathe slowly', can help you to stay focused. This is a technique used frequently in sport psychology.

Choose a movement or skill within your sport about which you think negatively. Think of three negative statements that you usually make and then dispute each of them, replacing them with positive ones. Here are some examples:

Negative thoughts	Positive thoughts
1. I haven't trained hard enough	1. Relax and follow the pre-competition plan
2. I hope I don't choke	2. I'll focus on what I can control
3. I am really nervous	3. I'll mentally rehearse my pre-routine
4. Why did this happen now?	4. I'll follow my strategy for this event
5. I'm not ready	5. Just go for it

Make your own lists, and work through them between and in the build-up to meetings/matches/competitions.

BUILDING A ROUTINE

The aim of a good strategic routine is to help you to be focused so that your mind and actions are consistently doing the same thing. The techniques above can be implemented into a routine. As you know, if you have a routine, then you have a habitual way of carrying something out. Your routine may mean practising before the task, either in your head or physically utilizing your focus techniques. In basketball, it may mean bouncing the ball three times before taking a free throw; in tennis, it may mean bouncing the ball while preparing to serve; as a kicker, it might mean taking some practice kicks at the side of the field. The good thing about routines is that they can be altered and adapted when necessary. When you go on holiday for instance, you can change your routine and still be happy and productive.

Going through a routine is much more effective than relying on a lucky penny! What happens if you lose your lucky penny or if it lands on tails when you needed it to land on heads? If you rely on it, superstition can be a coping mechanism for relinquishing control. Rather than you having to focus, it means that you are excusing yourself from taking responsibility. Are you waiting for signs that your superstitious routine causes a particular response or outcome? If the superstition doesn't work, then that can place doubt into your mind. Remember that routines can be changed and that you can have different routines for different situations.

A consistent routine will help you to access a strong mindset with a firm focus. A 'pre-routine' plan can minimize your focusing on distractions on the day. Experts and elite athletes admit to having well developed routines, which help guide them through pressurised situations.

Top Tips for Creating a Routine

- Begin with a physical and psychological warm-up
- Remember that attention is deliberate
- You choose whether to focus on diversions or not
- Use your energy to balance more than one focus at a time, if necessary
- Use breaks to shift your focus but maintain a relaxed focus
- Develop your sense of awareness; do not rely on superstition
- Understand that your emotions can interfere with performance
- Be careful not to use all your energy trying 'not' to think about something
- Remember you are the director of your focus, which is selective and allows you to multitask

'One size does not fit all', nor does it fit all sports.

CONCENTRATION GRIDS

When used as a visual search task, concentration grids can help improve focus. The objective is to find as many numbers as possible within a given time. There isn't a lot of theoretical evidence to support how it works, though focus skills in sport are similar to brain training apps and appear to indirectly improve your overall attention span. In my experience, the more specific the skill and situation, the better it is for training. Both practice sessions and simulation experiences, which are virtually like a real competitive situation, are beneficial; e.g. practising tiebreaks at the end of a table tennis set or a penalty shoot-out at the end of a football match. You can use a sodoku puzzle to view numbers or create your own such as the one I put together below.

A CONCENTRATION GRID EXERCISE

1	30	10	32	18	28	3	13	34	11
21	25	37	4	44	38	42	48	6	24
14	41	46	23	50	12	20	40	45	17
36	29	2	39	7	33	47	22	49	31
9	16	35	8	26	19	15	43	27	5

1. Time yourself. Concentrate on finding all the numbers in order from 1 to 50.

   The first time will be hard and you may want to quit, but keep going until the end. The second time will be a lot easier and so on. Some of this is due to the fact that you will learn the grid; however, you will get the experience of how intense focus really works.

   Try the grid in other ways to give yourself a new challenge:

2. Time yourself. Concentrate on finding all the numbers starting from 50 working backwards.

3. Time yourself. Concentrate on finding all the even numbers in order.

4. Time yourself. Concentrate on finding all the odd numbers in order.

Practise these exercises daily and see if you can improve your concentration skills. Record your times for a week as follows:

Monday   Tuesday   Wednesday   Thursday   Friday   Saturday   Sunday

Further Reading

There are a number of free articles on this subject available on the internet (e.g. by Robert Nideffer, on TAIS):

1. www.epstais.com/articles/tais.pdf.
2. www.enhanced-performance.com/articles/optimal.pdf.

5 MENTAL TOUGHNESS

'The most important attribute a player must have is mental toughness.'
Mia Hamm (American soccer player)

'Being mentally strong we have to see as a skill. It's high. We talk a lot about the technical things on the ice but definitely your attitude and mental toughness are a huge factor.'
Antoine Vermette (Canadian ice hockey player)

'Mental Toughness is essential to success.'
Vince Lombardi (American football coach)

Objectives

1. Defining mental toughness
2. Characteristics of mental toughness

The media promotes players as mentally tough. Viewers, therefore, connect mental toughness with the profile of a winner. In fact, when spectators are asked to describe their favourite sporting heroes, one of the most extensively used expressions is 'mental toughness'. Examples of this are demonstrated throughout sport. For example, in the FIFA World Cup 2014, the Brazilian player Neymar was described as 'mentally strong'; baseball player Chandler Taylor was described by his coach as 'dedicated, mentally tough and a leader'. In an article about the NHL draft, the San Jose Sharks were challenged to find mentally tough players. Mental toughness is on every coach's checklist. The question is, what is it?

WHAT DOES IT TAKE TO BE MENTALLY TOUGH?

To be mentally tough you need to have a psychological edge, which enables you to cope better with the demands of your sport, including essential training, competitive events and lifestyle factors (e.g. eating, sleeping). It specifically means being more consistent and better than your opponents in remaining determined, focused, confident, resilient, and in control under pressure (Jones, Hanton and

Connaughton, 2002). Mental toughness is a consistency to perform towards the upper range of your talent and skills regardless of competitive circumstances (Loehr, 1995). It is a perseverance to achieve a goal even in the face of adversity (Middleton, Marsh, Martin, Richards and Perry, 2005). Mental toughness is a quality that enables athletes to respond well to challenging situations and to persevere in the face of setbacks (Smith, 2006). Mentally tough athletes are people who have a 'high sense of self-belief and an unshakeable faith that they can control their own destiny' and who can 'remain relatively unaffected by competition or adversity' (Clough, Earle and Sewell, 2002).

The concept of mental toughness has been explored in research though it remains an abstract one. There is no uniform agreement of what is meant by the term between media, players, psychologists and researchers. Definitions are general so as to be inclusive in representing an assortment of personality characteristics. In fact, many psychologists say that the concept tends to be anecdotal rather than empirical. Research has identified four common categories or dimensions: attitude/mindset (self-belief and focus); training (including motivation); competition (including coping with pressure); and post competition (including perceptions of success and failure) (Jones, Hanton and Connaughton, 2007). It highlights how there must be a multidimensional characteristic, which supports previous definitions. Even though there is no unanimity, what does transpire is that these mental toughness skills are incorporated into all aspects of our lives. In addition, in sport, mental toughness is something especially needed in order to reach the top and remain there.

> *Are you hardy? Hardiness is having commitment, control, accepting challenge (Kobasa, 1979) and being confident (Clough et al., 2000).*

The four Cs

The following four Cs are useful for remembering what it takes to be mentally tough:

The first component of hardiness is *commitment*, which is a readiness to become involved and deal with situations as they arise. It is useful if you like clearly measured objectives. Objectives or goals help you to stay focused and to be motivated in being committed. I would also say that this includes a commitment to practice and choice of lifestyle. Once you arrive at your place of practice then make a commitment to listen, learn and apply everything you experience. If you are easily distracted and easily bored, then you may have more of a tendency to give up.

The second is *control*, which is the degree to which you feel you can have an impact on the situation. Some of us feel that we can influence our circumstances and make things happen. Others feel that they lack control and that life just happens to them. Being able to manage your time and your life as well as multitask helps in establishing the necessary control.

The third is *challenge*, which is the propensity to perceive unexpected and uncertain situations as non-threatening. This idea comes out in relation to other topics, such as anxiety and stress. There is an importance in seeing challenges and problems as positive opportunities as opposed to threats. Improving athletic performance is more difficult for people who don't like change than for those who enjoy problem solving.

The fourth is *confidence*. This is having a self-belief that keeps you going even when things are tough. Without this, athletes may give up when experiencing a setback in performance or when injury occurs. Having confidence means that you can reframe negativity and frustration rather than let it bring you down.

Jones et al. (2002) proposed that athletes have a psychological edge when they can manage the demands of a pressurised sporting situation. An illustration of their concept of mental toughness highlights four pillars, which lead to sustained high performance (Jones and Moorhouse, 2007). This theoretical framework of mental toughness is based on personal construct psychology, which relies on the unique ways you interpret your experience:

Pillar 1. Manage stress when things are tough. Stress and anxiety are inevitable in sport and always in competition, so develop good coping skills. Thrive on the pressure rather than letting it distract you.

Pillar 2. Stay strong in your self-belief to reach your goals.

Pillar 3. Keep motivated and resilient when you are not successful. Use lessons from poor performance to accelerate your determination.

Pillar 4. Keep focused on what is important. Engage in the task at hand and limit distractions. Master an ability to flick a switch to focus and refocus when required. Don't let negative internal thoughts and beliefs distract you.

In addition to these key aspects, psychologists have attempted to identify additional characteristics that you need in order to be mentally tough. Loehr (1995) identified seven characteristics as follows:

1. self-confidence
2. negative energy control
3. attention control
4. imagery control
5. motivation
6. positive energy
7. attitudinal control

Middleton et al. (2005) developed a model that identified 12 characteristics of mental toughness, including the concept of the positivity of your thoughts, attitude and beliefs:

1. self-efficacy
2. a belief in one's own potential
3. a positive mental self-concept
4. task familiarity
5. task value
6. intrinsic motivation to achieve one's own personal best
7. goal commitment
8. perseverance
9. task specific attention
10. positivity
11. stress minimization
12. positive self-comparison to opponents

The concept of mental toughness does have limitations. For instance, what psychological edge is needed within each of these characteristics? Can you still be considered mentally tough even if you don't achieve your objectives or if you lose? If it is something stable, then are you born with it or is it learned, or both?

The importance of all of this is that if you understand what is required it can help you to identify what you need to work on in order to improve or develop a mental toughness mindset. Some of you can cope and some of you struggle even though you have a good level of skill, and you do not achieve what you want, as something seems to hold you back. Mental toughness is about understanding what it takes and then programming your mindset to work for you. You know what you need to be mentally tough so try the mental toughness quiz below. This is a short version, which is also useful for children, and will enable you to compare yourself to top players.

Questions to consider

1. Does each sport share the same mental toughness package, or does it vary?
2. Do you need to be good in all aspects of mental toughness, or can you be stronger in one or two characteristics to make up for a lack of toughness in others?

REFLECTIVE PRACTICE: MENTAL TOUGHNESS QUIZ; REFRAMING; ABCD

MENTAL TOUGHNESS QUIZ

How do you know if you are mentally strong?

Consider your answers to the following questions to help identify where you are mentally strong and where you could improve:

1. Do you worry in advance about something which probably won't happen?
2. Do you find you can usually cope in a stressful situation?
3. Do you find it very difficult to know where to start when there are several demands at the same time?
4. Are you enthusiastic and passionate?
5. Do you stand your ground if there is a contentious point in conversation?
6. Do you think of the cup as being half full rather than half empty?
7. Do you find it hard to push yourself, especially when you are bored or tired?
8. Do you spend time worrying after you have made a mistake?
9. Do you tend to learn from mistakes?
10. Do you generally have a positive outlook on life?
11. Do you stick to things rather than give up?
12. Do you get easily distracted?

If you are mentally strong, then you would have answered yes to questions 2, 4, 5, 6, 9, 10 and 11, and no to questions 1, 3, 7, 8 and 12.

Your answers will have demonstrated various characteristics, such as whether or not you have a positive attitude, a sense of control, an ability to manage stress or utilise coping strategies, how you feel about motivation and commitment, whether you learn from your mistakes, worry unnecessarily or focus on the task at hand. Think about your answers: the process will help you decide what could be holding you back from being mentally strong.

The Mental Toughness Questionnaire (MTQ) (Clough et al., 2002) is a validated test, which contains questions that measure the strength of your answers on a 1–5 scale. If you want to test your mental strength, try this test online (www.aqr.co.uk). However, do remember that any test that produces an overall score can mask the fact that you are high on some characteristics yet low on others. As a consequence an average result does not necessarily balance you out as an overall strong person.

Assess yourself on where your strengths are and whether you need to develop these characteristics further. Consider those areas that you feel you need to strengthen, and which may be holding you back. Not everyone needs all the mental toughness characteristics, so don't dwell on what you are not good at. Commit to practice, play and lifestyle (healthy eating, relaxation and productive sleeping patterns).

REFRAMING

Framing is the meaning that you attach to your experiences. When you experience something, do you think it's good, bad or ugly? Particularly useful for those who think their glass is half empty, reframing is a technique in which you isolate a negative thought and look at it again in a more positive light.

For example:

Your frame: I can't make that basket, no matter how hard I try.

Your reframe: get a good look at the basket – see it, feel it, trust my shot.

Your frame: I can't make that hole, with the water being so close.

Your reframe: get a good look at the hole – see it, feel it, trust my swing.

Your frame: I can't make this serve, as I am just too tired.

Your reframe: keep my eye on the ball – watch the throw and trust my serving strength.

Your frame: Training is too hard.

Your reframe: at least the team and I will be fitter later on in the season.

REFRAMING THE SITUATION

The coach strongly nods at you after you perform your skill during practice. What could this mean?

- You put a negative spin on it – why did I only get a nod? Where are the comments? Perhaps it wasn't very good; perhaps he prefers someone else's movement? Perhaps he just isn't that confident in my abilities to perform this skill?
- You put a positive spin on it – he is pleased with me and knows I can do it. It is understated, however, he believes in me.

If it doesn't work, try it again later. Another simple way to change a context in reframing is to add the word 'yet'. 'I can't get a shot in from this distance or a goal in from here, yet'; or, 'I can't get a kick in martial arts, or lift that heavy a weight, yet'; 'I can't do a backwards flip, yet'. It keeps the door open to the fact that you will do it eventually, just not yet.

Another example might be that your teammate is shouting at you during the match. This annoys you so you reduce your effort out of anger. However, if you reframe it, then a better situation is created. To begin with, it is not abnormal to be shouted at in sport; your teammate is enthusiastic and passionate and wants the best for the team. He is being annoying or even aggressive; however, you also want the best so you need to keep pushing harder. Attribute the shouting as related to the passion in the game not to you as a person.

Reframing is about turning negativity into positive mental toughness. You may be a natural re-framer. If that is your strength, you can become even better at it. If it is not your strength, or it is new to you, then try it out.

ABCD

The meaning and feelings behind how you see things is under your control. One of the keys to mental toughness is to be able to see things in a positive light. When you limit your beliefs you will interpret things negatively.

In Rational Emotive Behaviour Therapy (REBT) (Dryden, 2011), there is a way of looking at problems called ABCD. This stands for the *Antecedent* or action or activating event – *Belief* (irrational thought) – *Consequence*. Then there is D, which stands for *Dispute*.

Something occurs (the antecedent or action or activating event) and there is a consequence (or outcome). For example, you throw the ball (A) and the result is that your teammate misses it (C).

The action of A results in the consequence of C. However, there is something in between which can impact on the result. This is B – your belief. Perhaps you were considering that s/he was not going to catch it because they are useless or because you are never successful in passing. This is interference and it is due to your belief. Perhaps you feel that you are useless because you missed a successful pass at some point before this.

If you dispute (D) that B is not accurate but irrational, then you can improve your performance.

ABCD is easy to remember. When you are playing a game and the consequence or outcome is not what you expected, then quickly check whether you were running interference with a 'belief'. Here are some sporting examples:

(A) ready to shoot (C) missed the hoop

(B) thinking that I am quite useless at shooting

(A) standing on the wing (C) plane banks and I miss my moment to jump

(B) thinking how I might die and what might happen if my parachute got tangled

(A) get dropped from the first team (C) start playing for the second team

(B) thinking I should probably quit, my coach does not think I have any value

Try giving two examples of your ABC and add a D:

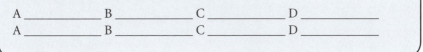

A _____ B _____ C _____ D _____
A _____ B _____ C _____ D _____

Further Reading

Dryden, W. (2011). *Dealing with Emotional Problems Using Rational-Emotive Cognitive Behaviour Therapy*. London: Routledge.

Gucciardi, D. F. and Gordon, S. (2012). *Mental Toughness in Sport: Developments in Theory and Research*. New York, NY: Taylor & Francis.

PART 3
SETTING SKILLS AND USING TECHNIQUES

Basketball star Michael Jordan

6 GOAL SETTING AND MOTIVATION

'Objectives should never be easy; they should force you to work even if they are uncomfortable at the time.'

Michael Phelps (swimmer – the most decorated Olympian of all time with 22 medals)

Objectives

1. The need for focus, effort, persistence, strategy
2. Understanding goals: process, performance and outcome objectives
3. The difference between task and ego orientation
4. Intrinsic versus extrinsic motivation
5. Autonomy, competence and relatedness

Goal setting can be used to provide direction, focus and motivation. This chapter will examine goal setting techniques and, as these concepts are linked, the theories behind motivation. Goal setting as a process is quite straightforward though it is not always done correctly. In order to be successful in setting goals, you need to be motivated.

Goal setting is the setting of specific and challenging objectives, which contribute towards an overall larger aim. According to Locke's theory of goal setting (1996), there are four factors that support it as a technique. These are: focus, effort, persistence and strategy. When you *set your goal*, you have *chosen your focus*. Then you *activate your effort*. This is as far as many athletes get. Where some may fail is that goal setting also needs continued *perseverance* based on an overall *strategy*.

For example, you want something in your sport so you establish a focus (e.g. improve fitness levels by being able to run 2 miles further in the same amount of time). Activation is set as you join a gym. Perseverance and a strategy are now needed. How many days will you go each week and at what time? How will you ensure that you attend these sessions? Without a plan, which requires continuously working towards your goal, it simply won't happen. You cannot just expect everything to fall into place. One trick is to write down these key words and place them somewhere prominent, so that every day you can remind yourself of your goal.

> *Make a note of the following key words:*
> *Focus   Activate   Persevere   Strategy*

WHAT TYPE OF GOALS SHOULD I SET?

In choosing specific types of goals, the way you set your focus is important. There are various types of goals, which have different results. These are outcome goals, process goals and performance goals.

Your *outcome goals* are what you would like to achieve overall, for example, whether you are looking to win a match or make the first team. These are often things over which you do not have control. *Process goals* are the 'how' in terms of technique and strategy. For example, to keep your arms bent, to stick to your pre-performance routine, to maintain a steady pace. *Performance goals* are related to the 'what' you hope to do en route. You set these by, for example, aiming to be two shots below par for the first three holes on the golf course or by reducing your running time. Process and performance objectives are usually cited as the keys to success, e.g. in *Fundamental Goal Theory* (Burton and Weiss, 2008). Outcome objectives are often not within your control as they may be related to other players, coaches, referees, etc. However, outcome objectives are also an important part of sport and therefore should not be dismissed. Setting objectives is also related to your achievement.

> *Make a note of the following key words:*
> *Outcome   Process   Performance*

WHAT TYPE OF MOTIVATION IS BEST FOR SUCCESS?

You now need to examine your motivation. One way to do this is to examine your achievement or motivational orientation (Needs Achievement Theory, McClelland, 1985): these are task orientation and ego orientation. *Task orientation* is when you are motivated to achieve or master the skill; you are keen to accomplish your objectives by optimizing your performance. *Ego orientation*, as the term implies, is linking your achievement into your own persona or ego, for example, going out to win and being better than the others. If you have to choose one orientation versus the other, then task orientation has been shown to be more effective. Ego on its own can be detrimental, especially when working with youngsters, as it doesn't provide a focus for skill development. In addition, it often results in wanting to quit when you discover that you are not as good as others. Coaches, parents or teammates unfortunately often reinforce this orientation when they fuel the ego through statements such as 'you are useless if you don't beat them' or 'you are a far superior player'.

There is no getting away from ego in sport. Everyone wants to win. Therefore it is unusual to be either 100 per cent task orientated or 100 per cent ego oriented. It is more likely that you will fit into one of these four categrories at any given time: high task/high ego; high task/low ego; high ego/low task; low ego/low task.

In most cases, depending on the level of sport you play, you need to balance both orientations. You want to do your best and you want to accomplish the sport skills required. You need to recognise that sport is task oriented; however, there are also ego-involving situations (e.g. 'I am going for a personal best'). You need strategies to deal with ego-oriented comments so that they don't interfere with your performance. A mindset called competitive performance mentality incorporates both orientations in terms of self-challenge and game challenge. Self-challenge is for your personal success and game challenge is when you are being competitive (Murphy, 2005).

To understand where you are in terms of achievement there are several tests available including the Task and Ego Orientation in Sport Questionnaire (TEOSQ) (Duda, 1989; Duda and Nicholls, 1992). (You can find this online at www.brianmac. co.uk.) In addition, there is the Perceptions of Success Questionnaire (POSQ) (Roberts, Treasure and Balague, 1998), which is useful for children and adults, and examines what success means to you (www.tandfonline.com). The test requires you to complete the statement: 'When playing sport, I feel most successful when...' There are 12 choices in which answers range from strongly agree to strongly disagree. For example, 'I beat other people' or 'I perform to the best of my ability'.

> *Make a note of the following key words:*
> *Task Orientation (Game Challenge)*
> *Ego Orientation (Self Challenge)*

Do you worry about failure? In addition to orientation, the Needs Achievement Theory identifies two independent constructs, i.e. the need to achieve and the fear of failure (Duda and Nicholls, 1992). Usually you start off in your sporting career with a high achievement orientation. You also begin with a low fear of failure, as you are not threatened by a competitive situation. However, you may become more proficient and start to win competitions. You may shift your perception and perceive a greater risk from becoming more concerned about what others, such as your coach and the spectators, think of your performance. You may be concerned with how capable you are, what your future holds. You may even have coping mechanisms where you try to get out of doing something (e.g. I am not going to be very good at this; I have a stomach ache; it is nearly time out anyway). How would you rate your need to achieve and your fear of failure?

Should you like to measure your fear of failure there is a multidimensional questionnaire called the Performance Failure Appraisal Inventory (Conroy, Willow and Metzler, 2002).

Make a note of the following key phrases:
Need to Achieve   Fear of Failure

Setting the difficulty of the goal is therefore an important part of the goal setting process. In controlling fear, and this varies between individuals, you need to set goals that are challenging though not overly difficult. Goals that are moderately difficult have a greater chance for success and can be increased progressively in difficulty. Accomplishing difficult objectives is rewarding; however, if the degree of difficulty is set too high then this could be counterproductive. Deciding on goals is something that needs to be negotiated and may be based on your confidence level. Even if a coach thinks the target is achievable, as an athlete *you* must also believe in *your* ability to reach that level and be aware if fear of failure, for example, is getting in your way.

DOES MOTIVATION ONLY COME FROM WITHIN?

Whereas goal setting is a technique that can facilitate your motivation, motivation is the driving force behind your behaviour. It is also a key component for success in sport. There are different types of motivation. Firstly, *intrinsic motivation,* which comes from within and is an internal striving to be good at something. Research indicates that those who undertake activities or exercise for their own self-satisfaction are happy, because intrinsic motivation is about passion and love for what they do. You are actually born to be intrinsically motivated with an innate drive towards achievement. If this motivation is reinforced through success and enjoyment, then there is a greater chance that you will maintain this behaviour throughout life. You also learn new habits through reinforcement, which strengthens the 'I am going to practise because I want to be the best I can be' behaviour. The more you want to continue with this behaviour, the more likely you are to reach your goal.

Extrinsic motivation is the drive from the outside rather than the inside. There are four types of this external motivation: external regulation, introjected regulation, identified regulation, and integrated regulation (Deci and Ryan, 2000). *External regulation* is being motivated through reward, financially or socially, (e.g. 'I am going to practise because I want the coach to let me play tomorrow'). It could come, for example, from prize money, getting paid, receiving a trophy, status or being praised. *Introjected regulation* is being motivated due to external pressure or even coercion (e.g. 'I would feel guilty if I missed practice'). *Identified regulation* is a type of external motivation where you choose to take part even though you are not really interested (e.g. 'I hate lifting weights but I know it is an important part of playing well'). Finally, there is *integrated regulation* (e.g. 'I won't go out with my friends tonight as I have a big game tomorrow and need to be in top shape'), which is a part of your values and belief system. External motivation does overlap with intrinsic motivation and may be about the reward of doing something that is valued in society by others. Intrinsic motivation is about being motivated for your own satisfaction rather than externally for the sake of a reward (Vallerand, 2007).

Amotivation is neither intrinsic nor extrinsic. It is a lack of motivation or absence of intentionality and motivation. You don't want to participate and really don't see any reason or benefit in engaging in sport or a physical activity. Behaviourally you may demonstrate lack of commitment and even competency.

When I am approached by someone who wants to improve a skill or take up a new fitness regime, one of the first things I ask is how much do they want to do it, what would it take to do it (a list including weeks and hours) and then how committed are they to doing it? Sometimes we are motivated by an idea but 'amotivated' about actually doing it.

In the majority of situations, intrinsic and extrinsic motivation will operate collaboratively. For instance, why would someone sign up to run an organised half marathon when they could just run 13 miles around their neighbourhood? You choose or feel you have to run a marathon, for example, due to a friend or family member's cancer diagnosis. You train and may not even enjoy having to push yourself; however, you keep in mind the goal of doing this to benefit other victims of the disease. You feel good about yourself when you finish and feel good when others praise you. Setting external objectives, such as events and challenges, is a highly effective way of keeping engaged and training for longer. You are driven to prepare for this event by a deep sense of intrinsic motivation.

When you set goals to achieve skills within your sport, you may be driven by either intrinsic, extrinsic motivation or by a combination of both. The only problem with extrinsic motivation is that when used as a part of goal setting you have to accept that certain aspects, for example the reward, may be out of your control. You may achieve the skill (e.g. knocking 3 seconds off your time), but you may not win the medal. When a reward is withdrawn, people can feel that they don't want to continue with this new behaviour. When this happens you need to reflect and evaluate your goal-setting plan.

Your motivation is also determined by three psychological needs, i.e. how you strive to be *autonomous (freedom of choice), competent (perceived ability to do well)* and show *relatedness (to get along with other people; shared experience)*. These factors are integral to the Self-Determination Theory (SDT) (Deci and Ryan, 1985; 2000), which explains how social factors either help or undermine actions and behaviours. The most important factors emerging from this theory are that your autonomy affects how intrinsically motivated you are. If you believe that the environment or other people have a stronger influence over your actions than you do, then you are less likely to be intrinsically motivated.

Learning to make decisions, feeling capable of doing things and being able to work with others are things that should be learnt at a young age.

With a stronger sense that you are in control you will feel that outcomes happen due to your effort and ability, then there is more chance that you have a greater sense of intrinsic motivation.

The Cognitive Evaluative Theory, one of the five sub-theories in the Self-Determination Theory, centres on intrinsic motivation or motivation for its own sake, in that it deals specifically with rewards and ego. When examining a sporting task, if you feel that you are competent and in control, you are intrinsically motivated to undertake the skill and you don't need any further external motivation. If it is extremely difficult to be good at a skill, then you may not feel competent. For example, setting yourself or an athlete an extremely difficult task without breaking it down to smaller objectives and achievements along the way could have the effect of frustrating you, or the athlete, so much that you/they give up. This suggests that the way in which rewards are viewed will play a role in determining motivation. If a coach asks you to join the team because 'they need your skills, talent and determination', you are more likely to be motivated to be a part of his/her team.

The type of feedback you give yourself, or that you receive from your coach, is related to your reward and this in turn affects your intrinsic motivation. Players may see that an external reward results in others having control over him/her or they may see the result as informational, meaning that it reinforces their feelings of competency and self-determination.

You may often wonder why you or others fail at goal setting. The key to successful goal setting is knowing how to set the right type of goals *and* understanding how to motivate yourself so that you don't give up on your dreams.

Questions to consider

1. Why is an outcome goal not as useful in improving performance as a performance goal?
2. Why would believing that you are in control of your efforts be more intrinsically motivating?

REFLECTIVE PRACTICE: SMART(ER) GOAL SETTING; MOTIVATIONAL SELF-ASSESSMENT

SMART(ER) GOAL SETTING

Goal setting is often referred to using the acronym SMART or SMARTER though the words are often modified in this procedure. Try this exercise:

1. *Specific* – Be specific as to the reason or purpose of the goal. Use the six W's to help you: *Who, *What, *Where, *When, *Which, *Why.

   e.g. 'I want to lose ½ stone (7 pounds/3kg) in one month. I plan to train/practise three days a week on Monday, Wednesday and Friday.'

2. *Measurable* – How will you measure your success? Set the criteria to measure your progress towards achieving the goal you have set. How will you know when the result has been achieved?

3. *Action* – Make a plan so you can see how you will accomplish this goal. You need to work out how you are going to do it so it is achievable.

4. *Realistic* – To be realistic, a goal must be an objective that you are willing and capable of achieving. Is it too easy or too difficult? Do you need to break it down into smaller achievable increments?

5. *Time* – Set the time aside to achieve this. Make yourself accountable by deciding when you are going to do it and by when you hope to achieve your goal.

6. *Evaluate* – After you have started make sure you review your goal regularly. Is it working? Do you have the right strategies in place? Are you achieving what you want to accomplish? Are you persevering?

7. *Revise* – Do you need to change anything in order to accomplish your goal?

MOTIVATIONAL SELF-ASSESSMENT

Look at the following statements. Tick those that apply to you. Be honest. Your answers will help you find out where you see yourself. What actions should you take to motivate yourself in designing your own goal setting?

1. *I feel ego oriented*
2. I feel task oriented
3. *I am intrinsically motivated*
4. I am extrinsically motivated
5. *I feel I control things*
6. I feel the environment and others control things
7. *I feel autonomous and able to make my own decisions*
8. I rely on others to help me decide what to do
9. *I feel I am competent*
10. I am not very good at what I do
11. *I feel that I can work well with others*
12. I don't work well with other people

Further Reading

Locke, E. and Latham, G. (2012). *New Developments in Goal Setting and Task Performance*. London: Routledge.

7 THE ZONE, FLOW AND MINDFULNESS

'I was trying to stay in the moment. I knew I couldn't think ahead.'
Eugenie Bouchard (Wimbledon Singles Finalist 2014)

'When I'm in this state, this cocoon of concentration, I'm living truly in the present, not moving out of it. I'm aware of every inch of my swing. I'm absolutely engaged, involved in what I am doing at that particular moment.'
Tony Jacklin, CBE (British golf champion, European Ryder Cup winning captain)

Objectives

1. The terminology of flow, zone and mindfulness
2. The importance of flow, zone and mindfulness
3. How to achieve the nine dimensions of flow

The sheer enjoyment from participating in sporting activities can provide you with a sense of wholeness. This sensation is often identified as a sense of flow, being 'in the zone' or mindfulness. All of these are often associated with peak performance.

Flow is a state of consciousness and focus where you are totally absorbed with what you are doing. Being in the zone is when your anxiety and emotions are in the right place for your best performance. Mindfulness is an increased awareness of the present.

Flow is the effortless collaboration of mind and body. You could say that sports are designed to flow. The skills are challenging and require intense focus and so you become completely absorbed. Sport seems to set you up for flow, which is a state of concentration so focused and directed that it results in a complete absorption of an activity (Jackson, Thomas, Marsh and Smethurst, 2001). Though there is a mixture of physical, psychological, technical and tactical aspects for players, coaches and psychologists, a heightened sense of concentration appears to be the key to getting in the zone.

You can achieve a joyous state when you feel you have the skills to meet an optimal challenge or you are working at something that doesn't exceed your capacity. This experience of flow is often described as being on autopilot. Athletes and performers say it is a totally absorbing experience where you may experience exhilaration, freedom from pain, fearlessness, being completely in the moment and using your skills at their best. Physically and mentally you may be so relaxed that negative thoughts and emotions are not evident and your confidence is high. You feel highly charged or energised and very much in control as you move effortlessly.

WHY IS IT IMPORTANT TO EXPERIENCE FLOW?

You are likely to get your best performance out of these peak experiences. In fact, this heightened state of awareness seems to differentiate elite athletes from novices. Elite players are better able to recognise and judge their anxiety levels prior to competition. They are in a high state of concentration. The concentration just before and during the sporting skill appears to be complete absorption. They are so involved in an activity that negative emotions and anxiety are sidelined, as they feel highly confident. They are attuned to cues and movement, resulting in quicker reaction times. It is an optimal state of intrinsic motivation or satisfaction. People report that they are at their happiest when they are in a state of flow, which is often described as the most outstanding and unforgettable highlight in life.

The state of mind associated with flow results when you push your boundaries towards your best performance. This state is, unfortunately, temporary and it does not seem to be something that you can force yourself into. However, the concept of mindfulness is something that you can incorporate into your training and this helps heighten your awareness of the state of flow.

Much of the research on flow is descriptive and anecdotal. However, studies suggest that flow is primarily due to your cognitive (i.e. thinking) resources and functioning. Research in this area does have methodological as well as conceptual challenges. For example, most of the information is self-reported by athletes and therefore hard to measure. In addition, the experience of flow is short-lived and fleeting during a game or performance and therefore needs to be captured somehow during or just after the event.

There are several key researchers who have dealt with this area. Csikszentmihalyi (1990) first coined the term 'flow', which originated as an optimal state relating to happiness, while Cratty (1983) identified four categories of flow:

- anxiety/arousal – positive or negative emotional experiences
- extremely good feelings
- mental escaping – associative or disassociate methods (thinking of something or separating yourself from it)
- post-contest mental break – the period after performance where it takes time to unwind and even to communicate

Hanin (1995, 2007) later designed the Individual Zones of Optimal Functioning model (IZOF), which explores how anxiety can positively affect performance, with Jackson and Csikszentmihalyi (1999) applying it specifically to sport in their book, *Flow in Sports*.

The IZOF is a model linking performance with anxiety. It identifies that you have your own zone for optimal functioning for both pre-competition and during competition. When your anxiety is outside this zone then your emotions can be detrimental to your performance outcomes. It is inaccurate to assume that the lower your anxiety the better you perform. Some of us are better at succeeding when anxiety is high. In fact, elite athletes are often more competent in their performance when they are capable of sustaining a desired level of anxiety, along with a perception that the anxiety is facilitative or helpful. In extreme sport, climbers with elevated levels of anxiety had more successful experiences when they also felt positive, happy and focused (Sanchez, Boschker and Llewellyn, 2010).

As it appeared evident that emotional states do impact on performance, the IZOF was refined to reflect a range of emotions besides anxiety. Emotions were also categorised in relation to performance: dysfunction-unpleasant emotions result from inadequate performance while facilitative-pleasant emotions emanate from successful performances (Pellizzari, Bertollo and Robazza, 2011).

Psychological and physiological measurements can be used to develop a greater sense of awareness of how emotional states affect you. There are several popular tests in the field, which examine state and trait anxiety, e.g. STAI, CSAI and SAS. These types of tests can help you to better identify your zone to enable your best performance (*see* an interesting PhD thesis which includes several of the tests and their references vuir.vu.edu.au/2048/1/09-04-01_thesis__bound_version_.pdf). There is a copy of the CSAI-2 on this site for you to have a look at. http://www.mrgillpe.com/uploads/1/2/9/2/12922833/csai2.pdf.

An important note - if you are every going to use tests with teams or as a consultant then I would recommend contacting authors who will usually supply them for free. However in some case there may be a cost. The references in this book, other books and articles are only a means of signposting what is available for free on the internet.

> *Flow is a change in consciousness where you are relieved from emotional constraints. You have clarity of vision where everything you do is effortless and perhaps even played out in slow motion.*

HOW DO YOU GET 'IN THE FLOW'?
The Nine Dimensions of Flow

You can't force yourself into a state of flow, but there are nine purported dimensions of flow to help you try (Martin and Jackson, 2008). I have added a key on how you can achieve this at the end of each dimension:

1. Challenge–skill balance
There is an equilibrium or balance between being challenged and feeling competent with your skill set so that you can cope with and address the challenge. As mentioned in Chapter 6, on goal setting, when objectives are realistic and/or somewhat difficult then you thrive on the satisfaction of meeting the challenge.

You feel good when you are able to find this balance. The challenge–skill balance is that you are in the flow or the zone when you have just enough of the right skills to meet the task.

The key: Train hard to get the right skills and build continually in terms of challenge. Learn to balance the two for a perfect combination.

2. Action-awareness merging

This is like an auto pilot setting, e.g. you drive without having to think about how you shift the clutch or you tee off without having to think about every aspect of your swing. Due to this merging, you effortlessly feel at one with your movements, which will be smooth and fluid. You may not even hear the noise of the crowd, as you are absorbed in the totality of the task at hand.

The key: Don't be distracted into thinking about the future or the past. Work on being able to place yourself in the present. Perhaps try mindfulness meditation (see page 61).

3. Clear objectives

This pertains to goal setting and having a keen sense of what you want to accomplish. Imagery can help here as you can develop a routine that includes visualizing the performance prior to the start of the match in order to help you keep focused on clear goals.

The key: Set achievable goals that can be accomplished, and which will lead to larger goals. Follow a goal-setting plan (see SMART(ER) Goal Setting in Chapter 6).

4. Unambiguous feedback

This means having a good radar through which you can feed back on how well you are doing so that you are able to adjust your performance, predominantly with a kinaesthetic (physical) awareness, while remaining in this state of flow; e.g. a slalom skier who when she passes a flag modifies her run back on course. It could also be when you need to adjust your grip on your bat or racquet during a competition.

The key: Use your sports' radar to provide you with feedback on how you are doing.

5. Concentration on the task at hand

This means you have to maintain an intense attention and focus on what you need to do. If you're a footballer and you are thinking about the after-game celebration, the chances are you will not be fully contributing to the game and may miss a great opportunity to score or make a goal-saving tackle.

The key: focus on the task at hand.

6. Sense of control

A feeling of being in complete control, with positive thoughts such as 'nothing can go wrong', or 'I am unbeatable'.

The key: Stick with what is controllable and let go of what is not.

7. Loss of self-consciousness

This is liberation of the self. You perform in a way that empowers you to feel strong and free from any sense of concern, fear or doubt. The automaticity of it means that it is closely linked with action-awareness. As a long-distance runner, you may feel completely free and unencumbered.

The key: Lose your restrictions and enjoy the rhythm of what you do.

8. Transformation of time

This is a change in the perceived speed of time. For some it seems that time passes slowly and for others it goes by quickly. It is the difference from the usual 'real time' to a new 'slowing down' of time, which identifies this experience. As you putt the ball, time seems to pass slowly as it makes its way towards the hole.

The key: Release yourself from real time.

9. Autotelic experience

This is an intrinsic experience as well as the exhilaration in doing something that makes you feel completely whole. It is the reward of feeling like a winner and being so high that it takes time to come down.

The key: Enjoy yourself.

You may even have an autotelic personality. This means that you have traits whereby you intrinsically enjoy an activity such as climbing. You may engage in this for the love of the experience, even if you get 'nothing' out of it (e.g. a trophy, medal, score, time). The autotelic personality is also known for its inquisitiveness, perseverance and humility.

There are several measures of flow. The Flow State Scale measures the nine components of the flow experience described above (Jackson and Marsh, 1996). The test requires participants to reflect on their experience but this is often criticised for being subjective. In addition, there are two flow scales for physical activity: Flow State Scale-2 (Jackson and Marsh, 1996) and the Dispositional Flow Scale-2 (Jackson and Eklund, 2002).

To summarize, in order to achieve a state of flow you need a balance between challenge and skill. When challenge is high (or realistic) and skills are also high, then flow occurs. If skill and challenge are both low, then apathy arises. If the challenge is high but the skills are low, then anxiety happens. If skills are high and the challenge is low, then boredom is apparent. Skills and challenges must therefore be appropriately matched. However, this relationship has been criticised. Contrary to the above theory, when there are high skills with a low challenge, enjoyment and relaxation may also transpire for some.

Mindfulness

Mindfulness is a technique to help remind you to focus on the present. It is described as a flexible state of mind where you are actively engaged in the moment (Hathaway and Eiring, 2012) or a purposeful state of attention (Kabat-

Zinn, 1994). Both ways of looking at mindfulness are about engaging in the moment, though the difference in these views is as to whether it is an active process or not. Early studies with rowers showed that mindfulness training does facilitate performance (Kabat-Zinn, Beall and Rippe, 1985). Research has also shown the effectiveness of mindfulness in the improvement of general sporting performance (e.g. Thompson, Kaufman, De Petrillo, Glass and Arnkoff, 2011).

The origins of the technique are derived from Buddhism where mindfulness is achieved through the practice of a type of meditation. You start in a quiet place where you can sit and relate to your body as well as the environment. You allow thoughts, breath, memories, plans and experiences to come and go. You attend to them in a non-judgmental way. The object is to accept and not to suppress or control thoughts. You simply stay in the present. Some studies show that mindfulness training enhances flow in athletes, though research is still limited and therefore inconclusive in this area. This is not about relaxation. It is about being in touch with where you are now, even if it is in a pressurised competition. It is designed to help develop a sense of awareness in the present moment, whatever that moment entails.

Mindfulness seems to work in all sports. Several protocols, such as Mindfulness Sport Performance Enhancement (MSPE) (Kaufman, Glass and Arnkoff, 2009), have been designed to integrate the discipline into sports skills training. A follow-up study conducted by Thompson, Kaufman, De Petrillo, Glass and Arnkoff (2011) substantiated the effectiveness of mindfulness with archers, golfers and runners. The MSPE protocol includes sets of exercises designed to increase your state of mindfulness. These range from a chocolate-eating experience, meditation, body awareness, yoga, walking meditation, to a sport-specific meditation. Another programme, Mindfulness Meditation Training for Sport (MMTS), which concentrated on psychological skills training was launched in 2012 (Baltzell and Ashtar).

A large majority of the research on being in the zone, the flow experience and mindfulness encompasses the idea that being in touch with the present contributes to your state of mind and to your overall success in performance. Though this is very much an individual experience, when you are operating in the flow you will find yourself on an autopilot setting where your radar for feedback is effective, the perceived pace of time can accelerate or decelerate and you can feel freer as well as less self-conscious.

Questions to consider

1. Remember a time when you were in flow or 'in the zone' in sport. How do the dimensions of flow help prepare an athlete for flow?

2. How can personality impact on flow and how could you compensate for various aspects of personality?

3. Can you say whether or not mindfulness could help in your sport?

REFLECTIVE PRACTICE: RECALLING FLOW; MINDFULNESS EXERCISE; FLOW STRUCTURE FOR THE SEASON

RECALLING FLOW

Consider a game or an event (or a situation) when you were completely engaged in what you were doing. It should be a time when you felt confident, successful, positive and able to do anything. Try and imagine yourself back there, run the pictures through your mind and consider the following questions: When was it? Where are you? Who is with you? What does it feel like? What do you see? What do you hear?

MINDFULNESS EXERCISE

Practise this daily. Spend 1–5 minutes sitting upright and comfortably in your chair. Be aware of your body and of your breathing. Let your mind settle down. Focus on your breathing. If you become distracted, bring your focus back to your breathing. Breathe and be in the moment.

Do this exercise when you go out running or work out in the gym. Be in the moment. Be aware of your environment.

FLOW STRUCTURE FOR THE SEASON

Look at the statements below. Become familiar with them. Read them again at the appropriate times during the season and check on your progress towards peak performance:

The week or weeks before a competition
'I am training and/or practising appropriately'
'I am eating well'
'I am sleeping well'
'I am reminding myself of my goals and objectives'
'I see the upcoming competition a positive challenge'

The day of the competition
'I see the competition as a challenge'
'I am as prepared as I can be'
'I am looking forward to the competition with enthusiasm'
'I am ready to take on the competition'

Arriving at the venue
'I am getting used to the atmosphere surrounding the event'
'I am remaining in an excited yet relaxed state'
'I feel confident in myself'

'I am reviewing my goal-setting objectives for the competition'
'I am using my positive self-talk'
'I am ready to take on the challenge'

During the competition
'I am giving it my best'
'I am using my trigger words'
'I am not concerned with small mistakes'
'I am confident'
'I am enjoying the challenge'

Post-competition
'I participated and gave my best'
'How well I did was down to me (and my team)'
'I will learn how I can improve from this experience'

Further Reading

Deci, E. L., Ryan, R. M., Schultz, P. P. and Niemiec, C. P. (2015). 'Being aware and functioning fully: Mindfulness and interest taking within self-determination theory.' In K. W. Brown, J. D. Creswell and R. M. Ryan, *Handbook of Mindfulness: Theory, Research, and Practice.* NY: Guilford Press.

Hathaway, C. and Eiring, K. (2012). *Mindfulness and Sports Psychology for Athletes: Consider awareness your most important mental tool.* Madison, WI: Lulu Press.

Jackson, S. and Csikszentmihaly, M. (1999). *Flow in Sports: The keys to optimal experience and performances.* Leeds, Yorks: Human Kinetics.

8 COGNITIVE INTERVENTION: NLP AND CBT

'*I've missed more than 9000 shots in my career. I lost almost 300 games. Twenty-six times I've been trusted to take the game winning shot and missed. I failed over and over again in my life. And that is why I succeed.*'

Michael Jordan (acclaimed American basketball player)

Objectives

1. Life coaching to augment learning and coaching

2. NLP: Neuro Linguistic Programming – principles for success and presuppositions

3. CBT: Cognitive Behavioural Therapy

Life coaching is about developing general and specific cognitive skills, which reduce your stress levels and enable you to experience a harmonious balance in your life, including your sport. Life coaching provides you with a set of basic tools and approaches, which enable you to respond appropriately to your sporting experiences (Tosey, Mathison and Michelli, 2005; Linder-Pelz and Hall, 2007). In fact, the popularity of life coaching and counselling certification is such that the British Psychological Society (BPS) has established a special interest group in coaching psychology in order to accommodate the rising numbers of psychologists and practitioners practising these techniques.

Two of the most popular techniques used in sport are Neuro Linguistic Programming (NLP) and Cognitive Behavioural Therapy (CBT). These tools can help you to expand your understanding of how the mind processes information, particularly in sport.

NLP AND SPORT

NLP is about the mind (neuro) and language (linguistic). It examines how language affects the way you perceive and interact with the world. The techniques are adapted to change behavioural patterns so that you can process information more effectively. NLP is the integration of concepts related to a variety of psychological approaches, such as psychodynamics, cognitive behaviour and humanistics (Hill, 2001). Unfortunately, however, there is little academic research on the effects of NLP in sport primarily because NLP focuses on individuals' subjective interpretation and perceived reality (Tosey, et al., 2005; Deeley and Tod, 2008). Research is often qualitative and often challenged within the scientific field (Culver, Gilbert and Trudel, 2003). Debate around the validity of subjective areas, such as NLP, is not new, though researchers such as Holstein and Gubrium (1997) acknowledge the importance of analysing the subjective experience. Phenomenological research, which examines subjectivity in sport psychology, is a useful way to examine thought, behaviour and emotions (Dale, 2000).

NLP is based in psychology and was developed initially by John Grinder and Richard Bandler (1981). They explored how 'successful people became successful' and clinically researched 'the difference that made the difference'.

> Grinder and Bandler studied leading therapists at the time, such as Virginia Satir (family therapy), Fritz Perls (Gestalt therapy) and Milton Erickson MD (hypnotherapy), who were recognised as excellent communicators. From their initial and subsequent studies, they were able to identify communication patterns and to develop a series of approaches and techniques, which formed the basis for NLP. Many of these techniques are being utilised in sport (Lazarus, 2014).

The Metamodel in NLP is a model of communication. It examines your use of specific language and consciously challenges distortions and generalizations. It has been found in sport to increase confidence. Canoe slalom performance imagery using the NLP Metamodel demonstrated successful results (Grinder and Bandler, 1981). NLP aims to improve communication skills, to change behaviours and beliefs and to help model excellence. It is built on two foundations, 'the principles of success' and 'presuppositions'.

NLP principles for success

These are all about knowing what it is you want, being able to change through feedback, being flexible in your approach, establishing rapport with others, having a good mind–body connection and taking action.

1. Goal setting. Be SMART(ER)!
This principle is all about goal setting, which is a motivational tool to encourage you to become more productive. Understanding the different types of objectives encourages you to focus on what you want to achieve. An outcome goal focuses on results, e.g. winning the game. This is not always within your control and it is relatively ambiguous in how you need to achieve it. Outcome objectives are therefore more effective in combination with setting performance goals. Performance objectives are what you are attempting to achieve. A performance goal, such as making three successful passes or trimming a second off your time,

is specific and measurable. These incremental steps facilitate being able to reach your outcome goal. Process objectives are completely under your control. They are the small steps you take to get to the performance and outcome objectives by, for example, incorporating two days of strength training into your training routine.

2. Learn from feedback

Being able to understand feedback is an active process, which empowers you to take responsibility for your actions and performance. In sport, as an athlete or coach, you need to attend to results, assess what is effective and evaluate what doesn't work. You also need to notice the subtle physiological shifts when performing and the psychological impact that these changes have on performances. Change revolves around your awareness and your process of reflection. The challenge is to find ways to learn: from success, being able to celebrate success, learning from non-success, not getting stuck and making judgements. This, in essence, is learning through the process of reflection.

3. Be flexible

Flexibility requires evaluation of strengths and weaknesses within performance. Doing the same thing over and over again and expecting a different result is basically unproductive. If you know what you want and are prepared to take feedback, then being flexible enough to amend your behaviour is a natural progression. Knowing exactly what to change may not be evident, but at least your mental skills can direct your attention to finding something that could work, perhaps something that works for someone else, or something you've read about.

4. Build and maintain rapport

Rapport is a feeling of mutual trust between two or more people. The deeper the rapport, the more people will unquestioningly follow your guidance and instructions. Carl Rogers (1954), the father of counselling psychology, emphasised the importance of rapport as a foundation to any (therapeutic) relationship. Rapport between a mental skills coach/sport psychologist and player is essential. It is also useful in a team context (Turman, 2003). Where a team really bonds, i.e. builds great rapport, results are normally far superior to those of a group of individuals who may be technically better but who haven't bonded.

5. Understand your mind–body connection

The mind–body connection is acknowledged as important within psychobiology and has been researched in areas such as stress, arousal and anxiety. In NLP, positive thoughts along with body movements and posture are appropriate for someone seeking optimal results.

6. Action learning

In NLP, there is a difference between 'knowing what to do' and 'doing what you know'. 'Knowing what to do' can be facilitated through action learning, which involves learning from others. Action learning is a theory, a methodology and a technique of learning.

> *Make a note of these key principles of success:*
> *Goal setting   Feedback and reflection   Flexibility*
> *Rapport   Mind–body connection   Action learning*

NLP 'Presuppositions' – key underlying beliefs

NLP presuppositions are not truths, but a series of beliefs and assumptions, which you may often assume and act on as if they were true. Here are some of the presuppositions that are particularly relevant in sport. Please also note that these presuppositions are most useful when combined, rather than taken in isolation:

1. Respect other people's points of view
One aspect of communication is that all of us delete, distort and generalise information. This is based on numerous reasons, which include our varying life experiences, beliefs and values. In his theory of flow Csikszentmihalyi (1990) explains how and why information is deleted. A coach wanting to create change effectively in a player does not need to believe what the player believes. However, by respecting their outlook of the world, change will occur more rapidly. When you respect another person's point of view, even if you don't agree with it, then co-operation is more likely.

2. The meaning of communication is related to the response
Conventional wisdom suggests that by clearly communicating your thoughts and feelings in words, other people should understand the meaning. However, others respond to what *they* think you said, not what *you* think you said. You can determine how effectively you are communicating by the response you get from the person you are communicating with. In addition, when you accept this presupposition, then you are taking 100 per cent responsibility for all of your communication rather than blaming others. You are in charge of changing the way you communicate. If you or others do not do what was expected, then the fault is due to miscommunication and misunderstanding. Try saying things a different way, especially if your recipient doesn't get it the first or second time (note: apply this in conjunction with point 4 on the next page).

3. There is no failure, just feedback
If you do not succeed in something, this does not mean you have failed. In essence, you have not succeeded *yet*. It could be useful for you to do something differently. You can take the feedback, learn from the experience and vary your behaviour

in order to find a different way of achieving your outcome. Remember Michael Jordan's quote at the start of this chapter, 'I failed over and over again in my life. And that is why I succeed.'

4. Flexibility rules
The person with the most flexibility (choices) of behaviour will have the most influence on the situation. What this means is that the more options and techniques available, the more likely it is that an answer or an approach that works will be found. It means that you are more likely to be open to new ways of thinking. Adaptability is important within a skill set. It is essential in sport to adapt to the weather conditions, the opposition's tactics, the referee's decisions, the crowd, the atmosphere and the playing surface.

5. Be resourceful
People themselves are not un-resourceful, but they can experience un-resourceful states (state can be defined as feeling emotional at any given moment). When you change your state from negative to positive, you have access to all the resources within you to accomplish far more than you can when you are feeling un-resourceful, e.g. nervous, scared or under overwhelming pressure. You have everything within you to change; you just need to practise it so that you can use it when you need to.

6. Modelling excellence leads to improved performance
'Modelling' consists of observing the behaviour of others, and finding out how they think before, during and after an event or competition. Clearly there are limits to everyone's capability, but by modelling excellence, you can improve by taking the best from the best.

The presuppositions above can be usefully summarized by the concept of cause and effect. Something happens, which is a cause, and then there is a resultant effect. In NLP you can be categorised as a cause or effect person. If you are a cause person then you take full responsibility for what happens in your sport and respond to it. You don't make excuses and you tend to get better results in the medium and long term. If you are an effect person then you don't believe that you have control – everything happens to you as a result of someone or something else. Being an effect person is not comfortable – you have lots of really good reasons for not getting the results you want in sport, you feel that you usually don't get enough of what you want.

Take note of the following key concepts:

Respect other people	Communicate clearly	Feedback, not failure
Flexibility rules	Be resourceful	Model excellence

Are you a cause person or an effect person?

COGNITIVE BEHAVIOUR THERAPY (CBT)

CBT is a form of psychotherapy originally designed to help with depression. It is now known to help you understand how your thoughts and feelings influence your behaviour. It is generally a focused short-term intervention relying on incremental steps towards a behavioural change. The way you interpret your challenges impacts on how you behave. Understanding and modifying your issues means exploring several elements, such as: how you think, how your moods are affected, what your beliefs are, how you behave and how your body reacts.

> *Your thoughts influence how you behave/which impacts on the choices you make/ and the quality of your performance.*

The basic concept in CBT is that your thoughts and moods play a fundamental role in determining your behaviour. For example, you may spend a lot of time thinking 'what if'. This could mean: what if you lose, what if you are not physically fit enough, what if you come up against a particularly strong opponent, or what if other people do not think highly about you? You are using vital cognitive energy worrying and this will reduce the full effort you should be putting into your performance. The goal of cognitive behavioural therapy is to teach you that you cannot control every aspect of your environment. However, what you can control is how you interpret and behave within this environment.

Steps in CBT

The first step in CBT is *functional analysis*, which involves identifying ineffectual thoughts and behaviours. It is important to understand how these thoughts, feelings and situations can play a role in unproductive behaviours, e.g. 'I really don't think that I am very good,' 'I am probably at my peak,' 'I don't think I could ever be better'. The process entails introspection leading to insight.

The second step is examining the *actual behaviours*, which contribute to the problem. For example, if you are suffering from low self-esteem you might experience negative thoughts about your own abilities. As a result of a negative thinking pattern, you might skip training sessions or even use injury/illness as an excuse to avoid an upcoming competition. This will reinforce the thoughts that you are not so proficient and your skill deteriorates, thereby compounding the faulty thought process/situation even more.

There are a number of different approaches to CBT that are regularly used by mental health professionals. One such approach is Rational Emotive Behaviour Therapy, which uses an action-oriented approach to managing cognitive, emotional and behavioural disturbances. This is the technique used in the reflective exercise ABCD in Chapter 5 (see page 43). One of the advantages of CBT is that it is well researched because the approach is extremely focused on specific objectives, meaning that results are easily measurable. One hurdle for some is that it does require you to be introspective. You need to be able to examine your thoughts and feelings in order to learn more about your behaviour. In addition, recognizing negative patterns is not enough to make unproductive thoughts disappear. Strategies have to be put in place and practised. This may involve keeping a thought record, in which you record what you are thinking and feeling, rating your beliefs, monitoring an action plan, role-playing and implementing relaxation techniques.

Questions to consider

1. What kind of questions can help you or those you work with to become more aware of their thoughts and beliefs? For example, 'What do you mean when you say ... ?', 'What does this "thought" say about you ... ?'
2. Which of the NLP presuppositions would you rank as the most important and why?
3. Can the 'what if' way of thinking ever help in sport?

REFLECTIVE PRACTICE: CBT WORKSHEET; ANCHORING (NLP)
CBT WORKSHEET

Think of a sporting situation that causes a specific mood, which leads you to certain thoughts:

- situation – playing against the current club, county or national champion(s)
- moods – sad, depressed, apathetic
- thoughts – 'I am useless so I should give up', 'I am not very good at this' or 'Why do I even bother trying?'

Now answer the following three questions. Ask yourself as many times as you need until you get to your core belief and the assumptions that you are making about yourself. What does your answer say about you?

1. I am frightened by others whom I perceive to be more competent than me.

   What does this say about me?

   ⇩

2. I am not confident that I am good enough.

What does this say about me?

⇩

3. I am afraid of challenging myself so I give up.

What does this say about me?

⇩

Now, try some more positive thoughts. What evidence do you have that these beliefs are 100 per cent true? Be positive, say: 'I have played people at all levels, for example...', 'I do enjoy a challenge such as ...', 'I have won games against top competitors, such as ...'

⇩

'What have I learned from this and what could I do?'

'I could just go out there and give it my all, as you can always learn from playing with a really experienced player. If I tried for every point, rather than focused on feeling like a loser, then I could win a game or even the match.'

CBT – MORE QUESTIONS TO CONSIDER:

1. What do I mean when I say this?
2. Can I say it another way?
3. What does it say about me?
4. Are there any other reasons?
5. Why do I jump to this conclusion?
6. Are there other ways of looking at it?
7. Do I benefit from thinking about it this way?
8. How does this belief affect my life?
9. How would I benefit if I changed this belief?
10. What would I or the world look like if I changed my belief?

ANCHORING (NLP)

An anchor is something physical that you associate with a chosen state. The purpose of the anchor is to help you instigate an emotional state whenever you need it. It can be whatever you want and is usually not obvious to any onlooker. This is something that you can use in any situation to help you with confidence and motivation. It is a stimulus, which causes a response. It enables you to take control of your own emotions and state, e.g. builds your confidence, relaxes you and raises your energy levels.

- Start with a breathing exercise, e.g. count of four breaths in and then two breaths slowly out (there are more extensive breathing guidelines in Chapter 10 on Stress Management).
- Visualization: Recall a time when you were really in a state of complete confidence. Imagine yourself back in that situation – surround yourself with thoughts of it. How did it feel? What do you see/hear/smell?

Let's go over the anchoring procedure:

1. *Decide on which emotional state you would like to improve*, e.g. confidence.

2. *Choose an experience that represents an ideal state for you*, e.g. winning a particular competition really boosted your confidence level.

3. *Choose an anchor*, e.g. squeezing your fingers together, turning your racket around, tapping the ground with your bat, placing a tee in the ground before you tee off, etc.

4. Now, let's put it all together:
   - activate your anchor
   - visualise your state
   - as you near the peak of the experience, release, stop or free your anchor
   - now stop or clear your head
   - practise over and over again until you are able to control and to recreate the desired state by instigating your anchor

Further Reading

Greenberger, D. and Padesky, C. (2015). *Mind Over Mood: Change how you feel by changing the way you think*. (2nd ed.) New York, NY: Guilford Press.

Lazarus, J. (2014). *Ahead of the Game: How to use your mind to win in sport*. Penrith, Devon: Ecademy Press.

PART 4
STRESS, HEALTH AND INJURY

Baseball icon Yogi Berra

9 AROUSAL AND ANXIETY

'*I'm happy with nerves… going into matches being nervous is good… adrenaline gets your mind focused on the match.*'
Andy Murray (tennis player: Olympic Gold medallist 2012; US Open Champion 2012; Wimbledon Champion 2013)

'*You need some level of pre-race nerves to get the adrenaline going but it is crucial to keep it under control.*'
Christine Ohuruogu (Olympic, World and Commonwealth 400 metres Champion)

Objectives

1. Distinguishing between anxiety and arousal
2. Describing several key theories
3. Types of anxiety

An extensive amount of research has focused on the relationship between arousal, anxiety and performance. This is because in sport, competition can elevate arousal and anxiety and have an impact on performance. We vary in how much arousal/anxiety we need for our sport and how much we can tolerate. Therefore it is important to develop an appreciation of how you can manage it. This chapter is a theoretical underpinning to this topic; however, it is very important to understand these theories and models prior to the application. The reflective exercises at the end are very applied and firmly based on the discussion.

Although a great deal of sport psychology research has used the two words interchangeably, there are significant differences between anxiety and arousal, though there is some overlapping within their meanings. Arousal is a bodily energy that prepares you for action. As a general state of alertness it ranges from being asleep to being extremely excited. These physiological feelings are operated by your sympathetic nervous system, which releases hormones such as adrenaline and noradrenaline (aka epinephrine and norepinephrine) into the bloodstream, which energises you. Arousal is a generalised physiological energy. Anxiety, on the other hand, is a specific type of cognitive and somatic (bodily) experience. It is typified by worry and apprehension, though usually accompanied by physiological tension.

In examining sporting performance, it is evident that athletes differ in the intensity of their arousal and anxiety and in how much they can handle in order to achieve their best performance. Furthermore, the relationship between anxiety and arousal within performance is dependent on the type of task that you are engaged in. In sports (or with specific skills) that require sustained concentration, it is a disadvantage to have a high level of physiological anxiety and arousal, whereas with sports (or with skills) that utilise a complex motor response or a great deal of thought, i.e. information processing, anxiety has less of an effect.

Another important point is that athletes appear to vary in their perception of arousal and anxiety states. Individual interpretation of this experience has been found to make all the difference in relation to preparation, implementation and interpretation of performance. High levels of arousal or anxiety may be interpreted as facilitative or debilitative by players, though there is no commonality as to how much of this state affects performance.

Techniques for controlling physiological response are examined in Chapter 10. Here, we will examine some of the theories surrounding arousal, the anxiety-facilitative relationship and trait–state anxiety.

WHAT THEORETICAL RESEARCH UNDERPINS THE AROUSAL/ANXIETY QUESTION?

There are several key theories that have explored the relationship between arousal, anxiety and performance. These are the Inverted U Theory (Yerkes and Dodson, 1908), the Attentional Control Theory (Eysenck, Derakshan, Sanots and Calvo, 2007), Catastrophe (e.g. Hardy and Parfitt, 1991; Hardy, Beattie and Woodman, 2007), the Conscious Processing or Reinvestment Hypothesis (Masters and Maxwell, 2008) and the IZOF (Hanin, 1995; 2007).

The Inverted U hypothesis (Yerkes and Dodson, 1908)

The premise of this still-popular theory is that optimal performance is achieved with moderate arousal. When arousal is either low or high then performance is poor. A graph illustrating this relationship is therefore curvilinear or in the shape of an inverted U. When you are either under aroused (lethargic or drowsy) or over aroused (elated) it is harder to do your best. Therefore, increased arousal will enhance skilled performance up to a certain point after which further increases in arousal may be detrimental.

On complex tasks, the relationship between performance and arousal does seem consistent with the inverted U theory. In terms of skill level, as the difficulty or complexity of a skill increases, the amount of arousal that is needed in order to achieve your optimal performance decreases. As the level of difficulty reduces, your arousal level increases. On complicated cognitive tasks, however, too little arousal will result in a performance decrease. The best performance occurs when your arousal levels are moderate in intensity and match the task requirements.

The effects of arousal on performance, therefore, may vary depending on the type of tasks required. One of the distinctions made is the difference between *sustained concentration* and *sustained information transfer* (Humphreys and Revelle, 1984). Performance in tasks needing sustained concentration (preparation to respond) decreases as arousal increases. This is due to your inability to process too much with a limited active memory system. However, in some studies, performance in sustained information transfer (being able to manage information so that you can respond effectively when necessary) has actually been shown to improve as arousal increases. Of course, a number of sports require a combination of both effective working memory and sustained information transfer. For example, in tennis you need to respond to the opponent as well as anticipate their play, which is often based on previous experience or knowledge on the circuit (see Hardy, Jones and Gould, 1996).

Some criticisms of the Inverted U theory are that it fails to identify any theoretical mechanisms that could account for the link between arousal and performance. In addition, the theory doesn't address the issue of intensity, which can be facilitative in some athletes. Facilitative and debilitative anxiety interpretation will be discussed after the theories section. (If you are interested in learning more about arousal theory, read Landers and Arent, 2010.)

Attentional Control Theory (ACT)

This theory suggests that not only does cognitive anxiety (or worrying) reduce the available resources of the working memory; it also redirects your attention to irrelevant task-related information. ACT proposes that managing your attention is incumbent on two interactive processes, i.e. a goal-driven system that is influenced by salient information (Wood and Wilson, 2008). For example, when anxious penalty takers displayed an attentional bias towards a salient and threatening stimulus (the goalkeeper) rather than to the ideal target for their kick (just inside the goalpost), they failed to hit the target.

The Individual Zones of Optimal Functioning (IZOF)

This is a descriptive model (not really a theory) linking performance with anxiety (Hanin, 1995, 2007). It identifies that you have your own zone for optimal functioning for both pre-competition and during competition. When your anxiety is outside this zone then your emotions can be detrimental to your performance outcomes. The problem, of course, is that we all vary and if you were to position anxiety on a continuum, i.e. a visual line that extends from high to low, then each one of us would be at a different point on this line. In addition, the amount of anxiety that you can handle in order to achieve your best performance varies.

As it appears evident that emotional states impact on performance, the IZOF was refined to reflect a range of emotions besides anxiety (Hanin, 2007). Emotions were also categorised in relation to performance. Dysfunction-unpleasant emotions result from inadequate performance while facilitative-pleasant emotions emanate from successful performances (Pellizzari, Bertollo and Robazza, 2011). This model doesn't explain why some players perform better than others in particular emotional states.

The Conscious Processing (or reinvestment) Hypothesis (Masters, 1992)

This theory proposes that anxiety impacts on performance by increasing an athlete's consciousness of his/her actions. In Chapter 7 we discussed how being 'in the zone' requires an automaticity that limits consciousness and affords you the luxury of being able not to think about something, e.g. problems at home, a recent row or an ill parent. When athletes shift from automatic to conscious control of movements, they can experience a sensation referred to as 'paralysis by analysis', whereby performance substantially worsens (Masters and Maxwell, 2008). This theory postulates that when anxiety is high, you consciously process information, which requires you to 'reinvest' your cognitive processes into perceptual motor control. For example, in a study on golfers (Masters, Polman and Hammond, 1993), the explicit group learned through coaching manuals while the implicit group were not given any information to consider. Both had to undertake a secondary task. The implicit group (no information) were more likely to be successful because they did not need to consciously process and shift their resources. Those that had to revert to conscious control had more of a decline in performance due to anxiety-provoking or stressful conditions.

Catastrophe Theory

This differs from the previous arousal theories as it proposes a multidimensional construct, comprised of both cognitive anxiety and physiological arousal components (e.g. Hardy and Parfitt, 1991; Hardy et al., 2007). The physiological arousal element interacts with cognitive anxiety to impact on athletic performance. Central to this theory is the idea that arousal affects performance depending on the overall level of cognitive anxiety. For example, when you have a high cognitive anxiety, your arousal-performance pattern follows the inverted U curve up to the moderate point and then may follow a different route due to the increasing levels of arousal.

The theory supports the inverted U theory in suggesting that when athletes are in a low cognitive state anxiety, arousal is associated with athletic performance as illustrated by the inverted U curve. However, if cognitive anxiety is high, and increases beyond the moderate level then a catastrophic decline in performance as opposed to a gradual deterioration may be experienced. Having an elevated level of physiological arousal does not in itself instigate a downfall. These occur from a combination of high physiological arousal and increased cognitive state (situational) anxiety. Although many coaches and players may witness this on the pitch, it is difficult to test out and apply to a real game situation.

WHAT IS THE IDEAL COMBINATION OF AROUSAL/ANXIETY FOR BEST PERFORMANCE?

There is an ideal combination for each individual, though there is no set formula. Various factors can influence this link, for instance, whether it is an open or closed skill. Closed skills are discrete and require movements to be executed in a set way, like a flip in gymnastics or target shooting. High levels of physiological arousal have been found to be detrimental to closed skills and can cause a sudden drop in performance. Unlike closed skills, open skills are dependent on outside factors such as opponents and the weather. They therefore require flexibility in reacting to ever-changing situations. On the whole, if the skill or task requires a lot of information processing or needs complex motor responses, then performance is optimised when combined with lower physiological arousal, such as when a skill or task involves aspects of decision making or intense concentration.

Some sports, however, operate better when there are higher levels of physiological arousal present. For example, in weight lifting or rugby, increased levels of physiological arousal can enhance performance. It is, however, difficult to generalise this relationship between arousal and all strength and endurance sports. There are unique and specific differences between sports with regard to processing information and in the variations to which they require complex motor control.

Finally, once performance has slipped and is heading towards a downward catastrophe, it is difficult to retrieve. This may also be complicated by an additional factor, which is the reduction in effort from a player who sees the futility in being able to return performance to where it was previously.

WHAT ARE THE DIFFERENT TYPES OF ANXIETY?

The theories discussed above demonstrate the type of relationship that may exist between anxiety/arousal and performance as well as the impact that they may have in sport. As you can see, the words anxiety and arousal are often used interchangeably. This section will focus on the different types of anxiety used in research. Being able to distinguish between the terms can provide you with a clearer focus on which application is best to use in the reflective practice section. The following forms of anxiety will now be explained: trait, state, cognitive, somatic, behavioural, facilitative and debilitative.

The two most common forms of anxiety associated with sport are *state anxiety* and *trait anxiety* (Spielberger, 1966). State is a transient and less permanent condition of anxiety related to a situation. Playing sport in a high level elite competition or perhaps against a specific opponent can evoke feelings of worry and apprehension in players. This may be a temporary situation, which can easily change during the course of a match.

Trait is a predisposed personality trait of feeling nervous and apprehensive. It is a relatively stable trait so it is a general disposition to feel anxiety and is induced by situations that are perceived as threatening or anxiety provoking. Regardless of the importance or level of the competition, some athletes experience more state (situation related) anxiety before a match. This might manifest itself as stomach sickness or bowel problems or other forms of nervousness in the changing room prior to a game. Players who exhibit a high trait anxiety are more likely to perceive sporting situations as threatening than those who are less anxious. Some of us are more vulnerable to state anxiety, as we are born with the personality gene or trait anxiety.

As mentioned previously, anxiety can also be multidimensional (Gould, Greenleaf, and Krane, 2002). These include: cognitive (thoughts), somatic (body) and behavioural (action) and whether this is interpreted as facilitative or debilitative.

Cognitive anxiety involves worrying about an upcoming performance or situation. It can continue to affect performance during a game. It often centres on specific themes such as: performance failure, apprehension about negative evaluation by others, concerns about physical injury or danger and unspecified fear of the unknown (Dunn and Syrotuik, 2003).

Somatic anxiety is physical or psycho-physiological (combined psychological and physical). Somatic anxiety can be measured through various physiological markers such as cortisol, the stress hormone. It can be experienced through a variety of bodily functions such as a racing heart, butterflies in the stomach, or shallow breathing.

Behavioural anxiety produces ineffectual muscular movements. Examples of this include tense facial expressions, alterations in communication such as quick speech, agitation and restlessness (Gould, Greenleaf and Krane, 2002). There is limited research into these behavioural changes, mostly due to the lack of objective measures of these movements.

The final point to understand here is that it is not how much arousal/anxiety you have but rather how you interpret it. Somatic anxiety/arousal can either have a *facilitative* (helpful) or *debilitative* (detrimental) affect on performance depending on how it is perceived (Jones and Swain, 1995). If anxiety and apprehension affect you, then the chances are you will be distracted and unfocused. Anxiety and arousal in some athletes may be linked into whether or not they feel they have a sense of control over the situation in relation to how well they are playing.

Let's look at the positives. When you perceive anxiety/arousal as helpful or facilitative, you may, as a result, have a greater sense of confidence in your ability to play your sport. This may mean that you cope better with the arousal that you are experiencing, manage your anxiety better and therefore are more resilient (Thomas, Hanton and Maynard, 2007). In addition, players who believe that they can meet their objectives tend to interpret anxiety as facilitative, as they push to be more involved, produce more effort in their play and tend to persevere. Furthermore, athletes who are low on trait anxiety (predisposition) are more liable to perceive anxiety as facilitative than those who display higher levels of trait anxiety. Finally, in pre-competition, if you see anxiety as facilitative rather than debilitative then you are more likely to be energised before a game. This excitement and motivation is particularly useful for explosive sports such as rugby (more so for rugby league than union) and American football. Elite or professional sports players learn to use arousal as a tool in their success.

In conclusion, anxiety and arousal are distinct in meaning. Arousal is a natural bodily function. The interpretation of these bodily reactions can be facilitative or debilitative. If a player starts to worry about it, then this is negative and is what we classify as anxiety. However, in researching into this area it is important to remember that the terms are often used interchangeably.

You can, however, argue that anxiety and arousal are considered to be multidimensional constructs, which means that they operate on various levels. An elevated amount of somatic anxiety has been shown to impact on performance in complex tasks such as those requiring sustained concentration and decision-making. Arousal/anxiety and muscular tension can interfere with some physical skills or can even lead to an increased susceptibility to injury. But an increase in physiological arousal and anxiety does not mean that this will have to result in a poor performance. It is important to understand how to effectively manage your feelings of arousal and anxiety. This relates to your sport specifically as often there is both a need for energizing and calming down within a game or competition (e.g. decathlon or mixed martial arts).

The key to this area is to have a respect for how you interpret these situations. Perception varies among players, whether at a professional or recreational level. Coaches know that competition is vital to producing best performance because it causes arousal/anxiety; therefore it is essential that players see it as an energy, which can then be directed towards play.

Questions to consider

1. In comparing each of the theories for their strengths and weaknesses, which one do you feel is most useful in understanding anxiety/arousal?
2. Do you need anxiety in sport?

REFLECTIVE PRACTICE: ANXIETY ANTECEDENTS; COPING STRATEGIES; VERBAL NARRATIVE

ANXIETY ANTECEDENTS

The catalyst for anxiety can be identified through the points listed below. Do you share these anxieties in common with other athletes? Are there any additional issues that you can add to this list that would help you to better understand your performance anxiety?

Do you have a need to be perfect?
Setting very high standards for performance can interfere with success by increasing anxiety and decreasing accuracy. This could be due to parenting styles in childhood or the way you are coached. Due to the nature of sport, achievement is valued. However, some parents/coaches value achievement so much that they are highly critical of everything. By continually emphasising high standards they place an importance on what is lacking. Rather than positive reinforcement for the good skills they end up giving conditional approval based on perfection. Remember, no-one is perfect.

Is being anxious generally a part of you?
Having trait anxiety naturally predisposes you to experience more state anxiety in a perceived 'threatening' situation, like a competition. This can be managed, but recognise that high anxiety situations affect you even more than others.

Do you worry that the game is too important?
Perceived importance can make you anxious, so concentrate on the match. Otherwise you are diverting your attention to thinking about the outcomes instead of focusing on your game.

Do you worry that you will not succeed?
This is linked in with how you value and see yourself. Remember you are a good person and do have value that will help raise your self-esteem and self-worth. Do you believe in yourself? Those who lack confidence are more likely to have higher levels of anxiety.

How do you account for or attribute your successes and losses?
Do you see it as all down to others and to luck? If so, you are less likely to put in a lot of effort, as much of what you do is beyond your control. You are also more likely to be more anxious.

COPING STRATEGIES

Coping is about managing stress or anxiety. Research has traditionally examined coping strategies as emotion focused and problem focused (Lazarus and

Folkman, 1984). But there are many other types of coping strategies, such as social focus and avoidance focus (Chesney, Neilands, Chambers, Taylor and Folkman, 2006; Nicholls, Polman and Levy, 2010). In sport, problem focusing is quite prevalent, as it is based on the interpretation of your sense of control. Emotion control focuses on managing your emotions. A lot of elite teams use both problem and emotional focused coping strategies, but we will also discuss avoidance and appraisal.

Emotion-focused coping
This is managing emotion by interpreting the source of your anxiety. As previously mentioned, stress can be re-interpreted so that you flip your emotions to be more positive and see the stressors as a challenge – facilitative as opposed to threatening. In addition, you could also use appraisal focus as a way to interpret a situation more rationally. After losing a hole or shot you remind yourself that you'll get it next time, perhaps with a little less spin, which will help you keep your feelings in perspective. Using avoidance could mean that you either withdraw from an emotional arousing situation, e.g. bad tempers and a potential fight on the pitch, or minimize the importance of an inaccurate refereeing call. By avoiding, you are preventing yourself from escalating your anger. People with low self-esteem typically use emotion-focused coping strategies. Emotional focus can engage various techniques such as relaxation, meditation, exercise and emotional social support from other people.

Problem-focused coping
This is managing and mastering the problem in realistic ways. It is a productive method enabling you to take control of a situation. In general, problem-focused coping is about getting to the root of the problem and then eliminating the source. It can therefore provide a long-term solution. However, problem focusing will not work where it is beyond the individual or coach's control to remove or fix the source of stress. It works best when the person can control the source of stress (e.g. learn a new tactical skill, a more efficient engine, learn to kick more effectively with the left foot). Problem-focusing can include concrete techniques, such as goal setting, additional training and time management.

Social coping
This focuses on utilizing a network of people who can help relieve the pressure of an anxiety-evoking situation. Social support can include emotional support and information support. It could mean that someone is helping get you to practice or to the clinic or help to arrange sponsorship. All this is tangible support. It includes the help of your family and friends who are a great source of support, as they can provide you with the boost you may need in your self-esteem (Bianco and Eklund, 2001; Chesney et al., 2006; Freeman, Coffee and Rees, 2011; Rees and Hardy, 2004).

WHAT ARE THE KEY AREAS THAT CAN HELP IN THESE COPING STRATEGIES?

- Taking control – this is readjusting the relationship between yourself and the cause of the problem. Examples: If the stress is somatic (or bodily) then begin with breathing exercises or muscular relaxation techniques. If it is a technical problem then work on goal setting for the new skill and have a well-planned practice schedule.
- Information seeking – this is a rational approach, which empowers you to understand the situation and what can be done about it. With the advent of the internet it is really easy to find out everything you need to know in order to identify cognitive strategies to help improve your thought patterns. Information seeking is a cognitive response. Try out and practise different exercises and techniques in this book and from other sport psychology resources.

VERBAL NARRATIVE

Your coach's sayings can increase or decrease your anxiety.

SAYINGS THAT INCREASE ANXIETY:

- 'You must win (at all costs)'
- 'You're playing like a bunch of losers. The other team is so much better'
- 'Don't bend your knees when you kick'
- 'Don't give the ball away like that'
- 'What will everyone say when you lose? Everyone is counting on you'
- 'Remember your family and friends are watching'; 'Your country is watching'
- 'The referee/linesman is useless'
- 'Run round the pitch three times – that'll teach you a lesson'

SAYINGS THAT DECREASE ANXIETY:

- 'Let's practise this again so you are ready for the next game'
- 'Let's invite the parents in to watch you do your routine'
- 'This is a bit harder than normal, but I know you can do it'
- 'It's OK, we all make mistakes'
- 'It's OK to be nervous, we're all a bit nervous. Nerves will help you play better'
- 'Right, go out there and do your best, but above all enjoy yourselves'

As a coach it is essential that you accent the positive, keep errors in perspective, promote task familiarity, build self-confidence with realistic expectations, acknowledge that some players might be stressed and help them to use that stress in a positive way. Remember that some players need energizing while others need to relax.

KEYS WITH CHILDREN

- Ask them how they feel – acknowledge that feeling nervous is normal.
- Ask them how much time and effort they have put in, so that they can learn that there is a relationship between effort and performance.
- Ask them if any part of the event is worrying them. Ask them how they plan to cope with this and/or suggest ways they can cope.
- Confirm that you will always be there to support them.

Further Reading

Lazarus, R. S. and Folkman, S. (1984). *Stress, Appraisal and Coping*. New York, NY: Springer Publishing Company.

Nideffer, R. M. and Sagal, M. S. (2001). *Assessment in Sport Psychology*. Morgantown, MW: Fitness Information Technology.

Pargman, D. (2013). *Managing Performance Stress: Models and Method*. London: Routledge.

10 STRESS MANAGEMENT

'I have learned over the years that if you start thinking about the race, it stresses you out a little bit. I just try to relax and think about video games, what I'm gonna do after the race, what I'm gonna do to just chill. Stuff like that to relax a little before a race.'

Usain Bolt (six-times Olympic Champion and world record holder at 100- and 200-metres)

'A lot of emotional stress that people go through, some people figure out a way to handle it. They have a strong enough support system to keep going and keep moving. And some people, they feel they don't have that outlet.'

Terrell Owens (National Football League, wide receiver)

Objectives

1. The difference in terminology between stress, arousal and anxiety
2. Stress as environmental and perceptual
3. The use of stress in competition

Stress is often confused with anxiety, though stress is a much wider concept. Lazarus and Folkman (1984) saw stress as a specific relationship between you and your environment. It occurs when you encounter something that you feel is threatening to your well-being. Stress is when you perceive that the environmental demands on you exceed your ability to cope. You are in a state of flux as you consider whether your resources are enough to handle the situation or whether you are in danger. There are two key parts to this definition. Firstly, it emanates from the environment. Secondly, it is appraised or interpreted. The good news is that *you can manage your perception* and that there is always more than one way to consider the stressors (things that stress you) that come your way from any environment or situation.

Arousal is a response to a real threat. It is a bodily energy that prepares you for action through the sympathetic nervous system. It is also known as 'fight or flight'. If, in the middle of the night, you hear a loud and unusual noise, your body is put on alert. If you think that someone has invaded your territory, you prepare to fight or to leave the house quickly. If you can rationalise that it was just the neighbour's car door, then you can relax and return to sleep.

Anxiety is a negative emotional feeling of worry and apprehension, as well as body tension due to a perceived threat. Anxiety can also be a personality trait (trait anxiety). You are born with it and might have a tendency to get more nervous than other people in the same situation. Anxiety is also a transient mood state (state anxiety), so it changes depending on the situation. You may feel more anxious speaking in an interview for a job than speaking on the television where millions of people are listening to your words. A highly competitive situation may make you more anxious. Environmental demands may be based around your sport, though they could be personal or even logistical. You need to understand that focusing on the environment and all the excitement of a competition around you can contribute to this stress.

Competition can be perceived as threatening as well as challenging. For example, you may perceive a match as threatening because defeat will mean that your team doesn't progress in a competition. In doing so you are responding to the stress by worrying about the outcome instead of concentrating on the game. Alternatively, you could be worried about the importance of the game as a future threat and worry that your performance won't be good enough to make the first team or the Olympic squad. This type of appraisal also means that you are not putting your energies into the moment, as you are thinking about the future. Generally, emotions such as worry and anxiety are associated with this type of appraisal and will typically result in feelings of anger and sadness. Alternatively, your appraisal of the situation, though stressful, could be that you perceive it as a challenge, which may even provide you with opportunities. This would enhance your mood, increase your confidence, increase your excitement and improve your focus.

CAN STRESS BE GOOD FOR YOU IN SPORT?

Some psychologists believe that stress is a positive energy, which is required not only as an important life-skill but also as an essential skill in order to be a top player (Loehr, 1995). Without it, you cannot progress from amateur to elite. You have to be able to cope with a moderate amount of stress or arousal to improve your ability to deal with it. This means learning to experience stressful situations, yet continuing to concentrate on things that are relevant without being distracted.

Loehr points out that being stressed needs to be balanced with a recovery period. Recovery is about having a break and switching off so that you become re-energised by being distracted away from the intensity of the stressful experience. This is called oscillation. It is a planned way of training so that you can extend your chance of being able to endure pressure during competition, especially if you compete at high levels. For example, during the break after every two games at a tennis tournament, the players sit down, have a drink, wipe off the sweat (even if there isn't any) and switch off momentarily. Weightlifters (for physical reasons as well) may walk around the gym and go and have a chat or a drink at the water fountain. Mental stress may involve intense concentration, while mental recovery would be clearing your mind and thinking of something else, maybe reading a good book or listening to your favourite band. Emotional stress could be worry or sadness, while emotional recovery would take place during a break when you think of something enjoyable, such as a holiday. The point is that stress is a part of sport, as well as life, and it needs to be managed through the use of high and low periods.

In conclusion, there is a general consensus that stress occurs when you perceive something in the environment as 'threatening' and something that you are unable to cope with. Continuous stress can lead to physical and psychological problems and even burnout. However, stress is controllable by learning to recognise how you interpret events and by developing recovery and/or coping tactics. Being able to handle stress is a necessary skill in sport, particularly if you compete in high-level competitions.

Questions to consider

1. Which comes first, your body or your mind?

   Are you frightened because your body reacts to something fearful, do the symptoms of a racing heart cause you to be afraid?

   OR

   Are you frightened because you see or interpret something as fearful and this sets your heart racing and causes you to be afraid?

2. What is your trigger for fight or flight? Is it seeing the competition as too difficult, knowing that you will have to speak in front of a large group, others watching your performance ... ?

   • Do you meet things head-on in particular situations?
   • Do you run away when the pressure (fear) kicks in?

REFLECTIVE PRACTICE: BREATHING TECHNIQUES; STRESS INOCULATION TRAINING

BREATHING TECHNIQUES

Athletes from all sports can benefit from learning breathing techniques. A useful technique, and usually the first one I recommend, is stomach breathing. This involves the diaphragm muscle, a strong dome-shaped muscle located under your ribs and above your stomach. When you breathe in, you push this muscle down, activating your stomach to move forward. When you breathe out, the diaphragmatic muscle returns to its resting position and your stomach draws back in. There is limited, if any, upper chest movement.

To develop a good breathing technique, begin by taking long, slow and deep breaths. Place your hand on your stomach so you can feel your lungs expand and compress. Make sure you are inhaling through your nose. Try holding your breath for 4 seconds and then exhaling slowly (do not blow out the air) through your mouth for 2 seconds.

Practise the following:

- stand or sit comfortably; relax your neck, arms, shoulders and jaw
- focus on the movement of your abdominal muscles
- take a deep breath through your nose and feel the expansion of the lower part of your lungs
- hold your breath and count to 4
- exhale slowly through your mouth to a count of 2
- repeat the deep breaths 2–3 times
- practise this often and in a variety of places

STRESS INOCULATION TRAINING

The following exercise is based on Stress Inoculation Training (SIT). The objective is for you to learn to perform in a stressful situation. It is inevitable that you will experience stress in a competitive situation at some point. You may perceive it as threatening and consider an avoidance strategy. However, this is a way of accepting it and working with it. You can adapt and add your own techniques into this as well.

SIT is a training method under which you simulate stress so that the ability to manage it can later be transferred into a real sporting situation. Simulated stress can be induced in a virtual or experiential way. You may be able to catch your stress level as it elevates. However, you also need to be able to switch it off at any level you experience. This structure is a cognitive behavioural approach, divided into three stages, designed to bring about positive thinking and successful behavioural change (Meichenbaum, 1997). First, the conceptualization phase – recognizing the effect that stress has on you and knowing what it feels like. Second, the skills acquisition stage requires adding in a coping mechanism, such as deep breathing to relax, or self-talk to control negative thinking. Third is the phase of reflective practice and follow-through. Taking the skill into the field with you and applying it in a real situation.

1. Start by watching a video clip of one of your performances where you experienced a lot of stress. Alternatively, visualise a highly stressful situation.
2. The key is to be able to monitor the feeling of reaching a high state of arousal. Allow yourself time to experience this several times. Each time, switch off once you feel you have peaked and take a break. Distract yourself by doing something else momentarily and start again.

3. Let's add in a coping strategy now. Start with the breathing technique above and then add some self-talk (affirmation of statements) strategy.

4. Now begin again and take your stress level to pre-maximum; this could, for instance, be about 75 per cent. Then switch off and think of a distraction and begin your breathing or positive statements.

5. Once you have mastered this, for example at the 75 per cent level, practise taking your stress levels down to 50 per cent and then down to 30 per cent and even lower if possible. Each time practise how to stop and switch to a coping technique.

Further Reading

Rumbold, J., Fletcher, D. and Daniels, K. (2012). 'A systematic review of stress management interventions with sport performers'. *Sport, Exercise and Performance Psychology*, 1 (3), 173–193.

Seward, B. (2011). *Managing Stress: Principles and strategies for health and well-being.* Burlington, MA: Jones & Bartlett Learning.

11 STRESS AND INJURIES

'I didn't let anything in from the past, I wasn't scared, I was just excited to be back. I just don't think of "What ifs", I just get on with things.'

Lindsey Vonn (World Champion alpine skier;
Olympic Gold Medallist 2010)

'I go out and do the best I can in each game, and I don't think about the fouls other players will commit or whether I might be injured. It only does you harm to worry about those things.'

Lionel Messi (Footballer with FC Barcelona and Argentina;
regarded by many as the best player in the world)

'Some skiers do give up. I have found the length of their career is part of an odds game – the longer they compete or engage in the sport, the greater the chance of something serious happening.'

Dr Rhonda Cohen (Sport and Exercise Psychologist)

Objectives

1. Components of the cognitive appraisal model: personality, experience, coping and appraisal model

2. Understanding the emotional grief model

Psychology can be used to predict the likelihood of a sporting injury. This is important because sport has a higher incidence of injury than any other occupation; it is unavoidable that people who participate in sport will run the risk of frequent and regular injury. The evidence for this relationship is based on an extensive amount of research, of which 85 per cent of studies were in agreement. This research consistently demonstrates that athletes with higher stress levels are approximately 2–5 times more at risk of becoming injured than athletes with lower stress levels (Williams and Andersen, 2007). According to medical professionals working in sport, injury rates for elite athletes can peak at 50 per cent, meaning that at any given time 50 per cent of players in some sports may have some sort of injury (Brewer, 2009). The English Football Association (FA) audit of injuries in the professional leagues identified that 10 per cent of players are unable to train at any given time (Woods, Hawkins, Hulse and Hodson, 2002).

CAN PSYCHOLOGY BE USED TO PREDICT A SPORTING INJURY?

There are several classic and still prominent models illustrating the relationship between stress and injuries, such as Andersen and Williams (1988), William and Andersen (1998) and Wiese-Bjornstal, Smith, Shaffer and Morrey (1998). These models are consistent with the cognitive relational theory of stress. That is that problem and emotional focus coping strategies can address stress that is environmental and appraised as a demand that exceeds the ability or resources of the person to cope. Stressors can be seen as beneficial (could be a useful opportunity), challenging (could be an exciting achievement), threatening (could happen) or loss (if it has already happened) (Lazarus and Folkman, 1984). Key elements within these models show how the influence of psychosocial stressors – such as personality, history, coping techniques and life events – affect individuals differently. If stressors are not managed then you run a greater risk of injury or illness (Brink, 2010). In addition, as perception is an important factor, the way you think can increase your physiological anxiety causing muscular tension, which also leads to a reduced focus on what is important. However, the good news is that you can examine how altering cognitive patterns can reduce this susceptibility.

COMPONENTS OF THE COGNITIVE APPRAISAL MODEL

Your arousal levels are increased when you are faced with a stressful situation. As your body becomes aroused, you begin to assess the situation. You can perceive the occurrence as either facilitative (helps you) or debilitative (doesn't help you). The way you see it is based on your *personality*, *previous experience*, and *coping strategies*. Your *cognitive appraisal* of a situation, as either challenging or threatening, influences your stress and this makes you more or less susceptible to injury.

Personality

You are born with a genetic predisposition, which influences your behaviour. Specific traits, such as anxiety, sensation seeking, neuroticism and self-esteem can influence your stress levels. The reason for this is that certain traits make up the essence of who you are and this personality core is relatively 'unchangeable'. For example, you may have been born as someone who is naturally anxious and therefore measures higher in tests of trait anxiety. Though there are coping mechanisms for dealing with this, your anxiety can be exacerbated when you are confronted with a stressful situation. This could be a game, for instance, against a particular rival. Fortunately, not all of personality is fixed within your genetic pattern. You demonstrate behaviour in a typical way as a result of specific situations. For example, maybe you experience more anxiety in a highly competitive situation or when playing at home in front of your friends and family. This is a state anxiety, as it is based on the situation. It is important to distinguish between trait and state so that the reasons for your stress can be addressed and your overall stress levels can be reduced, making you less prone to injury.

Professional hockey players who tested high on sensation seeking, demonstrated a higher incidence of injuries during the season, though this is not unusual among higher risk takers in this fast and often aggressive sport (Osborn, Blanton and Schwebel, 2009). Rugby players who measured high in neuroticism and low in self-esteem, believed that they were more prone to injury (Deroche, Stephan, Brewer and Le Scanff, 2007). As you might guess, the lower your self-esteem, the more likely you are to feel stressed (Kolt and Roberts, 1998). At the start of a season, athletes possessing lower self-esteem as well as lower mood states were more likely to be stressed and injured by the end of the season (Williams, Hogan, and Andersen, 1993).

Another aspect of personality pertains to how able you are to feel in control of your environment (Pargman and Lunt, 1989). This concept is called *Locus of Control* (LOC) and recognizing this in yourself can reveal how empowered you feel. There are two types of LOC. Internal LOC means that you recognise that a sporting situation is within your power and that any success in it would be due to your effort and ability. An external LOC means that the situation is out of your control, perhaps because you feel your performance is related to luck or the difficulty of the task.

Previous Experience

Previous experience, such as losing in an important or highly publicised event that you expected to win, can impact on your future stress levels and increase the risk of injury. Evidence for this is supported in a review of over 40 studies (Williams and Andersen, 2007). It is fairly palpable that these types of major life events can impact on you. High levels of stress were a significant predictor for new injuries in female footballers (Steffen, Pensgaard and Bahr, 2008). However, minor stressors, e.g. having the game delayed, can also increase stress in an athlete (Fawkner, McMurray and Summer, 1999).

A study examining the history of injury in 470 rugby players found previous injury to be an important contributory factor (Maddison and Prapavessis, 2005) and made them feel more susceptible to further injury (Stephan, Deroche, Brewer, Caudroit and Le Scanff, 2009). In an eight-month study following the progress of adolescent female footballers, it was found that a previous history of injury increased the likelihood of a new injury to the same part of the body (Steffen, Pensgaard and Bahr, 2008).

A typical consultation for a psychologist includes a discussion on recovering from injury and concerns about re-injury. The perceived risk needs to be explored versus a real perceived threat. You can be intensely worried about the possible damage of playing with a previous injury and can be concerned over whether this injury could contribute to the end of your sports career. You may begin the season or enter an event after injury hesitantly with an elevated level of stress, which is liable to increase the likelihood of future injuries. Past injuries may represent a weakness or vulnerability for you. If you have this type of reservation, you are potentially more susceptible to re-injury (Petrie and Falkstein, 1998).

Coping strategies

Coping is how you respond to and deal with a situation based on what you think, feel and how you behave. There are three categories of coping resources: general coping behaviours, psychological coping skills and interpersonal coping (Chesney et al., 2006; Nicholls, Polman and Levy, 2010). *General coping* pertains to sleeping, eating and leisure-time patterns. *Psychological coping* relates to managing physiological arousal. *Interpersonal coping* consists of social support. You use a range of coping techniques in sport. Often the coping method you choose can be used to predict your risk of injury. By understanding which coping strategies you employ, you can better understand the relationship between coping strategies and sports injury (Williams, Tonymon and Wadsworth, 1986). Understanding this relationship can also help you to estimate how many and how severe the injuries may be in the upcoming season (Hanson, McCullagh, Tonymon, 1992).

Positive *psychological coping* strategies are negatively correlated with injuries (Noh, Morris and Andersen, 2005). Coping strategies can be problem focused, e.g. looking at alternative travel arrangements for getting to training on time so that you are less stressed during practice. They can be emotion focused, e.g. addressing the emotional impact rather than panicking, crying or getting angry. This is beneficial for dealing with persistent long-term emotional problems. An intervention programme focused on stress management could reduce injury if you are quite emotionally focused (Maddison and Prapvessis, 2005). The strategy can, of course, also be one of avoidance coping, which is associated with greater levels of negative moods (Gallagher and Gardner, 2007). Avoidance means escaping from a problem or difficult situation by not entering yourself into demanding competitions, only attending sporadic practice sessions or turning to drugs. Problem coping is often the most productive way of dealing with stress and thus avoiding injury. However, in order to problem focus there has to be tangible solutions for resolving the issues.

Interpersonal coping or social support can act as a barrier to protect you from aspects of stress. If you have inadequate coping skills and also limited social support then you will have an increased risk of injury (Johnson, 2007; Smith, Smoll and Ptacek, 1990; Hardy, Richman and Rosenfeld, 1991). Those with higher levels of social support had fewer injuries, regardless of life event stress (Yang, Peek-Asa, Lowe, Heiden and Foster, 2010). Therefore social support facilitates the management of stress, and you would be recommended to seek support, especially if not included in the team during injury.

We will now explore 'response', which is the central stress component of the model, comprising cognitive appraisal as well as physiological and attentional changes.

Cognitive Appraisal

Cognitive appraisal refers to the way you interpret a situation. It is a vital element in the stress-injury model. The way you perceive a situation can be facilitative (helpful) or debilitative (unhelpful) and impact on your stress levels.

If you are under stress, either real or perceived, then this impacts on physiological activation. Muscle tension is increased and this elevates the risk of injury. Cognitive appraisal also affects attention, as when you are stressed you tend to narrow or distort your focus. This distortion or narrowing can increase the likelihood of injury (Rogers and Lauders, 2005), as you may not be in tune with everything that is going on in your sporting situation (Andersen and Williams, 1988).

Emotions are also important in the stress-injury model. Five dimensions of mood (anger, confusion, fatigue, tension, depression) were examined through the Brunel mood scale and perceived stress scale in 845 athletes. The results indicated that mood was significantly related to orthopaedic injury (Galambos, Terry, Moyle, Locke and Lane, 2005) and that psychological measures of mood could predict injury though physiological indicators.

The cognitive stress appraisal model is helpful in delineating how the relationship between psychological factors and injury works. This model purports that the stress process is an interaction of biological, psychological and social factors. After injury, stress continues.

WHAT IS THE EMOTIONAL EXPERIENCE OF GRIEF FOLLOWING A SPORTING INJURY?

The emotional grief model

Grief is an emotional response to loss, predominantly associated with death. The emotional grief model developed by Kübler-Ross (1969) is often cited in sport for the way it parallels the loss experienced by athletes due to injury. It is seen as one of the most influential models in understanding athletes' reactions to injury (Brewer, 2001). This stage process follows the pattern of grief so many of us experience when someone close to us dies. Initially, when you hear the news of a death, there is a sense of *denial* where it is hard to believe. Next come *anger* and *depression*. Anger can also be directed at the person who died for leaving you behind, or even at the medical staff that treated them for not keeping them alive. Depression is sadness, but it is also an anger turned inwards. This means that it is a state of despair.

These stages of grief are similar for individuals who are terminally ill. On hearing the diagnosis there is a sense of a denial, anger and depression, during which the person wonders, 'why me'. There follows a bargaining stage, a negotiation or exchange for help – i.e. if you are allowed to get better or live then you will do something in exchange. This can be with medical staff, family or even a spiritual deity. Finally, there is the stage of acceptance.

What do you experience after an injury, according to the grief model? You can feel a sense of shock, denial, an unrealistic expectation of recovery, depression and stress. Heil (1993), in his affective cycle, said that athletes show signs of distress, denial and determined coping following injury. Tracey (2003) identified emotions, such as loss, lower self-esteem, frustration and anger not only as an outcome of injury but also as emotions that continue to be present during recovery.

Grief is obviously more likely when injuries are serious and potentially permanent. Loss as a result of injury may be perceived or real. Losing the ability to play competitive sport at that level ever again is usually a great loss to any athlete. Injury can also create a sense of loss of self. In other words, they may not really know who they are without sport and the camaraderie of their teammates. For example, you may hear them say things like, 'I am no one without my sport'. People working with athletes should encourage them to stay in touch with their team and the coach, as well as to use recovery time to explore other avenues. For example, the time of injury is a great time to strengthen one's mental skills, such as the effectiveness of goal setting, imagery and relaxation, for example.

A player's sense of loss when injured is associated with various factors, which range from a loss of identity, limited contact with teammates, less attention from the coach, reduced training and playing opportunity, change in status, reduced mobility, change in independence, reduced media attention as well as the possible end of a career. Though the stages within the theory are difficult to study scientifically (Brewer, 2009), this is still one of the most widely recognised theories of grief.

The grief stages in sport

It is likely that your thoughts following injury will probably follow a predictable pattern:

1. Denial
At first it is often difficult to accept that you have been injured. You may suddenly find that you are on the bench or back in the changing room. Phrases such as, 'Why me?' or 'I can't believe that this has happened' or 'this injury is nothing – I'll be fine' are quite typical. A sense of loss in terms of your identity as an active player can occur. Those working with you can assist by reiterating what has happened and slowly the reality of the situation will sink in.

2. Anger
You may become angry at yourself or with others. You may blame others for being at fault, e.g. 'The coach should not have allowed me to carry on with an injury.' Or you may suggest it is the physiotherapist's fault for not ensuring that a prior injury had healed to optimal recovery. You may be angry at missing playing time.

The most effective way for you to manage this anger is to defuse the situation by staying calm. You should never respond to anger with anger. You need to accept that you may need some time to express your feelings and that this is normal. It may help to remind athletes of previous times when they felt angry due to injury or illness and discuss how they got through it then. Try and suggest emotional controls they could use to get through it this time.

3. Depression
Depression is a sense of hopelessness, despair and sadness. You may say things such as, 'This is a pathetic situation,' and 'I will never be as fit again as I was previously,' or 'all my opportunities for success are gone.' You may not feel like attending recovery or training sessions. You may see your career as at an end. When you feel despair you need to be encouraged to take a more positive focus. For example, what will you do when you finish your recovery period? How will you celebrate your return to sporting activity? Can you envisage a time when you felt really happy in your sport? Goal setting with close monitoring, imagery techniques, relaxation and NLP techniques such as anchoring may be useful.

4. Bargaining
This is a stage where negotiation takes place. It may be between you, as the injured player, and your sport physiotherapist. It may be between you and your coach. It may be between you and 'something' spiritual. Standard comments might be, 'If I work every day on my rehabilitation, will it make me stronger than I was before?', 'Will my rehabilitation make you put me in the first team?', 'If I recover from this, I promise to be a better person and get involved with team activities in the community.'

5. Acceptance
The last stage is the appearance of acceptance. This includes statements such as, 'I am going to work out regularly and adhere to the recovery schedule.' It is essential that your 'important others', such as coach, psychologist, parent or team member, are supportive of you during the rehabilitative process. Remember the importance of interpersonal coping.

In summary, emotional reactions can vary both during and after injury. You may progress through all or some of these emotions, and not necessarily in the same sequence. You may not even experience any of these emotions. Injury may even benefit you by providing an opportunity to improve your mental skills and enhance your training (Urdy, 1999). The impact of emotional, behavioural and cognitive responses to injury and recovery from injury is complex (Walker, Thatcher and Lavallee, 2007). Carson and Polman (2008) propose that research is carried out in this area though it is often solely focused on professional athletes rehabilitating from severe injuries. They have designed a holistic module, which includes shock, depression, relief, encouragement and confidence development based on their work with anterior cruciate ligament (ACL) patients.

There is more research literature on the cognitive appraisal models than on the grief stage theory, though both have their admirers and critics. The importance of the models is how they capture the essence of how you or others differ in psychological response to being injured. This is useful to all those dealing with players as a way to assess possible likelihood for pre-injury and then how best to deal with players post-injury.

The grief model is centred on cognitive (conscious and unconscious) processes following injury. It is, however, limited to several key cognitive thoughts (e.g. anger and depression). The Cognitive Appraisal model purports that risk of injury is based on an interaction of biological factors, psychological and social factors, though cognitive appraisal is key. This model takes into account individual variations in reacting to injury (e.g. previous experience, personality). The grief model is 'somewhat' linear (e.g. bargaining happens after denial and acceptance comes at the end), so it is more restricting in identifying an order in which you as an athlete will experience certain emotions.

Scientifically, the grief model uses the word 'grief' in death as synonymous to 'loss' in sport, which is vague and probably inaccurate. Can grief in death and loss in sport be tested as interchangeable concepts? In addition, in the grief theory it is difficult to test all the variables, i.e. denial and bargaining. In the Cognitive Appraisal theory, it is difficult to test out how someone appraises a situation, though personality measures and qualitative measures based on one's experience can be utilised.

Both models are useful in examining the importance of emotional reactions on the propensity for, and the recovery from, injury. There are additional criticisms (e.g. Williams, 2001) that the Cognitive Appraisal Theory only illustrates an acute reaction to injury and does not address long-term chronic conditions. In addition it does not explain how emotions will impact on recovery. Finally, the lack of clarity of the mechanism by which psychological factors affect an athlete's development is also raised as an issue (Gallucci, 2014; Brewer, Andersen and Van Raalte, 2002).

The future, based on my own research and in agreement with others (Gallucci, 2014 and Williams, 2012), is that sport psychology studies need to be more scientifically robust in examining specific variables in sport, such as gender differences, level of performance (expert/novice), age, type of sport (including extreme sport) and seasonal play differences. From controlling these variables, you, other athletes and others who work in sport will be better able to derive benefits on predicting, and recovering from, injury.

Questions to consider

1. How can previous injuries impact on perception and stress in sport?
2. Not everyone feels that they go through the stages of grief in sport – is this normal or pathological?

REFLECTIVE PRACTICE: PERCEPTIONS; STAGES OF GRIEF

PERCEPTIONS

How can these ways of cognitive appraising have a detrimental impact on your performance?

- Catastrophizing – 'I left my favourite socks at home and therefore I can't possibly win'
- Personalizing – 'If only I hadn't been tackled then we would have won – it's all my fault that we lost'
- Negative labelling – 'I'm useless at scoring'
- Overgeneralizing – 'If I don't score this goal then my career is finished'

STAGES OF GRIEF

Reflect on a time when you went through all or some of the stages of grief with a sporting injury. How did you display the following: denial, anger, depression, bargaining and acceptance?

Further Reading

Brewer, B. W. (1994). 'Review and critique of models of psychological adjustment to athletic injury'. *Journal of Applied Sport Psychology*, 1041–3200, 6 (1), 87.

Wiese-Bjornstal, D. M., Smith, A. M., Shaffer, S. M and Morrey, M. (1998). 'An integrated model of response to sport injury: Psychological and sociological dynamics'. *Journal of Applied Sport Psychology*, 10, 1, 46–69.

12 INJURY INTERVENTIONS

'And at the time, it is funny how you can look at something and say, for example with my shoulder injury, when it first happened I said this is the worst thing that could happen to me. "Why me, why now?" Now I look back and say it was probably the best thing that happened to me.'
Drew Brees (NFL quarterback, New Orleans Saints)

Objectives

1. The use of Psychological Skills Training
2. Progressive Muscular Relaxation Technique
3. Combined techniques for recovery from injury: relaxation and imagery, goal setting, self-talk, social support
4. The injury recovery mindset: cognitive control, adhering, motivational orientation and coping

The unfortunate yet inevitable experience of injury can be detrimental to your physical and psychological well-being. However, it can also provide you with an opportunity to enhance your understanding of recovery as a process whereby you can grow stronger (Tracey, 2003). One way you can facilitate the journey to recovery is by developing a Psychological Skills Training (PST) programme. PST combines various psychological interventions into a systematic approach, for example, the use of imagery to guide you through a progressive muscular relaxation technique in order to reduce the stress of injury.

There are a number of positive benefits in using PST, such as reducing your injury time and expediting your recovery. In addition, PST used in a pre-injury period can prevent injuries (e.g. Johnson, Ekengren and Andersen, 2005; Kolt, Hume, Smith and Williams, 2004). For example, rugby players identified as having a 'high risk' of injury were given a stress management programme that resulted in shorter recovery times and fewer subsequent injuries than their counterparts (Maddison and Prapavessis, 2005). When they used psychological skills, such as goal setting, positive self-talk and healing imagery, they recovered faster from injury than those who did not (Ievleva and Orlick, 1991). The research has demonstrated that PST reduces stress levels, raises confidence, encourages involvement and helps you to improve your coping strategies (Cohen, Nordin and Abrahamson, 2010).

Studies have identified the effectiveness of PST in a variety of sports. Research has shown PST is successful, for example, in football (Johnson et al., 2005), gymnastics (Kolt et al., 2004; Kerr and Goss, 1996), rowing (Perna, Antoni, Baum, Gordon and Schneiderman, 2003), swimming (Davis, 1991), marathon running (Schomer, 1990) and alpine skiing (May and Brown, 1989).

The most popular psychological techniques used in PST for rehabilitation are: relaxation management, healing imagery, goal setting, positive self-talk, social support and constructive thinking, i.e. 'time out' to rest, re-clarify and re-group (e.g. Moran, 2012; Williams and Scherzer, 2010). The effectiveness of PST is supported by research as being beneficial during rehabilitation, as well as during pre-injury and post-injury phases of recovery (Cohen et al., 2010).

HOW CAN I USE THE VARIOUS TECHNIQUES IN PST TO OVERCOME A SPORTING INJURY?

Relaxation Management

Relaxation is a widely used technique for controlling anxiety and managing pain. It has a great appeal and is recommended by sport psychologists, though research into this area is somewhat limited. There are a variety of popular relaxation methods, including deep breathing (outlined in the reflective practice section in Chapter 10). There is also the autogenic technique, meditation, yoga or music. This section will focus in on one of the most established methods, Jacobson's Progressive Muscular Relaxation (PMR) technique (Jacobson, 1938), which is often used in psychological skills training.

PMR relies on learning to differentiate between tightness and relaxation within a muscle and muscle groups. Step 1 requires you to tense and then relax a particular muscle group for a set time. The muscle groups are then accessed in a particular order. You need to learn to distinguish between the feelings of tension and relaxation. Imagery can be integrated into this technique by using a relaxation script. For example, a script used by Gill, Kolt and Keating (2004) suggests to participants: 'Relax your feet and lower legs. Be aware of the tension being released. Release all the tension. As the tension fades away, focus on the new relaxed feeling in your feet and lower legs, continue to focus on this feeling.'

Guided Imagery

PMR and guided imagery are highly effective when recovering from anterior cruciate ligament (ACL) injuries, in reducing anxiety and concerns over re-injury (Cupal, 1998; Cupal and Brewer, 2001). In addition, a combination of relaxation and imagery has been shown to reduce injuries by 52 per cent in collegiate swimmers and 33 per cent in American football players (Davis, 1991).

Imagery techniques are useful in helping you to manage pain, staying motivated (Driediger, Hall and Callow, 2006), improving mood and confidence during rehabilitation. Healing imagery is a particular type of visualization commonly used by psychologists and sport medical teams during recovery (Brewer, 2009). You can concentrate on visualizing a specific movement, e.g. seeing the injured limb moving in the desired way, while regaining function. A badminton player remarked, 'I would try to imagine what the (muscular) tear looked like and think about how it feels and how it's going to heal' (Driediger et al., 2006).

Healing imagery can also use metaphorical images to facilitate your healing (e.g. Evans, Hare and Mullen, 2006; Green, 1992; Ievleva and Orlick, 1991; Korn, 1983). In metaphorical or comparison visualization you might imagine the hip joint moving as a wheel related to physiological processes, such as tissue repairing itself (Cohen et al., 2010). Healing imagery is illustrated in the following quote from a male semi-professional footballer with a cartilaginous knee injury:

'I can see the joint itself, I can see the bones, I can see the ligaments, I can imagine where the cartilage is. Once I've actually got that image in my mind I'll actually focus on the point where I feel the pain... I turn it into a colour... I usually see it as originally red, right, because that's where the pain is... it basically goes from red, to orange, to yellow, to green and through to blue. Once I've got that blue, I just imagine a cold icy feeling, which I think tends to help the actual pain at that particular moment.' (Evans et al., 2006).

The use of imagery during rehabilitation enhances your confidence (e.g. Law, Driediger, Hall and Forwell, 2006; Evans et al., 2006; Sordoni, Hall and Forwell, 2002). Even in chronic cases where treatment is prolonged, a combination of imagery with relaxation can improve your mood (Johnson, 2007). This may be because in using imagery and relaxation PST is effective in decreasing emotional reactions such as fear and anxiety, as demonstrated by gymnasts who often fear returning to their sport following an accident (e.g. Chase, Magyar and Drake, 2005).

Athletes who used imagery and relaxation while recovering from ACL reconstruction not only demonstrated greater knee strength but also showed less concern about re-injury (Cupal and Brewer, 2001). However, not every study is in agreement about the benefits of PST. In a study conducted on athletes with grade II ankle sprains, imagery and relaxation had no effect on their perceptions of pain, or range of motion. It is proposed that different imagery types need to be researched further (Christakou and Zervas, 2007). Understanding the nature of an injury is vital to its effectiveness. You are more productive during recovery when you understand the reasons behind your rehabilitation exercises and the estimated length of the treatment (Williams and Scherzer, 2010).

Goal setting

Goal setting is mapping your moves from your current location to your future position. When you are injured, the recovery route chosen is dependent on items such as the severity of the injury, previous injuries and the level of performance. A goal-setting plan illustrates the process from injury to recovery and should include physical and psychological development.

Goal setting results in an individual plan, though a range of people may be involved in the consultation, such as your sport physiotherapist, sports rehabilitator, fitness trainer or coach resulting in setting performance goals, process objectives and outcome objectives. One outcome objective could be to recover in time to return to the first team for the next season. The problem, as you can probably ascertain, is that to some extent this may be outside your control. Returning fully fit may take longer than you plan and the coach may not play you in the first team immediately following your rehabilitation period. Goal setting with only outcome objectives can result in increased levels of anxiety with reduced levels of self-confidence. Performance objectives, for example, of being able to lift a desired amount of weight as part of your strength training with a process of building up through a set amount of weights two or three times a week is more feasible. In rehabilitation, this is one of the preferred methods for you when on the road to recovery (Brewer, Jeffers, Petitpas and Van Raalte, 1994; Cupal, 1998), though goal setting does need to be used effectively.

Positive Self-talk

Self-talk is a technique using statements that can be motivational or instructional in nature. Statements can be positive, negative or neutral. Research has shown that positive self-talk is more effective than negative self-talk (see e.g. Hardy, 2006). Examples are, 'I have been injured before. I am going to return stronger than before when I finish my rehabilitative period,' 'I am going to be thrown off the team if I am not fit enough'. Statements can be relevant to the rehabilitative programme such as, 'I need to bend my arms more and keep my back straight, while performing a rehabilitation exercise correctly.'

By combining both goal setting and self-talk, athletes performed better on physical tests of their injured knee than those who were only given one psychological skill to use during the rehabilitative period (Beneca, Maliou, Theodorakis and Godolias, 2000). If you know how to practise goal-setting techniques then you will be able to demonstrate superior strength during your rehabilitative programme (Theodorakis, Beneca, Malliou and Goudas, 1997; Theodorakis, Malliou, Papaioannou, Beneca and Filactakidou, 1996).

WHAT DO YOU NEED SOCIALLY AND EMOTIONALLY TO OVERCOME A SPORTING INJURY?

Social support

Social support is based on social interactions, which can facilitate rehabilitation. When people are brought up 'rich in social support they develop expectations that stress is manageable and that they will be equal to many of the stressors they face' (Gallucci, 2014). Social support impacts on you in a way that creates a sense of self-confidence, which can get you through challenging times. Having social support can empower you to take responsibility to achieve your rehab goals. There are three types of social support: tangible, emotional and informational. These are often used in combination.

1. Tangible support is providing something substantive, such as money to live on during an injury or lifts to the clinic for treatment. This can be helpful when you need to get to a clinic miles away from home and travelling on public transport is no longer an easy option.

2. Emotional support includes being listened to so you can express your thoughts and feelings. It requires the listener to have an objective ear. When a coach or manager asks you how you are getting on, it can show that the coach is concerned (Bianco and Eklund, 2001) and that you are important. On the other hand, attention can be detrimental to recovery as demonstrated in a study on injured skiers and other athletes when coaches were more negative than positive (Brewer, 2001). Therefore, if you are experiencing a sense of loss (as discussed in the grief model in Chapter 11), you can benefit more from positive emotional support (Gallucci, 2014). An emotion-focused coping strategy during injury can help control anxiety, stress and pain and provide you with confidence in being able to handle stressful situations and intense pressure.

3. Informational support is about providing useful resources, materials or information about your situation. If you are focused on physical rehabilitation, then you may appreciate getting more than the usual amount of information on the nature of your injury. Players working with sport scientists, performance analysts, a medical team, several coaches, a psychologist, etc. tend to have an interest in understanding the information that is available (Bianco, 2001; Podlog and Eklund, 2007; Yang et al., 2010).

Players with low self-esteem need more social support, though they are not likely to ask for it. In a study on injured skiers, those who felt that they had not yet demonstrated their competence to a coach were less likely to seek his/her support (Bianco and Eklund, 2001).

Social support for injured youth and adolescent athletes is important. Parents acknowledge that injured children lose out on camaraderie with the team during rehabilitation. Adolescents admitted that they felt less concerned about returning when they had social support to guide them back to their sport (Podlog, Kleinert, Dimmock, Miller and Shipherd, 2012).

Constructive Thinking

A 'time out period' due to a sporting injury can provide you with the space to reflect and improve physically, technically and psychologically (Gallucci, 2014).

High performance athletes are more likely to engage in this process while younger athletes for instance may require more encouragement (e.g. Sordoni et al., 2002). Different cognitive techniques can be used and combined with various interventions to help this process along.

Frightening thoughts and images can perpetuate a traumatic injury experience, which can manifest themselves as flashbacks or nightmares. This can derail or decelerate the rehabilitation process. Substituting negative thoughts and images with positive ones helps change perspective, though it takes time. NLP (see Chapter 8) also uses a visual imagery technique called Visual-Kinaesthetic Dissociation Technique, which helps post-traumatic stress patients and can be useful in this situation.

Reframing can help you change your perspective from negative to more acceptable or even positive, for example, 'this is the end of my career' to 'this gives me an opportunity to work on my weaknesses'. There is a case of an injured female rugby player who worked with an integrated team, including a sport physiotherapist and strength conditioning coach, on her physical recovery and a psychologist on psychological enhancement. Utilizing a PST programme of reframing, imagery, relaxation and goal setting she went on to play in the 2006 World Cup with a stronger sense of self-confidence (Cecil et al., 2009).

Self-confidence is part of a mental toughness package that includes skills such as motivation, focus and stress management (e.g. Jones and Moorhouse, 2007). Mental toughness is a determination and commitment towards a goal regardless of the pressure or hardship (Middleston, Marsh, Martin, Richards and Perry, 2005). An increase in mental toughness can be stimulated through an imagery intervention. Developing this mindset is beneficial for you in recovering from injury and correlates well with adherence to a rehabilitative programme (Levy, Polman and Clough, 2008). (See also Chapter 5 on mental toughness.)

Motivational Orientation

Knowing your motivational orientation is also beneficial for rehabilitation. If you are *ego oriented*, then you are more centred on improving in comparison to others who are involved in the rehabilitative process. Working out with others who are at different stages of recovery is useful. You can see where you have come from and where you are going. On the other hand, if you are *task oriented*, then you are more concerned with your own progress and are more relaxed about going at your own pace while self-monitoring your physiological changes. Gilbourne and Taylor (1998) examined task orientation across the different rehabilitative phases and suggest in an article some guidelines for a task-oriented goal-setting programme. Others suggest that regardless of orientation, you can be trained in different psychological techniques to facilitate the rehabilitative process (Clement, Shannon and Cannole, 2011). (See Chapter 6 for more on task and ego orientation.)

Adherence

You can enhance recovery by encouraging adherence. Problem-focused coping helps you in working out exercise routine schedules and ways of getting to the physiotherapist or gym. However, adherence is then required. This involves sticking to an agreed plan, as opposed to compliance, which is a direct order that you need to obey. Adherence is one of the most researched areas in behavioural response to injury and should be used to encourage you to improve. One of the basic tools is a diary or log, which tracks daily and weekly progress. This can be done in a notebook, on a phone or any other device. It is a powerful way of empowering you to track your own progress. Of course, willingness to keep a diary in the first place is an indicator that you are serious about being proactive in the rehabilitation process. The results of a study examining adherence in athletes who had ACL surgery, demonstrated that there was a relationship between adherence to home exercises and knee function, especially in under 30-year-olds (Scherzer, Brewer, Cornelius, Van Raalte, Petitpas, Sklar, Pohlman, Krushell, and Ditmar, 2001). The researchers also found that goal setting and positive self-talk were beneficial in guiding athletes towards greater adherence and greater effort.

Adherence is a vital contributor to the outcome of the rehabilitative process and without it the effectiveness of the programme and its progress is likely to be compromised. This also applies to both under-adherence (e.g. not doing the exercises prescribed) and over-adherence (doing more than you should at the relevant stage of recovery). The cost of under-adherence is that you may lose your confidence in feeling that you will recover. You may receive more attention from coaches and family than you did prior to injury. You may not be at the point where you would like to be in your career. You may use under-adherence as a way to avoid the pain and perhaps even as an excuse to retire from the pressure of the sport. Alternatively, you may decide to over-adhere to a rehabilitation programme. You could work at twice the pace of a recommended programme in the hope of recovering quicker. This may be due to an intense athletic identity, not wanting to lose your place in an upcoming competition or a position on a team, perfectionist tendencies, or perhaps pressure from significant others. Unfortunately, over-adherence will often set you back, as moving more rapidly than is medically recommended frequently puts you at a greater risk of injury.

In conclusion, injury is an inevitable part of sport participation. Injury recovery is a skill in which you can become more proficient. Of course, returning to sport prematurely is also a danger, as it makes you more vulnerable to re-injury and to developing a future fear of re-injury. Use your team of experts, if you have access to them, or advice from your medical team or doctor in order to develop a strong, psychological readiness to return. To be a truly competent athlete requires having the right skill set for your sport, including injury recovery skills. PST is a combination of various approaches designed to make you psychologically stronger. Remember, however, commitment is essential to rehabilitation. Commitment helps you to accomplish your objectives and a lack of it is one of the few things that really blocks your way to achieving your dreams.

Questions to consider

1. Are there any other techniques that could be incorporated into a PST approach to recovering from injury?
2. Are athletes who have a strong mindset better able to take injury in their stride?

REFLECTIVE PRACTICE: JUDGING RESPONSE TO INJURY

Below is a series of questions that I have compiled, the answers to which will help you, a colleague or your coach understand your/their response to injury. They may have an NLP slant. For a standardised questionnaire on emotional response to injury see Smith, A. M., Scott, S. G. and Wiese, D. M. (1990), 'The psychological effects of athletic injury: Coping' *Sports Medicine*, 9 (6), 352–69 (*see* link.springer.com/article/10.2165%2F00007256-199009060-00004).

1. What sports do you engage in?
2. What are your reasons for participating in sport (e.g. enjoyment, fitness, social, competition, trophies, etc.)?
3. What type of injury do you have and how did it happen?
4. How do you feel emotionally since your injury (e.g. depressed, stressed, relieved)?
5. Has your injury impacted on the way you think (e.g. knocked your confidence) or on your behaviour (e.g. you don't go out with friends any more as they are all in the team)?
6. How do you manage your pain?
7. Do you have a support system in place?
8. What do you feel you need in order to recover?
9. How optimistic are you about fully recovering (on a scale of 1 to 10 or as a percentage)?
10. How committed are you to your recovery programme (on a scale of 1 to 10 or as a percentage)?

Further Reading

Cohen, R., Nordin, S. and Abrahamson, E. (2010). 'Psychology and sports rehabilitation'. In P. Comfort and E. Abrahamson (eds.), *Sports Rehabilitation and Injury Prevention.*, London: Wiley-Blackwell.

Scherzer, C. B., Brewer, B. W., Cornelius, A. E., Van Raalte, J. L., Petitpas, A. J., Sklar, J. H., Pohlman, M. H., Krushell, R. J. and Ditmar, T. D. (2001). 'Psychological skills and adherence to rehabilitation after reconstruction of the anterior cruciate ligament'. *Journal of Sport Rehabilitation*, 10, 165–172.

13 EXERCISE PSYCHOLOGY

'Some people start a sport just to reduce weight, some say, "My doctor ordered me to run and do exercise," and for others, they run for completely different benefits. But it is not like that with sport. We need to eat, we need to rest, but also we need to run.'
Haile Gebrselassie (Ethiopian long-distance runner; Olympic and World Championship gold medallist)

'Exercise is so difficult when you have to and so easy when you want to.'
Felicity Luckey (author of website, Great Minds Think Fit)

'I think exercise tests us in so many ways, our skills, our hearts, our ability to bounce back after setbacks. This is the inner beauty of sports and competition and it can serve us all well as adult athletes.'
Peggy Fleming (American figure skater, Olympic and World Champion)

Objectives

1. Benefits of exercise psychology

2. Exercise psychology models

3. Beliefs and attitudes in exercise

4. Reasons to exercise: competence, controllability of weight, fun and boredom

As you take part in sport, you require certain fitness levels in order to achieve quality performance. Regular exercise and physical activity can also reward you with significant physical and psychological benefits. Physically, exercise helps to reduce the likelihood of disease such as hypertension, osteoporosis, type 2 diabetes, obesity and heart disease. Psychologically, it helps with cognitive skills such as memory enhancement, mood improvement and aspects of the self (e.g. self-confidence, positive body image). The words exercise and physical activity are often used interchangeably yet exercise refers to movement (usually repetitive) specifically performed with the aim of health benefits, while physical activity generally relates to daily living activities, such as household chores and the physical demands of work.

Exercise psychology as a subject area has two intertwined goals. One is a focus on how you encourage yourself to exercise or increase physical activity. The second is towards research encouraging the benefits of exercise/physical activity. Recent research promoted in the news has demonstrated that those who keep fit tend to live longer, stay healthier and may even maintain a stronger cognitive ability, for example reducing the risk of dementia later on in life. In addition, exercise slows down muscle loss, which is estimated at between 1–2 per cent annually after the age of 50. The topic of exercise psychology is integral to sport and to those who wish to continue to play sport well into older age.

- Exercise psychology has an esteemed place alongside sport psychology.
- In 2006, the Health Care and Professions Council became the regulatory body with the protected title of 'Sport and Exercise Psychologist' in the UK.
- The British Psychological Society (BPS) established the Division of Sport and Exercise Psychology (DSEP) in 1998.
- In 1987, the *Journal of Sport Psychology* was renamed as the *Journal of Sport and Exercise Psychology*.
- The American Psychological Association (APA) established Division 47, Exercise and Sport Psychology in 1986.

WHAT ARE THE PSYCHOLOGICAL BENEFITS OF EXERCISE?

Exercise and physical activity have a strong effect on enhancing your mood (Berger and Motl, 2000) and reducing depression. One reason for this is that exercise releases endogenous opioid endorphins (produced in the body), which are similar to morphine. These endorphins make you happy as well as provide you with pain relief. Exercise also stimulates the brain to release neurotransmitters called serotonin. Serotonin upkeep medicines are popular in treating clinical depression as they stimulate the release of serotonin, which improves mood. Exercise does this naturally and has a quicker effect than anti-depressant medicine (Knubben, Reischies, Adli, Schlattmann, Bauer and Dimeo, 2007). A regular routine of exercise enhances mood and relieves depression (Annesi, 2005) and should include a moderate combination of both aerobic and anaerobic exercise (Dunn, Madhukar, Trivedi, Kampert, Clark and Chambliss, 2005; Singh, Stavrinos, Scarbek, Galambos, Liber and Singh, 2005). Physical activity such as walking, running and playing sports has this same effect on mood (Rethorst, Wipfli and Landers, 2009). If you are physically fit and exercise regularly, then you are less prone to depression. Being task oriented, i.e. doing something for the sake of your best performance, is also good for you (Grant, 2000) as it provides you with a great sense of well-being. In addition, motivational music can also enhance positive emotions (Karageorghis, 2008).

Exercise is anxiolytic meaning it has an anxiety lowering effect (De Moor, Beem, Stubbe, Boomsma and De Geus, 2006; Goodwin, 2003). Even one session of aerobic exercise can decrease anxiety, though the effect only lasts for 2–4 hours (Martinsen and Raglin, 2007). Therefore, regular or continual exercise is required to reduce trait or chronic anxiety. Anaerobic exercise, e.g. weight training, can also be anxiolytic, especially if carried out with moderate intensity (Arent, Alderman, Short and Landers, 2007).

Exercise psychology, therefore, can positively change your mood and benefit you if you suffer with depression or anxiety. On a more negative note, however, you can get so hooked on exercising that you find it difficult to control your exercise schedules to an acceptable amount (Cohen, 1995). You may persist regardless of injury, time restrictions and/or other obligations. This can lead you to exercise addiction or dependency. Similar to other addictions, as a chronic exerciser you can experience symptoms of withdrawal when you are unable to exercise. You may feel a loss of control with an urge to continually exercise, resulting in isolation from social contact with friends and family. Finally, you may or may not need to increase levels to experience the same good feeling (i.e. tolerance). You may be more prone to exercise dependency if you have a particular personality type, i.e. perfectionist, extravert, or intravert (Hall, Hill, Appleton and Kozub, 2009; Hausenblas and Giacobbi, 2004). Women tend to be exercise dependent if their sense of self-esteem is linked with their physical appearance.

An exercise dependency, along with a distorted body image, can lead you to a greater propensity towards an eating disorder (Meyer and Taranis, 2011; DiBartolo, Lin, Motoya, Neal and Shaffer, 2007). There are ways of measuring this addiction. The Exercise Dependence Scale – revised (EDS) was developed to measure exercise dependency. It is based on criteria for substance dependency in the DSM-IV-TR (Symons Downs, Hausenblas and Nigg, 2004). There is also the Exercise Dependence Questionnaire (EDQ) (Ogden, Veale and Summers, 1997). Interestingly enough, males score higher on EDS while females score higher on the EDQ. Exercise dependency is more common in competitive and elite athletes (McNamara and McCabe, 2012), as is overtraining syndrome.

Overtraining can result from excessively high exercise and training programmes without adequate recovery periods. Symptoms include low mood states, chronic fatigue, reduced appetite and a suppressed immune system. Appropriate exercise and training programmes are therefore extremely important to all those who are serious about health, fitness and sport (Biddle and Mutrie, 2008; Landers and Arent, 2007; Berger, Pargman and Weinberg, 2002; Buckworth and Dishman, 2007).

Exercise and Health Models

Research has resulted in the publication of several exercise and health models. Examining these is helpful in understanding what underlies the motivation to exercise.

The Health Belief Model (Becker, 1974) highlights the relationship between information and behavioural change. You need a strong belief, based on evidence, in order to take on a new way of being. Knowing how the benefits of exercise will pre-empt or avoid disease will impact on your beliefs and push you towards developing a new behaviour. You need to know that exercise will help you avoid illnesses by which you feel threatened, such as diabetes and cardiovascular disease. Your beliefs can be altered by health campaigns, educational material or annotated stories on other people's adversities. Self-talk statements such as, 'I can do this' and/ or 'I am improving my chances of good health' are useful in altering your perceptions.

The Transtheoretical, or 'Stages of Change', Model (Prochaska and DiClemente, 1982) is often used to teach fitness instructors. It illustrates the shift in mindset that we go through from the pre-contemplation of an exercise plan to action (Prochaska, J. O. and Marcus, B. H., 1994). This is an intentional way of altering behaviour, which develops slowly. The stages of change are as follows: *pre-contemplation* (there is no serious intention to change); *contemplation* (the idea of changing is considered); *preparation* (the planning stage to action taking place); *action* (the initiation of the behaviour); *maintenance* (the regular occurrence of the behaviour measured for more than six months); *termination* (signifies that the behaviour is now incorporated into the person's repertoire and there is no temptation to return to old behaviour). Relapse is, of course, also possible. This model shows that there is a decisional balance and also a confidence at each point that you can take on each stage.

The Theory of Reasoned Action (TRA) (Ajzen and Fishbein, 1974) is based on your intention towards an action. This is based on your attitude and subjective norms. You also take into account beliefs about what those who are important to you want you to do. However, this theory does not take into account those things that may not be under your control. One of my students once mentioned that she wished to exercise though she was limited by the fact that she was suffering with chronic fatigue syndrome.

The Theory of Planned Behaviour (TPB) is a modification of the TRA. It addresses the criticism stated above on accountability and includes perceived behavioural control as a factor, which can impact on your intentions (Azjen, 2005).

The Self-Determination Theory (SDT) (Deci and Ryan, 1985; 2008) is based on three factors: *autonomy* (controlling your actions), *competence* (being proficient in your outcomes) and *relatedness* (feeling connected with others) (see also Chapter 6). When an environment provides freedom, it enables you to develop a sense of autonomy, which encourages competency and relatedness. In a study with overweight adults, competence was helpful in forecasting exercise behaviour (Gay, Saunders and Dowda, 2011).

A subsidiary of the SDT theory is the *Organismic Integration Theory* (Ryan and Deci, 2007; Ryan, Williams, Patrick and Deci, 2009). This identifies the motivational orientations that impact on your choice of activities. Intrinsic motivation is self-generating, and therefore you choose what interests you. Extrinsic motivation is influenced by external factors. It is subdivided into four types: externally regulated behaviour, introjected regulation of behaviour, regulation through identification and integrated regulation. When you are motivated by external factors, such as winning a trophy or a medal for competing, then you are *externally regulated*. When you participate because you believe you have to or you may feel guilty if you don't, then this is *introjected (internalised) regulation*. An example of this is feeling that you have to exercise in order to lose weight, in order to lower your blood sugar levels because you are borderline type 2 diabetic. If you engage in exercise because you desire a certain outcome, such as you want a six-pack or toned arms, then this is *identified regulation*. Finally, if you participate because it brings everything together for you then this is *integrated regulation*. The latter two represent a type of self-determination.

Can these theoretical constructs help you in understanding the reasons behind exercise? The 'Stages of Change' (Transtheoretical Model) illustrates the journey you may make from non-activity to regular exercise. It demonstrates how you can't necessarily push someone into an exercise mode until they are ready to take on the planning and the action themselves. Collectively, these theories also identify key factors such as belief, attitudes, intentionality, motivation, autonomy, competence, social support and information. These are the different steps that can be used to promote exercise.

The first step towards changing behaviour requires having an insight into your own beliefs on exercise and health. The importance of this stems from the Health Belief Model, which stresses that your beliefs and attitudes affect your behaviour. What you need in order to change your thinking is information. This is a powerful tool, which can push you towards positive health behaviour.

Where does this information come from? Educational material is available through various sources, such as health and specialist magazines, e.g. *Women's Running* or *Men's Health*. Exercise clubs often provide free reading material on a variety of topics. Specialist journals are also available to trainers and those in the management of clubs, e.g. *Fit Pro Network*. Internet sources include forums and blogs catering to those exercising at every level. Even sites with specialist equipment or clothing (e.g. Kora) have information – I was quoted there once on the psychology of an ultra marathon.

Educational material can develop intrinsic motivation. Information gives you a sense of self-control and perceived competence. You may identify with something you read in a magazine or 'like' a Facebook page that promotes your specialist activity. This can intrinsically motivate you through identified regulation. You may watch an emotive story, which feeds into your sense of introjected regulation (guilt) in wanting to avoid a particular illness.

The theory of reasoned action says that your intentions are then based on these beliefs. Age is a distinguishing factor in your beliefs and attitudes towards why you exercise. Younger adults acknowledge that they see activity as important for perceived health benefits while older adults exercise due to health benefits such as reducing high blood pressure, reducing obesity and preventing diabetes (Biddle and Nigg, 2000). These models provide you with an underpinning to the importance of attitude, belief as well as intention in deciding whether to exercise or not.

WHY DO PEOPLE EXERCISE?

Competence and controllability

The TPB theory identifies the importance of control in changing your exercise strategies. The SDT theory also shows that you have a need to feel competent in exercising. Research using meta-analysis (the term used when a researcher analyses several studies and comes up with a numerical figure that identifies a statistical effect) reveals that there is a greater probability for participating in exercise when interventions focus on self-regulation strategies (Carver and Scheier, 1998; 2011).

What can you do if you want to do it yourself and maintain a programme? First, there is goal setting, which has proved to be highly effective when used appropriately. A goal-setting app or a watch that monitors your statistics, an online blog or a hardcopy plan will ensure that you are keeping track of what you are doing (see Goal Setting in Chapter 6). Goal-setting advice often suggests that objectives should be challenging but realistic. Make sure they are specific and that they are recorded with a time plan. Half of the exercisers who join a gym drop out within six months (Linke, Gallo and Norman, 2011). Exercisers report that they leave because they do not feel that they have achieved their goals. You seldom persevere when you feel inadequate, so setting high, unachievable objectives will lead to perceived low competence.

A feeling of low competence can be based on becoming continually injured, which is another reason to drop out. This can also be controlled with a good goal-setting plan. Personal trainers can provide instructions on how to avoid injury, as can YouTube videos, which demonstrate how to use equipment. Gyms that can utilise apps or internet instructions can be linked into an individual plan with an overall monitoring system. Exercise impacts on your thinking and memory. Regular exercise improves decision-making and problem solving.

Confidence

Confidence underpins competence. If you are a highly confident person (high self-efficacy), then you are more likely to exercise and to continue with exercise. Confidence provides you with the means to face obstacles and challenges in maintaining your effort, whether it is due to a bad day at work or the fact that there is something interesting to watch on the television. Even though there is convincing evidence on the link between developing chronic health conditions and lack of exercise, not everyone takes up the call. And if they do, they often find difficulty in maintaining the effort and can have several break periods from it.

Weight

Your body image is based on your perceptions and beliefs. Women in particular may exercise to control their weight and enhance their appearance. The strategies mentioned above, i.e. information, competence and control, are all important in encouraging exercise for weight loss, as is the use of goal setting. An important addition is to consider the beliefs behind your weight loss. If the ideal look for you is a model on the cover of a magazine or a highly unrealistic weight loss, then you may feel let down when you are unable to meet that challenge. Individually or with the help of a trainer, you need a goal that concentrates on how clothes fit as well as a toned body shape and improved cardiovascular fitness. The key here is to revisit your goals and make them more realistic. A useful tool is to look again at your body image, perhaps judging your progress not by how much you weigh but rather how your clothes fit.

Fun or Boredom?

The fact is that you are more likely to exercise if it is fun and interesting. What are the reasons behind you feeling motivated to exercise? Is it enjoyable? Is it to get a reward, to belong to a community club, so that you don't feel guilty or because it gives you loads of energy? Breaking down the reasons behind this statement will enable you to put the right motivation in place. Music can be motivating and even enhance performance (Karageorghis, 2008). Motivating tunes on a phone or piece of equipment you use in the gym can be arousing and lead to greater endurance in your exercise routine. It is a distraction from boredom. Those who admit to dropping out of exercise programmes due to psyching up uncontrolled anxiety can consider either more emotion-focused music or activities, such as yoga or Pilates, which reduce stress levels. The strategy here is also not to encourage negative self-talk. You can measure the extent of your desire to exercise on the Exercise Motivations Inventory (Marklan and Hardy, 1993; Markland and Ingledew, 1997) (*see* http://www.livingstrong.org/articles/ExerciseMotivations.pdf).

Rewards, feedback, achievement

If you like rewards, as in external regulated motivation, then goal setting with short term and intermediate rewards is for you. It is important that you are provided with feedback on how you are exercising and progressing. There are great apps for this, which send you reminders, congratulate you on achievements and monitor your progress. The Needs in Achievement theory is not specifically a health model; however, it does also illustrate your desire to feel a sense of accomplishment. Set yourself up with a system of rewards, such as a new water bottle, a new song download, a healthy lunch or a pair of new trainers for each time you meet your target. There are so many ways to monitor physical activity, with different walkmeter apps, pedometers, step counters, accelerometers and dedicated fitness watches/monitors, that achievement is easy to monitor.

However, you may be the type of person whose reward is a sense of achievement. According to the needs achievement theory, developed by Mc Clelland (1961), your motivation is linked with your sense of accomplishment.

If you are an achievement motivated individual then you look for opportunities where there are challenging yet realistic goals. You get great satisfaction out of becoming fitter or healthier as this gives you a personal sense of satisfaction in meeting your goals. You like feedback so having scheduled meetings with a personal trainer who can give you an indication of how well you are getting on is helpful and you will appreciate seeing how you have met goals more than being praised.

Social Support

You are more likely to drop out of an exercise programme if you do not seek social support. Social support is useful, and you may prefer it when this takes place face-to-face with a personal trainer, for example. If so, then it is important to get to know the staff at your gym. Adherence improves if you are reminded to exercise by phone, mail or internet. Internet forums and blogs can also be useful. As mentioned previously, information can help. Monitor attendance and share your successes with a community, by using social media, such as Facebook or Twitter.

Exergaming

In 2006, Nintendo Wii transformed exercise when it introduced active video games (AVG). Research shows that the effectiveness of these games depends on the type of game and for how long it is played. Exercises that focus on lower body movements (e.g. jogging in place), as opposed to upper body movement (e.g. boxing), are better (Biddiss and Irwin, 2010). Though AVG is not better than the real thing, it can begin to turn your sedentary leisure time into something more physically challenging.

Questions to consider

1. How can you maintain or increase adherence and prevent boredom when using a fitness app? For example, did you do 10,000 steps every day for a month using your fitness watch and then lose interest?

2. How do you move extrinsic motivation (such as receiving a medal, raising money for charity or flashing words of congratulations on your app) to intrinsic motivation (wanting to do it because you care)?

REFLECTIVE PRACTICE: CHANGING EXERCISE BEHAVIOUR IN THE TRANSTHEORETICAL MODEL

ENCOURAGING EXERCISE

Try to change your exercise behaviour according to the Transtheoretical Model (Auweele, Rzewnicki and Van Mele, 1997). Use the box below to remind you of the stages as you progress through them:

Stage	Goal	Strategy	I am here – Self-evaluation
Pre-contemplation	I am starting to think about changing	Think about perceived benefits	
Contemplation	I would like to exercise regularly	Read up on the importance of exercise	
Preparation	I am joining a gym or club	Check all barriers to avoid problems	
Action	I am attending 3 days a week	Reinforce yourself	
Maintenance	I am monitoring my progress with a trainer once a month	Evaluate	
Relapse	Time to start again – what went wrong	Re-evaluate	

Further Reading

Anshel, M. (2005). *Applied Exercise Psychology: A Practitioner's Guide to Improving Client Health and Fitness.* New York, NY: Springer Publishing Company.

Edmunds, J., Ntoumanis, N. and Duda, J. (2006). 'A test of self-determination theory in the exercise domain'. *Journal of Applied Social Psychology.* 36, 9, 2240–2265.

Linke, S. E., Gallo, L. and Norman, G. (2011). 'Attrition and adherence rates of sustained vs. intermittent exercise interventions'. *Annuals of Behavioral Medicine,* 42(2), 197–209.

Prapavessis, H., Gaston, A. and DeJesus, S. (2015). 'The Theory of Planned Behavior as a model for understanding sedentary behavior'. *Psychology of Sport and Exercise.* 19, 23–32.

PART 5

UNIQUE AND INDIVIDUAL ASPECTS

Long-distance runner Haile Gebreselassie

14 TALENT IDENTIFICATION

'Personality makes the difference between the best and the rest in just about any field of human endeavour'

Eugene Aidman (researcher into personality in sport at the University of Sydney, 2007)

'Elite junior to elite senior is very poor, we have a massive dropout rate and a large talent pool wasted.'

(UK Athletics website, 2003)

Objectives

1. Identifying and measuring talent

2. Models and structure in identifying and developing talent

3. The difference between experts/elite and amateurs/novices

Talent recognition in sport has become a mainstream business. Millions of pounds are spent helping those with realistic medal-winning capabilities for the next major events, such as the Olympics and Paralympics. Appropriate talent identification and development can make a significant contribution to sport in any city or country.

Talent identification is about finding someone with a special aptitude for sport with a potential to be developed. It is beneficial to search for players who provide a team with an advantage by adding special or needed skills to the team's portfolio. Effective talent identification can also help in producing long-term success (Gee, 2010).

Many psychologists, coaches and sports teams are wary of whether it is possible to predict talent and success, as there are inconsistent findings in the research (Deaner and Silva, 2002) and also because it is difficult to know how best to support the development of talented individuals.

This chapter will look at some of the empirical findings in talent identification and development, which can help you in supporting talented athletes and in gaining insight into the differences between experts and amateurs.

HOW CAN YOU MEASURE FUTURE TALENT?

Personality

Personality tests for selection and talent search in sport have risen in popularity since the start of this century, due to recent successes in predicting the likelihood of achievement (Aidman, 2007), performance motivation (Judge and Ilies, 2002) and leadership (Judge, Bono, Ilies and Gerhardt, 2002) see http://www.truity.com/test/big-five-personallytest.

How useful is personality selection testing? Eugene Aidman achieved a 84 per cent success rate in predicting the transition of athletes from junior to senior teams over a seven-year period using personality tests. These results were supported by another longitudinal study (Gee, Marshall and King, 2010), which confirmed the importance of personality testing in predicting achievement with professional ice hockey players. A meta-analysis provided evidence that some personality traits were consistently associated with leadership emergence and effectiveness (Judge et al., 2002). Despite continuing concerns over methodology (Cohen, 2012), the importance of personality as a viable area in sport remains both for its value in predicting sporting success and also because of its strong link with performance (Raglin, 2001).

Psychological Attributes

Recently, there have been several measurements developed to help assess and research this field of talent development and identification. First, there is a template to assess open skills in football (i.e. strategy and decision making) designed by Waldron and Worsfold (2010). In their study, results indicated that elite footballers scored higher on the test than sub-elite footballers, though in comparison there was little difference between them. Secondly, the Psychological Characteristics of Developing Excellence Questionnaire (PCDEQ) (MacNamara and Collins, 2011) was designed to facilitate the compilation of information on psychological characteristics needed for progressing talent. Another factor thought to be important for talented athletes would be stress management, so that they can cope in increasingly competitive situations and avoid an overtraining or burnout situation.

Finally, though these are not a measurement of talent, Pankhurst, Collins and MacNamara (2013) conducted a study identifying key constructs on talent identification and development and a study on whether one's place of birth is an indicator of talent. This study revealed that those who live in larger cities (i.e. with a population over 500,000) are more likely to be talented players (MacDonald, Cheung, Cote and Abernethy, 2009) than those who do not.

Place less stress on identifying talent and more on the importance of essential general skills, which combine psychological, physical and behavioural components. (Martindale, Collins and Abraham, 2007)

Coaching and Social Support

Coaching is obviously important in the development of talent. Providing training and empowering coaches to research with universities is a way forward. There are other significant people in every athlete's life, such as the team, friends and parents, who would also benefit from training on how best to support a talented athlete. Clubs also need to know how to work with National Governing Bodies (NGBs) so that talent is discussed at governmental level and within sporting policies. According to an elite coach, 'One of the things that is very obvious in looking at young players is that 90 per cent of the time the ones that make it through have got good solid advice at home,' (Martindale et al., 2007).

The Environment

Understanding what impacts on the environment of future talented athletes may be a key to understanding how you can best support their progression and ensure their talent is committed towards achievement (Abbott and Collins, 2004). The Talent Development Environment Questionnaire (Martindale, Collins, Wang, McNeill, Lee, Sproule and Westbury, 2010) was designed to measure the athlete's experiences relative to ideal environments. Researchers concluded that there was a 77.8 per cent accuracy in what were identified as influential discriminators that exist between high quality and low quality environments (Martindale, Collins, Douglas and Whike, 2013).

DO YOU NEED A STRUCTURED SYSTEM TO IDENTIFY TALENT?

A structured system for the development of key mental skills is recommended for talent development (Bloom, 1985; Gould, Dieffenbach and Moffett, 2002; Talbot-Honeck and Orlick, 1998). This would be a system established to: set clear goals, monitor procedures and evaluate progress. The development of individual plans to monitor skills and experience where individuals develop self-awareness and responsibility would also be key. Systematic monitoring should include individual players/performers, their parents, teammates, role models, coaches and a range of medical and sport science specialists (including, of course, sport psychologists). It would offer a complete education package to athletes, parents and coaches. UK Sport and Scotland Institute of Sport (SIS), for example, already have a variety of educational workshops covering specialised topics, such as performance profiling and monitoring progress, which are specifically geared towards coaches and managers who work with developing elite athletes. They even offer workshops on transitioning from juniors to seniors, which is particularly relevant to those working at academies of excellence.

Successes around the world as records are continually broken and athletes improve both physically and psychologically. Different countries establish different systems, although one that includes schools or clubs is essential in terms of the development of all students. At that level it is not necessary to work on technical specialist skills; instead it is helpful to work on productive life skills that are more generic and can help with those who wish to pursue high-level sport. Entry should be at various points and those supporting the system, e.g. parents, coaches, managers and schools also need support. The sport student experience should be an enjoyable one where one can feel empowered to devote oneself to the pursuit of excellence. The UK Sport and the SIS websites have some excellent resources on this.

Becoming the gold medal winner at an international event is often measured in microseconds. Organisations and clubs strive to recruit talented future contenders by assessing physical as well as psychological attributes. UK Sport and the English Institute of Sport (EIS) have developed a strategy aimed at identifying talented athletes so as to provide them with a supportive structure in order to reach their full potential (www.uksport.gov.uk/our-work/talent-id). The USA Olympic Committee (USOC) subsidises sporting programmes to identify talent (teamusa.org), the SIS has an extensive website and football clubs (like Tottenham Hotspur) and rugby union clubs (like Saracens) all organise their own youth sporting academies.

Some countries identify and then train children from a very young age (e.g. in Germany children from the age of six are selected for tennis). Many countries also use the school system, which feeds into youth clubs and college competitions (e.g. the USA). By choosing talent at a young age, it is easier to manage environmental factors. The literature on talent suggests the importance of manipulating the quality of the environment. However, there is limited research on how to facilitate a successful transition from junior to senior level.

At the moment, talent selection includes performance indicators, though the decision on final selection often comes down to some subjectivity. The importance of the development of generic skills i.e. commonly used skills such as kicking and throwing is identified in research (e.g. Wolstencroft, 2002), which suggests that the majority of children are not given the opportunity to develop basic motor ability. The New Zealand model recognises young talented athletes and includes generic sport skills for those who have shown an aptitude. However, selecting children at a young age doesn't allow them to explore different sports or activities because it forces them into a specific sport early on in their development. Many countries are limiting the types of youth sporting options and PE due to poor world economic factors, at a time when children can learn a wide range of sports (Wolstencroft, 2002). An additional problem with basing selection on early success is that young children are often taught to focus on winning, which isn't an entirely healthy perspective in sport psychology (Abbott, Collins, Martindale and Sowerby, 2002; Abbott, Colins, Sowerby and Martindale, 2007).

WHAT ARE THE MODELS OF TALENT?

One significant model in talent development (TD) is Bloom's Model of Staged Talent (1985). It was based on interviews with a range of high performing individuals such as those in sport, music, medicine, etc. A key aspect of the model is that it is based on stages related to task completions rather than a chronological (age) development approach.

Bloom's Model includes three stages for the achievement of excellence:

Stage 1 – the initiation
Stage 2 – the development
Stage 3 – the perfection

The roles of those involved with this process, the athlete or performer, mentor and parents, are identified.

Stage 1 is when talent is first noted and the child is rewarded for their efforts. The focus is on sport as fun with little emphasis on winning. All significant others (e.g. mother, father) are involved in being supportive of the child. Continuing on into Stage 2, the child takes on the identity of an athlete. They recognise themselves as footballers or swimmers and not just as someone who happens to play these sports. There is intrinsic motivation from the child and enthusiastic social support from others. Parents also play a role in limiting the outside activities of the child so as to enable them to grow in their sport. There is a new coach in Stage 2 who is able to progress the child further with more advanced technical skills. S/he provides strong guidance and has an interest in the child's development.

Finally, Stage 3, perfection, recognises a shift from a reliance on coach and parents towards the athlete taking on his or her own responsibility. This stage involves the athlete putting in the time for training, practice and competition. The role of the parents is reduced and the role of the coach is stronger in terms of pushing and moulding talent. There may be a fear and love-hate relationship between coach and athlete.

A follow-up study confirmed a similarity in the stages identified with 75 per cent of the 26 elite USA figure skaters interviewed (Scanlan, Ravizza and Stein, 1989; Scanlan, Stein and Ravizza, 1989b; 1991). The model describes cognitive, behavioural and social factors. It characterises the support needs of the performer and the importance of transition. It is, however, typically American, as the system involves schools, high school, college and then professional teams. It has been criticised for concentrating on individual performers and not recognizing the differences with team sports. In addition, it is based on only one pathway to excellence, when sport psychologists and coaches believe there are various pathways (Tebbenham, 1998).

There are other models, such as the British World Class model of TD (1993). This one pathway is illustrated as a pyramid. It begins with a world-class start at grass roots level, progresses to a 'world-class potential', which includes support programmes, and finishes with 'world-class performance' where the most talented are helped. Many local councils and sporting organizations use this approach. Unfortunately, it does not distinguish between athletes who operate at different levels of competition. It also only highlights one route to the top with limited information on how transition is achieved.

The Canadian model, Cooke's House of Sport, incorporates two pathways. The athlete acquires skills on a foundation and then on an introductory level, before moving on to either recreational or performance sport routes, which lead to elite and gold status. It is possible in this model for movement between the different pathways. In New Zealand (McClymont, 1999), the TD model emphasises the idea of social support from the family, coaching and education system. It is a series of six levels, as follows:

Level 1: Physical education system and recreation
Level 2: Selection for sport
Level 3: Selection to generic sporting discipline
Level 4: Selection to specific sports
Level 5: Selection for high-level training
Level 6: Selection for national teams

Schools in Canada, as in the USA, play an important role in offering youth skills training and experience in competitive sport up through college (university).

The German method also includes anthropometrical data, looking at the body and the physicality needed for the particular sport. It includes basic skills, such as coordination and general physical state. Some models specify how many training hours must be undertaken, e.g. British LTA starts with 1–2 days a week, increasing during basic training to 2–3 times per week, build-up training 3–4 days per week, performance training 4–5 days per week, ending with perfection and top performance 1–2 days per week.

All in all, some models are based on the age of the athlete rather than which skills need to be developed. Psychological traits to support skills are often missing or not identified. Of course, funding needs to be in place to support transition in any model, which can be an issue. Longitudinal studies would be beneficial in tracking the progress of athletes and relating it back to the models. TD models should be developed based on research and not just previous experience, i.e. 'it worked before'. There needs to be various pathways, with different entry routes. Psychological support should be available to support athletes with their sport as well as with life needs.

WHAT DO EXPERTS HAVE THAT NOVICES DON'T HAVE?

You admire sporting heroes for the expertise they have achieved in sport. You also live vicariously through them, as you imagine their every movement while watching them perform and share their feelings of success. Secretly, you wish or wonder if you could accomplish the superhuman feats that they do.

There is an abundance of research coming through on investigating the differences between experts and novices, though the definition of what constitutes an expert is somewhat sketchy. Expert samples in research sometimes constitute university or collegiate players and other times they are Olympic gold medallists. In extreme sport, identifying an expert is even harder. Are they experts because they compete at levels similar to traditional sport or because they are still alive, e.g. after ten BASE jumps?

Studies show that professionals have more sophisticated and elaborate knowledge of their sport than amateurs. Moran (2012) classifies this knowledge into three areas: *declarative knowledge* (factual information pertaining to the sport), *procedural knowledge* (technical aspects of the sport) and *strategic knowledge* (recognition of patterns within a sport). This section will examine these differences between experts and novices.

What do elite/expert performers do well? Elite participants recognise (Allard and Starkes, 1980) and recall more proficiently than amateurs (Williams, Davids, Burwitz and Williams, 1994; Starkes and Ericsson, 2003). Expert karate practitioners are highly proficient at memorizing strategic patterns (Bedon and Howard, 1992). They are quicker problem solvers, particularly in their sport (Woll, 2002). Experts are more consistent as well as accurate (Starkes and Ericsson, 2003). Research comparing elite to amateur has shown that the elite are quicker in anticipatory skills than the amateur. However, this is not always consistent when tested, as sometimes practice alone does not develop this skill.

Thompson, Watt and Liukkonen (2009) noted that the differences between elite and amateur in studies on reaction time need further investigation. Kioumourtzoglou, Kourtessis, Michalopoulou and Derri (1998) reported significant differences between samples of elite and novice volleyball players in the mean estimation time of speed and direction of a moving object using computer-based stimuli. However, differences were not found between the groups in relation to the number of correct responses associated with the identification of speed and direction of the moving objects. As yet no researchers have found a clear pattern of differences in the perceptual cognitive processing skills of athletes involved in different sports (Williams, 2002).

Elite athletes demonstrate superior anticipatory skills, although there is no evidence that they were born with a faster processing nervous system (Abernethy, 1987). Professional tennis players, for example, can anticipate the spot where an opponent's ball will land even before the opponent's racket has touched it, and can judge the direction of a serve better than novices (Williams, Ward, Knowles and Smeeton, 2002; Jackson and Morgan, 2007) by picking up subtle motion cues in their opponent. Elite cricket batsmen were far more proficient at speed, accuracy skills and pre-empting information than novice players (Stadler, 2008; Muller, Abernethy, and Farrow, 2006).

Experience and training can improve reaction and decision-making on complex tasks as well as improving accuracy (Visser, Raijmakers and Molenaar, 2007). In karate, experienced performers had quicker reaction times than less experienced performers. However, in volleyball, inexperienced players were shown to have quicker reaction times than experienced players though they were lower on accuracy (Fontani, Lodi, Felici, Migliorini and Corradeschi, 2006).

In his book entitled *Talent is Overrated* (Colvin, 2008) the author states that anyone can be a top performer if they work extremely hard at it. It negates the idea that individuals are born with a natural talent and an ability to be successful. Of course, being born with certain physical attributes may give some individuals the winning edge in certain sports. However, you can be exceptional at something if you devote approximately 10,000 hours of 'deliberate practice' (Ericsson, 2006) to developing your talent. Many athletes come into sport later on in life and just practise a lot. Anyone can be talented if they want to and this is somewhat supported by the fact that few top athletes were talented youth players (Abbott et al., 2002).

In summary, research on sporting performance has provided evidence of differences in levels of performance between expert and novices with regard to strategic thinking, cognitive processes and perceptual abilities. This confirms the importance of isolating level of performance in sport (Duffy, Baluch and Ericsson, 2004). There is much evidence from the literature that the expert–novice relationship is indeed a useful division to learn from and that therefore this focus on the elite–amateur comparison may contribute to the better understanding of athletes and improve ways of identifying what is needed by elite athletes.

Models of talent and ways of identifying talent are available and there are many comparisons in world sport that can be considered. The importance in recognizing how to support talent in a psychological environment, however, is vitally important.

Questions to consider

1. What psychological skills do young players require if they are to make the shift from reliance on coaches and family to being independent players on professional and semi-professional teams?
2. How could you best implement a shift from novice to expert?
3. What model of talent would suit your sport?

REFLECTIVE PRACTICE: TAP INTO TALENT

Developing talent takes lots of hours of practice; however, with motivation, commitment and a good plan, it is possible. Work through all three sections in the following exercise:

PART 1: THINKING OF OTHERS' TALENT

Think of a person, possibly in your sport, that you admire.

1. What type of skills and characteristics do they have?
2. What do you know about how they have developed these?
3. Did they work through hours/years of practice?
4. Do they watch sport, read sports books, work with other sporting professionals... ?
5. What are your thoughts about their journey to the top?

PART 2: LABELLING YOURSELF

How you label yourself may be preventing you from moving ahead with your talent. Do you fall into any of these categories?

1. The Fatalist – 'I attribute my successes and failures to luck or fate or poor referees or coaches' (read up on attribution theory). If you blame things on external factors, you are not really relying on your own effort to do things. Try to attribute your success and failures as predominantly based on ability and effort. This is positive.
2. The Defender – Do you get angry when things go wrong? Perhaps you are just being defensive, acting as though you feel that you know exactly who you are. This could be useful if you are successful however, if you are less successful it could be keeping you in a fixed state of mind where you defend your every thought and behaviour. This may indicate that you don't think you should, or could or want to change. This could be holding you back.
3. The Blamer – Do you blame others for everything that doesn't happen? Take responsibility. Face up to the fact that you can change your life if you want to, that it's not always because of everyone else.
4. The Non-Adherer – Do you set yourselves goals and then not stick to them? This shows a lack of adherence or stickability. You need to think strongly about how committed you are. Where do you rate yourself in terms of adherence on a range of 0–100 per cent?

5. The Know-it-all – Do you learn from mistakes? Do you go further than accepting them? Are you open to new ways of doing things? Or do you know it all – obviously you don't need to improve as you are already at the pinnacle?

6. The Talent Stunter – Do you label yourself as not being able to go any further because you don't have the 'hidden' factor – e.g. you are too short, tall, overweight, slow. Consider whether you might have plateaued because you're stunting your own talent growth for some reason?

PART 3: ENHANCING YOUR OWN TALENT

Answer the following questions now, if you want to change:

1. How motivated am I to change – 10 per cent, 50 per cent, 100 per cent? If it's not 100 per cent then is it really going to happen? Do you really want to change? Are you up for a challenge or would you prefer to avoid having to do something different?

2. How would I rate my commitment to change – 10 per cent, 50 per cent, 100 per cent? If it's not 100 per cent then is it really going to happen? Are you realistically going to make a plan that fits in with your life, or are you lazy, lack any sense of planning, give in too easily, don't have the time to put into change?

PART 4: TAKING STEPS

1. Start by deciding how you would like to improve your talent. What would you like to change?

2. Think about your goal – why are you stuck? Do you want to achieve your goal and be proactive or are you trying to avoid a potential problem and being reactive? Use the goal setting techniques in Chapter 6.

3. What will the pitfalls be and how will you handle them (are you a yo-yo or binge committer – go fully into it and then out of it then full into it and then out again ...) when it comes to change?

4. What skills do you need to cope with this change?

5. How will you learn from your mistakes and take criticism so that you can change? Can you be flexible?

6. What will your success look like? Can you visualise how you will look, feel and think? Can you put this image 'somewhere' as a constant reminder?

Further Reading

Colvin, G. (2008). *Talent is Overrated: What really separates world-class performers from everyone else.* London: Nicholas Brealey Publishing Ltd.

Martindale, R., Collins, D. and Abraham, A. (2007). 'Effective Talent Development: The elite coach perspective in the UK sport'. *Applied Sport Psychology*, 19:2, 187–206.

Syed, M. (2010). *Bounce: The myth of talent and the power of practice*. London: Fourth Estate.

15 EXTREME SPORT

'Everyone has limits, but not everyone accepts them. We want to push mankind's boundaries out a little further.'

Felix Baumgartner (the first person to break the sound barrier, free falling from over 128,000 feet).

'I am riveted by extreme sports like big-wave surfing, "megaramp" skateboarding and half pipe snowboarding. I am fascinated partly because the sports are so exhilaratingly acrobatic. But I am also captivated by the fear that a terrible accident might happen at any moment. And accidents do happen.'

Lucy Walker (Director of *The Crash Reel*, the dramatic story of snowboarding athlete Kevin Pearce).

Objectives

1. Defining extreme sport
2. Motivation in extreme sport: pathological, personality, culture, arousal, stimulation, sensation-seeking, thrill, experience, boredom, uniqueness
3. Risk in extreme sport: calculated, homeostasis, zero risk
4. Accuracy and speed; occupational risk

What motivates you to ski down an icy mountain with two wooden planks attached to your feet at over 100 miles per hour? What drives you to drag race at speeds of over 300 miles per hour? Extreme sport is increasing in popularity. It is estimated that one in seven adults in the UK, i.e. 14 per cent of the population, participate in extreme sporting activities (Campbell and Johnson, 2005). The death rate from extreme sport is also increasing. BASE jumping, for example, has seen 200 deaths since 1998 and 75 per cent of these have occurred since 2000.

In America, marketing specialists are capitalizing on a growing interest among young people. For example, 25 per cent of under-25s express an interest in being involved with extreme sport (Alliance Leisure, 2006). Having an extreme sport experience is easy enough, as these can be bought through gift days. In addition, many charity organizations now host extreme challenges as fundraisers. Businesses also support their staff in hard core obstacle events as a staff development tool.

These challenges teach staff to step out of their comfort zone, to take calculated risks and to persevere in the face of adversity. Even Age UK promotes extreme sport to older people, as it espouses the virtues of continuing to experience the thrill that these extreme activities can provide.

Of course, extreme sport often appears in the news especially when you do the unthinkable or push the boundaries into new realms, such as skydiver Felix Baumgartner. He broke the sound barrier, achieved the fastest speed of free fall at a rate of 843.6 miles per hour (1,357.64km/h), and at the time (2012) the highest free fall, estimated at 24 miles (39km), until surpassed by Dr Alan Eustace's highest free-fall parachute jump two years later.

TV documentaries such *Daredevils: Living on the Edge* (C4, 2012) showed the sports of high liners, TT racing and BASE jumping. Newspaper articles, such as 'The pursuit of flying just a stone's throw from a tragic fall', look at why people, even in the wake of death, continue to engage in extreme sport (*Canadian National Post*). With all this publicity, whether good or bad, everyone wants to know why people are doing it. Is it something to do with your personality? Does it mean you are a thrill seeker? Is it about facing your fears and challenging yourself? Is it because you are a risk taker?

Let's quickly begin with a definition of what actually constitutes extreme sport. In the past, it has been equated only to high risk. Literature sees it as a collection of activities that predispose you to a high chance of injury compared to sports with a normal risk where you are 'relatively safe' from serious injury. I don't feel that risk is the only factor. I see it as both a mental and physical challenge, with competition from the elements – unlike traditional sport where you compete for a score or time – and in which there is high possibility of injury. My full definition is as follows:

> 'Extreme sport' is a 'competitive (comparison or self-evaluative) activity within which the participant is subjected to natural or unusual physical and mental challenges such as speed, height, depth or natural forces and where fast and accurate cognitive perceptual processing may be required for a successful outcome. An unsuccessful outcome is more likely to result in the injury or even fatality of the participant than in a non-extreme sport' (Cohen, 2012).

Though there is some risk involved, this is not the most important aspect of the sport. It is about the challenge of competing against the elements, which may be natural or contrived.

WHAT MOTIVATES YOU TO UNDERTAKE EXTREME SPORT?

Early psychological research linked risk (although not necessarily related to sport) to a *pathological condition*. It concluded that taking extreme risk must somehow be a sign of mental illness. The psychoanalytic view regarded physical risk-taking as the expression of a death wish, though Anna Freud stated that high-risk activity served the function of mediating anxieties. Have you gone crazy if you take up an extreme sport?

Instead of admitting that it is a mad, mad world, you could attribute participation in extreme sport to your *personality*. Your genetic make-up programmes you to behave in a certain way. Personality is one of these programmes that you are born with. One of the key dimensions with personality is *Extraversion–Introversion* (Eysenck and Eysenck, 1985). Extraverts are people who seek excitement, often via the company of others. They are recognised as friendly and assertive. Introverts on the other hand, are less outgoing, more reserved and less sociable, requiring less stimulation from others, though this may be because they are content with their own thoughts. Is the need to take part in extreme sport therefore due to your personality?

As an extreme sport participant, you would tend to score higher on tests of extraversion than non-participants though the extent of extraversion is largely dependent on the type of extreme sport that you are involved in. If you are an elite alpinist, you should be lower on extraversion than a skydiver. The difference in levels of extraversion may also be related to your *cultural background* (Breivik, 1999). If you are English or Italian, you may be more introverted than if you are Norwegian or Slovakian (Breivik, 1999). Norwegians and Slovakians therefore undertake greater risks. If you are a drag racer, you are lower in extraversion than if you are a sport science student who engages regularly in sport (Cohen, 2012).

Neuroticism, another trait in Eysenck's personality theory, is concerned with the tendency to experience negative emotional states. Individuals who play sport are attributed with having lower neuroticism or anxiety. However, overall research examining this as a personality trait is inconclusive. Findings in extreme sport have suggested that participants have lower levels of neuroticism than other groups, though this has not always been consistently demonstrated (e.g. Goma-i-Freixanet, 1991). My research found that there was a significant difference in neuroticism with regard to gender among drag racers, archers and sport science students. In addition, if you are female, then you are identified as being higher in neuroticism across the different sports.

Do you undertake extreme sport because of a *physiological need for arousal and stimulation*? Extreme sport personality is also linked with two other concepts: optimal level of arousal (OLA) and optimal level of stimulation (OLS). If you already have a satisfactory or high level of arousal (OLA) that meets your needs, then you would not look to undertake more activity. In others words, if your glass is already full, you don't need any more to drink! If your levels are low, however, then you require more input, so you would seek more novel and intense situations of stimulation in order to reach a higher OLA and function more efficiently. So, some of you already have a full glass or usually full glass in terms of arousal. You therefore keep out of extreme sport or perhaps only go for the occasional experience. Some of you find that your glass is often empty and needs a greater level of stimulation to keep it full. This would identify you as a sensation seeker and influence your choice of sporting activities (Zuckerman, Kolin, Price and Zoob, 1964).

If you participate in extreme sport, you are more likely to be an extravert and a sensation seeker. *Sensation seeking* is a 'trait defined by the seeking of varied, novel, complex and intense sensations and experiences and the willingness to take physical, social, legal and financial risks for the sake of such experiences' (Zuckerman, 1994). Sensation seekers have a need for 'novelty' or something different, 'complexity' of challenge and intense experience. This trait can be satisfied through various activities such as extreme sport or through lifestyle choices or job choice (Zuckerman, 1994).

Sensation seekers, like extraverts, need more arousal. Zuckerman et al. (1964) justified that sensation seeking is integral to personality and reflects individual differences in biological functioning. If OLA gets too high, individuals display greater levels of stress. OLS is when individuals look for sensory experiences that are beneficial to optimal functioning (Zuckerman et al., 1964). Sports increase levels of stimulation and excitement especially if they are extreme sports such as snowboarding or motor racing. According to this research, athletes who are sensation seekers crave high levels of arousal and stimulation.

MEASUREMENTS FOR SENSATION SEEKING

Sensation seeking is a personality trait 'defined by the seeking of varied, novel, complex and intense sensations and experiences, and the willingness to take physical, social, legal, and financial risks for the sake of such experience' (Zuckerman, 1994, p. 27). Sensation seeking is not purely about risk taking though you may be inclined to ignore or underestimate the risks associated with pursing these experiences. This behaviour of minimising risk can also be part of the attraction.

The measurement of sensation seeking began in 1964, when Zuckerman et al. developed a sensation seeking scale (SSS), which has subsequently been refined and is still in use today (there are six forms). This scale, though not developed specifically for measuring sensation seeking in sport, has been used in numerous studies in sport science research. The scale has demonstrated that 'extreme sport' participants score higher than participants of lower risk sports on sensation seeking and the various subscales.

The SSS-V subscales measure four sub-factors: *thrill and adventure seeking, experience seeking, disinhibition* and *boredom susceptibility* that combine to provide an overall sensation-seeking score. The thrill and adventure seeking (TAS) subscale reflects the desire to be involved in physical activities that provide unusual sensations and experiences, such as mountain climbing or skydiving. Experience seeking (ES) concerns the pursuit of new experiences where you like using your mind and senses, such as music, art and reading (though these could also be extreme activities as well). The disinhibition (DIS) subscale indicates whether the extent of sensation seeking you want is through other people. These activities include socially 'deviant' behaviours, such as wild parties and binge drinking. Some extreme sports, such as urban climbing and BASE jumping, can have an element of illegality.

Finally, the boredom susceptibility (BS) subscale represents an aversion to a repetitive situation. The monotony of being in a sedate job may bring out the extreme sport enthusiast in you at the weekend or on holiday. Research has shown that this trait can be linked with those high in psychopathological personalities. Extreme sport participants, however, do not fall into this boredom susceptibility category nor do they appear to 'predominantly' participate in order to be anti-social (DIS). Overall, these components add up to a total sensation score that is indicative of how much of a sensation seeker you are. In extreme sport, the thrill and adventure seeking score and then the overall sensation seeking score are particularly relevant. What has been discovered once again is that there is a strong positive correlation between the sensation seeking trait and the extraversion trait (Zuckerman, 1994).

A great deal of research has supported the relationship between sensation seeking and participation in extreme sports. However, in examining sensation seeking as a personality trait, my own research (Cohen, 2012) showed that those with high extraversion tend to be high in sensation seeking and this is more typical in those who engage in traditional sport – not in extreme sport.

There is an alternative test to Zuckerman's Sensation Seeking Scale called the Arnett Inventory of Sensation Seeking (AISS) (Arnett, 1994). It measures the novelty and intensity of the activity. However, it does not consider socially unacceptable norm breaking behaviours nor does it focus on sport. There is also the Need Inventory of Sensation Seeking (NISS) that assesses motivational disposition though, again, this was not developed specifically for sport (Roth and Hammelstein, 2012).

Risk Perception

What else could motivate you or others to participate in extreme sport? Risk taking does imply that there are elements of uncertainty with possible negative outcomes. Whether this is healthy or pathological can be debated. As an extreme sport participant are you deliberately seeking danger? Let's consider risk perception. Several studies have suggested that an athlete's ability to participate successfully in an extreme activity outweigh the risk factor. The athletes I have spoken to about it say they understand the risks. However, they feel they are well trained and have a great thirst for life and challenge. BASE jumpers in particular know that there is a very high risk of fatality. *Taking a risk is calculated.* During filming for a documentary on BASE jumpers, the crew were not able to witness a jump by Jokke Summer and others due to the extremely poor weather conditions. The jumpers waited quite a while to see if the snowstorm would pass; however, they decided against taking the risk of jumping because of the limited visibility. In extreme sport, risk does not appear to be the primary motivator in behaviour, though some research suggests that extreme sport participants tend to underestimate the risk involved; this tendency has been well correlated with sensation seeking (Zuckerman, 1994; Rossi and Cereatti, 1993).

The *theory of risk homeostasis* (Wilde, 1982) explains that you have your own acceptable level of perceived risk with appropriate benefits. If, however, the perceived risk becomes too great, then you will take action to reduce that risk in order to return it to an acceptable level (Napier, Findley and Self, 2007). A balance or homeostatic effect is achieved by continually adjusting how you perceive risk. As a sport psychologist, I have met extreme sport participants for whom the risk factor is counter-intuitive to being safe. Some of these athletes report how their fear grows in direct proportion to how much they participate in their sport. This linear relationship continues until such time that they withdraw from the sport or suffer from an accident or worse.

The *zero risk model* explains that when you go above your threshold, which is set at zero, you inhibit your actions. It doesn't, however, explain why your threshold levels vary on an individual basis. Another theory is threat avoidance (Fuller 1984). This is based on 'stimulus-response' or 'cause and effect' relationships. For example, a stimulus or event (a dangerous snow storm) causes a response resulting in either approach or avoid behaviour (no wingsuit flying today). The Reversal Theory (Apter, 2007) identifies you (an extreme sport player) as an arousal seeker who seeks out extreme situations that enhance your mood. This can be measured using the arousal avoidance subscale of the Telic Dominance Scale (TDS) (Murgatroyd et al., 1978).

Could it still be pathological? It has been suggested that perhaps you undertake a high-risk sport because you have emotional difficulties, in particular with relationships (Woodman et al., 2010). It does seem that this may be the case with some of the urban climbers (see *Don't Look Down: The exploits of an urban free climber*, www.sportpsych.co.uk/latest-news/2014/3/23/dont-look-down-dr-rhonda-cohen-interviewed-on-60-minutes-abo.html). Speaking to BASE jumpers, however, there appears to be a bond or sense of camaraderie among them rather than an emotional gap. But there is no doubt about the presence of an escalating experience of anxiety among those who continue to participate in high-risk sports, particularly after the injury or death of another participant, that you are gambling in a numbers game and that you could be next.

Having a *risk-taking nature* is not what you need to be safe and proficient but rather a commitment to years of dedicated training. Indeed, you may be devoted to engaging in extreme sports, and possess a real sense of 'courage and humility' (Brymer, 2009). Some research has taken this even further to say that you 'engage for the holistic experience as a positive way to charge your batteries' (Willig, 2008). This may be true in some extreme sports where there is a spiritual focus, such as an endurance marathon through the Himalayas or perhaps mountain climbing. In fact, this altered spiritual state of consciousness is motivating, and may be a driver in you continuing your chosen sport. It is also reinforcing in itself so it may not be a personality trait that predisposes you to participate in extreme sports.

Quick and Accurate Reactions

According to my research, personality extreme sport often requires athletes to have quick and accurate reactions while maintaining high levels of motor skill. If you do not have quick reactions or are not trained in the advanced skills required, then you need to avoid the risk. Being able to achieve certain skill sets will either encourage or exclude you from participating.

Risk outside of sport

As an extreme sport participant do you also work in a job where there is a high occupational or emotional risk? Various studies have been undertaken to examine occupational risk takers, such as those in the police force or bomb disposal experts and those that take anti-social risks such as lawbreakers/offenders/prison inmates. The general and unsurprising result is that if you do hold one of these jobs or fit into one of these categories then you are a risk taker and therefore some of your personality is similar to those who engage in extreme sport. However, it seems there is a difference between participating in high risk sport and undertaking risk in other aspects of your life. Having spoken to a soldier who had returned from a dangerous mission, the thrill and excitement of the risk seemed to be a catalyst towards his future involvement in extreme sport. He took risks on the job and when the job ended he got involved in extreme sport, which most of his friends noted as a personality change. So, the extreme occupation came before the extreme sport.

Research has so far identified that if you are an extravert you will tend to search for stimulating events. As the environment does not always provide you with a choice of socially acceptable sporting activities in order to satisfy your need for stimulation, you will seek out risky behaviours through career choice or anti-social means. The general consensus is that if you are involved in such high-risk activities you will score higher in sensation seeking tests. Therefore extreme sport may be an outlet for satisfying this strong need for stimulation and a way of raising your arousal levels through socially acceptable means. While much of the early research (e.g. Eysenck et al., 1983) suggests that there is a very strong link between sensation seeking and extraversion in sport, the results of studies into sensation seeking have generated mixed findings.

Finally, risk of injury is an accepted part of any sport. However, risk on its own infers that there is uncertainty and a lack of control, not necessarily of oneself but of environmental or external elements. If you are in extreme sport, you are most likely a calculated risk taker. Risk in extreme sport is not a driver.

Extreme sport events, such as ultra-marathons, may even be seen as holistic and a way of becoming re-energised through an intense experience. Extreme sport may be a useful outlet for emotions. Extreme sport is different from risk in occupation or through anti-social behaviour. Having the right skill set seems vital and an ability to react quickly and accurately is essential.

Questions to consider

1. What personality traits do you share with those in your extreme sport?
2. Can you turn someone into a thrill seeker?
3. Do you take risks or are you trained and prepared for what you do?

REFLECTIVE PRACTICE: DO YOU SEEK ADVENTURE AND THRILLS?

How much of an adventurer or thrill seeker are you? Answer the questions below to find out. These are based on my own questioning as well as discussion with those in extreme sport. It is not a standardised test, like the SSS-V (Zuckerman et al. 1994); however, you can see whether you prefer any particular type of risk or thrill seeking. You may do these things because you are excited by thrill and risk. You may enjoy the excitement by watching others do it and so live vicariously.

1. I enjoy climbing and hiking because of its novelty. That is, it is unpredictable in terms of what you may see or experience along the route.
2. I enjoy reading a book or watching a TV series where the ending is unexpected.
3. When I travel I never take a guidebook, as I prefer to wander around and explore (sorry *Lonely Planet*).
4. I enjoy riding roller coasters and rides at the funfair because they are thrilling.
5. Since I was a child, I have always enjoyed jumping off things, even from 'great' heights.
6. I enjoy booking a day of new experiences such as white-water rafting, a helicopter ride or an off-road experience.
7. I like watching scary TV shows and films.
8. I have tried or would like to try surfing, parachuting or off-piste skiing.
9. I love trying new food and combinations of food, such as salty chocolate.
10. I find noisy clubs, parties and raves very exciting.
11. I don't mind if something is somewhat illegal.
12. I get tired of going out to eat at the same restaurants with the same people all the time.

How many of the questions did you respond to with a yes? The higher number of yes answers, the greater your sense of thrill, risk and adventure.

Further Reading

Apter, M. J. (2007). *Danger: Our Quest for Excitement.* Oxford, Oxon: Oneworld Publications.

Zuckerman, M. (1994). *Behavioural Expressions and Biosocial Bases of Sensation Seeking.* Cambridge, Cambs: Cambridge Press.

Zuckerman, M. (2007). *Sensation Seeking and Risky Behaviour.* Washington DC: American Psychological Association.

16 REACTION TIME

'You can't think and hit at the same time (you need to react)'
Yogi Berra (Major League Baseball player and manager)

Objectives

1. The impact of gender, age, physical activity, exercise, training, fatigue, lifestyle and personality
2. Reaction time: salient features (movement) and reaction features (duration, signals, options, emotions, decision making)

Training in cognitive skills can teach you how to better anticipate what is going to happen, how to attend to relevant and critical cues, and how to be a more effective decision maker. Furthermore, cognitive skills are the very foundation required for the development of successful motor and tactical skills, so an athlete needs them to become an expert.

WHY ARE QUICK REACTION TIMES NEEDED IN SPORT?

Reaction time training in sport can facilitate and improve your decision-making skills. The use of performance analysis (e.g. analysing your movements mathematically through filming) can identify when you make your decisions and how it links to success in your performance. Virtual reality or computer programs can enhance decision making, especially when they are designed to be sport specific. For example, I created a program for drag racers using *Superlab*, which measured reaction time in response to the different coloured lights used at the starting line of a competition. You or your coach can design these types of programs or utilise the expertise available from commercial apps or university research in doing so.

Improving your reaction time can help you develop from a novice into an expert. Research has found that if you are an expert athlete then you tend to have advanced perceptual skills in sport specific tasks. For example, in a study comparing basketball players to non-players, experienced players were significantly better than non-players at recalling structured game information. The interaction between high-level perceptual skills and sport specific structured displays suggests that an encoding of structure is vital to your successful performance as an elite (expert) athlete. The rate of visual processing in reaction time can also differentiate between you as a top ranked athlete or a bottom ranked athlete in sports such as basketball and hockey.

WHAT KEY FACTORS AFFECT YOUR REACTION TIME AND HOW DO THEY IMPACT ON YOUR SPORTING PERFORMANCE?

There are a variety of key factors that affect your reaction time and impact on your ability to perform well, such as gender, age, physical activity, exercise, fatigue, training, lifestyle and personality.

With regard to *gender*, if you are male, you are more likely faster at detecting signals, as well as more vigilant at looking at a cue for a longer period of time without being distracted. As a female, on the other hand, you tend to be more sensitive to stimuli. With *age*, the younger you are the better you are at responding to selective attention. You are better able to ignore distracting stimuli and stay focused. This would imply that training at a young age and with other young players in academies where reaction and attention is required could be key to the future success of players and of a team (see Chapter 17 on gender differences). Evidence for whether *physical activity* or *exercise* can affect your reaction time is mixed, i.e. it is not supported by all research. If you are physically fit, you should have faster reaction times than those who are not. Easterbrook's Cue Utilisation Theory (1959) was devised to account for how differences in physical activity produce variations in cognitive functioning, such as attention and decision making. With low levels of exertion, cognitive processing may be weak, as both relevant and irrelevant cues are attended to. As your exertion levels increase, your attention narrows until it reaches the point when it is directed only towards cues that are relevant. If the physical requirements are so demanding that you are over-extending yourself, then your ability to focus on what is relevant may be difficult and impact negatively on your thought process.

However, there is limited evidence to indicate that just exercising will make you quicker. Generally, if you are an older person or a mature athlete who exercises regularly, then you probably have faster reaction times than those who do not. This may be due to the effects of exercise on cognitive functioning. Some studies have shown that when implementing an exercise programme (water exercise in particular) there was no improvement in reaction time among the older participants.

Other studies show that when you have to discriminate between the speeds of moving objects following exercise, improvements in decision making are demonstrated in terms of speed but not of accuracy. Some studies have found that vigorous exercise helps improve your reaction time on tasks that require a choice of response.

Contradictory results have been shown in various other studies. There was no significant improvement in reaction time demonstrated in football skills in testing for choice in reaction time. In runners there was no post-exercise effect, though exercise improved reaction time while exercising.

However, physical activity/exercise increases arousal, which may enhance your reaction time. The results of a recent study measuring arousal in a continuous performance showed that some participants' results matched the classic Yerkes Dodson inverted U curve which demonstrates that a moderate amount of arousal leads to the greatest performance while other studies (e.g. Hull, 1943) demonstrated a linear relationship between arousal and reaction time. In a study of footballers, cognitive results were enhanced while they undertook both moderate and maximal exercise, though this was attributed to enhancement in decision making rather than improved accuracy. This is supported by a study conducted with Polish footballers where improvement in choice reaction times occurred as a result of increasing workload while cycling.

An organised exercise programme as part of your *training* should allow you to gain maximum benefit in developing the endurance needed to maintain quick reaction-time skills. In many sports, there is an endurance element that requires you to engage in play over a long period of time or to compete in several qualifying competitions over a period of days. This element necessitates you having to sustain high levels of both motor performance and perceptual skill. It is also expected that *fatigue* can hinder your performance, once again illustrating the benefits of an appropriate exercise training programme.

Being fatigued slows your reactions, especially if your task is complex. Studies on the effect of fatigue in sport have shown that being tired places limitations on both physical and perceptual skills. Muscular tension due to fatigue reduces your brain's ability to work quickly. However, tasks that included exercise resulting in voluntary exhaustion haven't produced any significant improvements in cognitive performance.

Lifestyle factors, such as smoking, can also affect your reaction time. Smokers who were abstaining from cigarettes and wore a nicotine patch had faster reaction times on recognition reaction time tasks than non-smokers who, while wearing the patch, also demonstrated better accuracy. Drinking coffee or moderate amounts of caffeine will decrease the time it takes you to find a target stimulus and the time needed to prepare a response for a complex reaction time task. Caffeine was useful in enabling sleep-deprived soldiers to maintain their reaction times and marksmanship. In fact, moderate amounts of caffeine decrease the time it takes to find a target stimulus and to prepare a response for a complex reaction time task. Sleep deprivation affects cognitive functioning and many who travel to competitions may experience the impact of changing time zones or lack of sleep.

According to the majority of research, mostly conducted through studies in the last century, if you are an extravert *personality* type then you will have faster reaction times. My research confirmed that sport science university students were significantly extraverts. However, I found low extraversion in female archers. A link that was demonstrated in my studies was that there was a positive correlation between extraversion and percentage accuracy on a specific sport test. High extraversion and fast reaction times were only evident in the students.

Previous research also demonstrated that those who were higher in neuroticism or had more anxious personality types demonstrated slower reaction times. You might expect that if you are an introvert, as you rely on feedback as a corrective measure. A study of drag racers showed that the higher the neuroticism, the slower they were on measures of reaction time. However, female university students who played high-level sport showed the opposite relationship, which was that the higher the neuroticism the faster the reaction times.

Throughout sport science literature, the relationship between high extraversion and low neuroticism with quick reaction time has been supported. However, the research used in these studies has predominantly included measurements from participants engaged in many sports as one sample group. When you analyse the cohorts or participants separately there are distinct variations according to different sports. Don't assume that because you play a particular sport that you must be outgoing as a person and that means you are naturally fast. The relationship of personality and reaction time depends on specific variables such as your sport and your position within a team.

Finally, Eysenck stated that extraverts tend to trade accuracy for speed. You may be fast but not necessarily accurate. In relation to sport, Eysenck identified baton passing, football passing and returning a serve in tennis as examples of activities requiring quick reaction times. Students studying sport science at Middlesex University were high in extraversion, fast in reaction times yet also high in accuracy. There wasn't a speed/accuracy-trade off, which is often discussed in the literature. You can be fast and accurate in sport. In the same study, archers who were high in extraversion also tended to be higher in accuracy. Those who were high in neuroticism, e.g. drag racers, were less accurate. Elite or professional drag racers were fast and accurate and this was not related to an extravert personality. It is clear therefore that the relation between personality, reaction time and accuracy is not universal and that it often depends on the sport that is being played.

HOW CAN YOU IMPROVE REACTION TIME?

Your reaction time can improve in two ways. First, you must become more aware of salient features, such as the spin of a ball, the position of a bat or racket, or a sudden movement on the track. When salient features are unusual or new then they will require your attention. Later on, once you have habituated or become used to them and what they mean, then you can often process them automatically. In tennis, for example, the position of the racket and the spin of the ball are important to you while you prepare to return the ball. The more you practise responding to these cues, the quicker your anticipatory response becomes and the faster you react.

The second thing you can change is the nature of your reaction, such as the duration or length of the stimuli, strength of the signal, reducing the number of options being offered, the level of emotion needed and the efficiency of your decision making. In some sports, of course, visual displays are of a very short duration, such as in the reaction time needed in response to the start lights in motorsport. People vary in their ability to process these short duration visual displays. Short-term visual storage or iconic memory is often debated in psychology; however, it is usually agreed that these memories last for approximately 4 seconds. In sport, your success may also be linked to the ability to process visual information quickly. In cricket, for example, successful batsmen were faster and more effective at picking up information from rapid visual displays than less successful batsmen.

Your reaction time also varies with different signals and whether or not you need to make a simple or a complex response, e.g. the weaker the signal, the longer the reaction time. The more consistent the intensity of the signal (moderate or strong), the more consistent the reaction time. When you don't need to process a player's movement visually or hear what is happening, then you should be quicker in your reaction.

The time needed to prepare a response may also depend on how many options or choices you need to process. In the 100-metres you may be listening for the starter's voice, waiting for the sound of the gun, hearing the buzz from the crowd and feeling the presence and pressure of the other runners. Similarly in golf, this experience can occur at each hole, choosing your club, assessing the wind, deciding how hard to hit the ball and so on. These stimuli can be paired with the necessary physical response, such as assuming the starting position, getting set or on the mark, shifting your weight from the front foot to the back foot, etc. An overwhelming amount of information can therefore be sharing your attention and thereby preventing you from achieving your best performance, especially if you are an amateur or novice. For example, in motorsport, in addition to external stimuli, vehicles have numerous dials and digital readouts that drivers need to react to using both hands and feet. In some extreme winter sports, there can also be a long duration while waiting for the start of a race with long periods between runs.

Of course, emotion can affect your reaction and response. When anxiety is high and the sport skill is demanding, you only have a limited amount of resource with which to respond. When demands are exceeded, your performance efficiency as well as your effectiveness can decrease. Whether you are born with the anxiety trait or are anxious due to the competitive nature of a sporting event, you need good coping strategies, as high levels of anxiety have a negative effect on performance efficiency unless you also have high levels of confidence. Self-confidence along with an ability to see anxiety as facilitative rather than debilitative can be positive. In extreme sport, continually pushing the boundaries of human limitations can create high pre-anxiety. However, it doesn't necessarily impact on performance.

Decision making can be strategic or selective. You may be thinking five steps ahead on your decision-making plan, deciding whether to pass a ball or how to take a penalty kick. Decision making, or when you are being selective, is an important part of understanding motor skills.

What methods are used to study decision making and how can you improve?

Within the information processing approach, decision making involves visual search, recognition, recall and anticipation. You start off by scanning the environment, ignore things that are irrelevant, use advance cues and then engage in anticipation. Then you react. Experts seem to collate information into relevant groups better, put together cues and responses and use a memory bank of decisions in similar situations.

If time is limited, experts are in a better position to take a quick decision more automatically using the cognitive and motor systems along with knowledge store and motor schema. This is studied through response accuracy and response time where players can watch static or dynamic situations and are required to make a response. It can also be studied through examining perceived meaning in the sporting environment.

In conclusion, studies on perceptual skill development for sports often vary according to the requirements for particular sports, e.g. ball skills, target skills and so on. To date, no distinct pattern of difference has been established in the perceptual-cognitive processing skills of athletes participating in various sports. The focus of sport research, often based on visual processing in relation to performance, varies. For instance, some research has examined choice reaction time in sports, which has shown a positive relation with increasing exercise intensity until energy expenditure levels reach a maximal point.

Alternative studies have utilised speed discrimination e.g. tennis players outperformed triathlon competitors. In volleyball, significant differences were demonstrated between beginners and advanced players in estimating the speed and direction of a moving object. However, no differences were shown in relation to the number of accurate responses associated with the recognition of the speed and direction.

In one of my studies, the reaction time of students who played sport showed that they had faster reaction times than non-sport students. When given specific tasks related to sport, once again those who played sport had faster reaction times than those who did not.

Questions to consider

1. What factors can be identified and modified in order to enhance reaction time?

2. Which sports can benefit from reaction time training and how would you go about developing this kind of training?

REFLECTIVE PRACTICE: IMPROVING REACTION TIME

TRY AN ONLINE REACTION TIME TEST OR APP

There are quite a few out there. https://faculty.washington.edu/chudler/java/redgreen.html, http://www.humanbenchmark.com/tests/reactiontime raction and excitement.

ANALYSE HOW REACTION TIME AFFECTS YOUR PLAY

The purpose of this exercise is to understand that how you react in different situations can impact on your performance. We need to manage how we react and we can only do this by understanding how we react. Then we can improve.

This questions below is just a way of demonstrating how many things you can change to improve your reaction times. One of the best ways to use this list is to video your performance and then go back and try to analyse how you could do things differently. Watch a professional golf swing and then watch your own. How do they compare? What can you do different.

Another way to progress is to find a trainer or coach to advise. Professional and semi-professional teams and athletes often have access to a sport science team or a University department where there are performance analysts who look at your movement according to mathematical perturbations, biomechanics, gait analysis etc. (some companies that sell trainers /sneakers do this). Of course there are also bachelor and masters degrees in these areas so you could study it yourself.

1. *The way you position your equipment*: the angle of a bat or racket, the surface I am on.

   How can I change or improve my reaction to this?

2. *Movement*: the spin of a ball, a movement of the shoulder, eye contact, body angle, head position.

   How can I change or improve my reaction to this?

3. *Unusual features*: a large crowd, vuvuzelas from South Africa ... a sudden movement on the track.

   How can I change or improve my reaction to this?

4. *Unusual environment*: Olympics, World Cup, a new golf course.

   How can I change or improve my reaction to this?

5. *Duration or length of the stimuli*

How can I change or improve my reaction to this?

6. *Strength of the signal*

How can I change or improve my reaction to this?

7. *Number of options*

How can I change or improve my reaction to this?

8. *Level of emotion*

How can I change or improve my reaction to this?

9. *Decision making*

How can I change or improve my reaction to this?

Further Reading

Schmidt, R. and Lee, T. (2014). *Motor Learning and Performance: From principles to application* (5th edn.). Champaign, IL: Human Kinetics.

Vickers, J. (2007). *Perception, Cognition and Decision Training: The quiet eye in action.* Champaign, IL: Human Kinetics.

17 GENDER DIFFERENCES

'I think the key is for women not to set any limits. People ... used to think
that if girls were good at sports their sexuality would be affected.'
Martina Navratilova (Multiple Grand Slam tennis champion)

'The 2012 London games fostered a generation of hope. I witnessed
women participating for the very first time, representing every nation.'
Jackie Joyner-Kersee (regarded by some as the greatest
female athlete of the 20th century)

'God made me the way I am and I accept myself.'
Caster Semenya (South African middle distance runner,
won gold in the 800 metres at the 2009 World Championships,
after which some people questioned her gender)

Objectives

1. Gender issues in sport: historical, physiological, nutritional, cultural, religious
   and media related
2. Psychological differences in gender: reaction to injury, success orientation,
   motivational orientation, personality, risk, sensation seeking, reaction time and
   developmental
3. Gender testing, transgender criteria and homophobia in sport

Female participation in sport has risen in popularity and, in fact, for the first
time ever in the history of the Olympics, all countries included at least one female
competitor in their team for the London Olympic Games 2012. If you are a woman,
you can now compete in combat sports such as boxing (Olympic Games 2012) and
extreme sports, such as women's ski jumping (Sochi Winter Olympics 2014). In
Rio 2016, there will be a new contact sport, rugby sevens, open to both male and
female teams.

This chapter examines a number of issues, which range from the historic reasons
why women may or may not participate in sport to performance variations by
gender. It will identify the criteria for transgender competitors and discuss tactics
being used to combat homophobia in sport.

WHY DO WE HAVE SEPARATE SPORTS FOR MEN AND WOMEN?

The segregation or exclusion of women from sport is a *historical* issue as it was thought that if you were a woman then you would engage in resplendent activities, which were portrayed as graceful and elegant (e.g. gymnastics or ice skating), while if you were a man then you could compete in sports bursting with speed, physical contact and strength (e.g. speed skating, wrestling or weightlifting). In a male-oriented society, where the female body was held up as an aesthetic icon, sports that offered an aesthetic impact matched the stereotypical ideas of femininity of the time (Koivula, 2001). In addition to appearance, there was also concern that, as a woman, sport could impinge on your menstruation processes and interfere with your reproductive processes at a time when child bearing was considered the primary role for women.

There are also particular *physiological* issues in working with women in sport, known as the 'Female Triad'. The American College of Sport Medicine (ACSM) identifies the triad as an interrelationship between energy availability, menstrual functioning and bone mineral density. Energy availability is calculated as dietary energy intake minus the energy you expel through exercise. Not eating appropriately combined with the extensive demands of exercise or training for sport can lead to poor reproductive and skeletal health (i.e. osteoporosis). ACSM therefore advocates the importance of healthy eating in promoting good health. Low bone mineral density can result in injuries such as stress fractures. Menstrual irregularities are often associated with intense sport participation and result in reduced oestrogen levels.

There are more *nutritional* issues relating to eating and weight issues with female athletes compared to male athletes. Female athletes are more likely to be junk food addicts than their male counterparts. Eating disorders, such as anorexia and bulimia, are prevalent among women in sport especially when there is a specific desirable body form, such as in gymnastics, ice skating, swimming and diving. This does not mean, however, that females should be at a high risk from an eating disorder. If you are in a team that has a nutritionist, then you could benefit from healthy eating advice. Sport nutrition is growing in popularity along with regulation, so look for a sport exercise nutritionist who meets professional competencies and is on a register such as the Sport and Exercise Nutrition register (SENr). All team members need to understand healthy weight management rather than pathological weight loss.

In addition, *cultural* issues play a role in sport as it reflects the idealization of beauty and femininity. Physically fit celebrities and female sport stars are often used to advertise new ranges of clothes. This stimulates an aesthetic interest in the female form, which has most likely led to an increase in women exercising in gyms. Levels of exercise can, however, be age dependent. More adolescent boys participate in organised sport and physical activity than girls (Coleman and Brooks, 2009). Adolescent girls often drop out of sport and structured physical activity, as they don't want to be sweaty in front of boys. Young working women, on the other hand, are increasingly attracted to physical challenges such as marathons, which have the additional altruistic attraction of raising money for charity.

There are religious considerations too that may divide men and women. Some religious groups will only allow men or women to exercise or participate in sports if they do so separately. They may or may not allow women or men to watch the opposite sex play sport. In addition, wearing religious clothing may not be suitable in sport, e.g. a hijab, although there are innovative companies that are designing clothing to enable women to exercise or play sport. There are also popular women-only sessions in some gyms.

There are fewer female role models in sport, which makes it predominantly a *media* issue. A career in women's sport is not particularly profitable, as women are underrepresented as coaches and women athletes receive less funding (Kremer, Moran, Walker and Craig, 2012) and less prize money. When a woman does succeed in landing a sport position, the media sees it as a field day. Interestingly enough, I was invited by a radio station to discuss gender issues when Andy Murray hired a female coach. I declined, as I didn't see what difference gender makes to a coach's competency. The reason for the male/female divide and the lower rates of participation by women in sport is therefore directed at the media. According to Cooky, Messner and Hextrum (2013), the media is largely responsible for the slow growth in women's sports because television coverage is limited and there is an inferior quality of coverage resulting in less exciting footage and clips to show. On the other hand, the Women's World Cup (WWC) was televised in 2015 and WNBA basketball is continually gaining popularity in the USA. However, there is still a large discrepancy between the coverage of men and women's sport.

WHAT ARE THE PSYCHOLOGICAL DIFFERENCES BETWEEN FEMALES AND MALES IN SPORT?

According to research there are varying gender differences in relation to emotion, success, motivational orientation, personality, risk, culture and age.

For example, following an injury, females feel less contented with the emotional support that their coach provides, though they feel satisfied by the encouragement from their friends and family (Granito, 2002). This is most likely due to the fact that females, particularly those who are sub-elite to elite and those who are adolescent, tend to implement emotion-focused coping strategies (e.g. Anshel, Porter, and Quek, 1998; Hoar, Crocker, Holt and Tamminen, 2012). Cognitive interpretation of a situation affects stress, which can lead to injury. Interestingly enough, females do not differ from males in whether they perceive physiological anxiety as facilitative or debilitative (Jones and Hanton, 1996).

In terms of success, females admit to lower expectations of success and score lower than males on tests of mental toughness, i.e. confidence, stress management, focus and motivation (Nicholls, Polman, Levy and Backhouse, 2009). They worry more about achieving personal objectives and being adequately prepared for competition. Males agonise over the difficulty of the competition and the outcome (Jones, Swain and Cale, 1991).

The female tendency to avoid success was first identified in the 1970s (Horner, 1973). The evidence for this psychological barrier to achievement, however, has not been consistently supported. In studies into motor activities, for example, females did not demonstrate any more fear of success than their male counterparts (Conroy and Metzler, 2004). Unfavourable and critical self-talk can result from elevated levels of fear of success and this can jeopardise an athlete's opportunities to achieve. Negative self-talk was especially evident in a study examining female junior tennis players (Van Raalte, Brewer, Rivera and Petitpas, 1994).

Motivation orientation varies between the genders in many studies. There are two types of orientation: task orientation and ego orientation (see Chapter 6 for more on this). Task orientation is considered in relation to one's own baseline of performance. Ego orientation is focusing on your performance in comparison to other competitors. Most literature recommends that females and males derive benefit from being task orientated (Petherick and Weigand, 2002). Elite British adolescent female athletes demonstrated high levels of task orientation with low ego orientation (Harwood, Cumming and Fletcher, 2004). Female basketball players (aged between 10–14 years) showed higher task orientation and lower ego orientation than their male counterparts (Grossbard et al., 2007). However, elite Norwegian athletes, male and female, showed relatively high levels of both task and ego orientation (Abrahamsen, Roberts and Pensgaard, 2008). Junior elite female gymnasts with task-oriented coaches demonstrated more enjoyment, more positive body image and higher self-esteem (Duda, 2001). Those who trained with coaches who encourage ego orientation were more likely to experience competitive stress.

The fact that there are significant gender differences in personality trait scores is not new to psychological literature (see Costa and McCrae, 2001; Chapman et al., 2007) though very little of the research in psychology has examined the differences between personality and gender in a sporting context. Various personality tests exist and two key variables continually emerge.

Firstly, there is neuroticism which is a display of worry. Secondly, there is extraversion which is being outgoing and in need of high levels of arousal (Eysenck et al., 1983).

One study on gender differences in personality (O'Sullivan et al., 1998) showed that sportswomen followed the typical trend of being higher in neuroticism than sportsmen. Males were measured as being less neurotic than females among a sample of rock climbers (Feher, Meyers and Skelly, 1998). Female bodybuilders were less neurotic and higher in extraversion than the population norms

(Freedson, Mihevic, Loucks and Girandol, 1983). Contrary to this, Fuchs and Zaichkowsky (1983) found that males and females had similar personality profiles in bodybuilding

Those who play in a team sport scored higher on extraversion than those who participate in individual sport (Eagleton, et al., 2007). When comparing gender in team sport, females scored lower on extraversion than males (Colley et al., 1985).

Evidence for potential moderators of personality with regards to gender and physical activity were inconclusive. Rhodes and Smith (2006), in a review of 33 studies conducted from 1969 to 2006, did not conclude with any significant findings. The authors of this review paper attributed the lack of findings to the small number of studies available that have controlled-for-gender differences. Traits such as extraversion were evident, though a link between personality and physical activity was not concluded. The researchers suggested that future studies are required before any conclusions can be made.

Men and women are different when deciding whether or not to engage in risky behaviours. Kerr, Au and Lindner (2004) conducted a survey, which concluded that there were significant differences between men and women on the desire to participate in high- and low-risk sport. Males are typically more willing to engage in risky behaviour than females and concurrently perceive these risks as less serious (Spigner, Hawkins, and Loren, 1993). Kontos (2004) attributed this to the fact that females possessed a higher perception of risk, therefore participated in fewer risk-taking behaviours, while males demonstrated a greater propensity for sensation seeking than females (Ballet al., 1984). In my research, I found that female students who engaged in various sports such as athletics, netball and football were higher risk takers than females in archery or drag racing (Cohen, 2012).

On measures of sensation seeking, males have demonstrated higher scores than females. The largest gender differences as measured by the sensation seeking scale have been shown on the sub-scales for thrill seeking and disinhibition (Zuckerman, 1994). However, studies have not considered whether women who compete in high-risk sport alongside men, for example in drag racing or motor racing, have the same level of sensation seeking as each other.

Personality studies have demonstrated that those high in extraversion have faster reaction times though are less accurate than those high in neuroticism who have slower reaction times and are more accurate (Brebner, 1980). With regard to gender, studies have predominantly shown that males have faster reaction times than females even when training or practice is increased (Welford, 1980; Thomas and French, 1985; Adam et al., 1999; Dane and Erzurumluoglu, 2003).

A warning stimulus improves reaction time, although research on whether this differs between the sexes is very limited. Research examining the effect of warning stimuli on gender differences in reaction time, (Philip, 1934), shows that girls were quicker than boys, although the differences were not significant. In a review paper, Silverman (2006) speculates that an impending stimulus or warning would appear to slow down females or those who are already slower respondents more than the affect on males or faster respondents. Boys were faster than girls without a warning stimulus.

Does the gap in reaction time between the genders appear to be changing? In the Olympics of 1928, the 100-metres record was 10.8 seconds for men and 12.2 seconds for women, representing a difference of 1.4 seconds. The current record (at time of writing this book) set by Usain Bolt for the men's 100-metres is 9.58 seconds. The equivalent record for women, set by Florence Griffith Joyner, is 10.49 seconds. The difference between the world records is therefore reduced to 0.91 seconds. However, the women's record has fallen by 22 per cent since the beginning of the 1900s compared to a fall of 9 per cent in the men's record.

There are also diminishing time differences between the genders in swimming, specifically in the front crawl (Guttmann, 1991). The discrepancy between males and females has decreased from a 12.41 per cent difference in 1936 to a 5.2 per cent gap in 1980. In the 100-metres freestyle (long course), the fastest time as of 2014 is 46.91 seconds for men and 52.07 seconds for women – a difference of 5.16 seconds. However, in shooting sports research has found that men were quicker than women in aiming at a target, though women were more accurate (Barral and Debu, 2004). This may be due to more modern sport science training. However, if it were just due to training then the differential between men and women would have stayed the same. Alternatively, the reduction in reaction time between the genders may be due to an increase in participation of females in sport (Silverman, 2006). Studies that do not account for gender can have inaccurate results. For example, a study by Christenson and Winkelstein (1988) on testing reaction time in visual performance can be criticised for having twice as many males in the 'athlete' group as opposed to the 'non-athlete' group.

Developmentally, there are differences between girls and boys. Thomas and French (1985) carried out a meta-analysis examining differences in gender for reaction time across childhood and adolescence. They concluded that there were no significant differences in these age groups between girls and boys. However, in a more recent study of handball players, boys demonstrated faster visual reaction times than girls (Dane and Erzurumluoglu, 2003). Some recent studies find females to be quicker in reaction time than males within certain age brackets (e.g. Hommel et al., 2004).

Culturally, Silverman (2006) in his meta-analysis of reaction time studies, found a difference between women living in the United States of America (USA) and women from 11 other countries. Silverman speculated that this difference could be due to the fact that American women are more actively engaged in motor performance activities, such as driving and fast-action sports, than women outside the USA. Silverman predicted that continuing at the current pace, this differential could narrow substantially.

In studies on risk-taking, adolescents perceived situations as less risky than adults (Kontos, 2004). However, as age increases, reaction time decreases for both men and women and the differential between the two is maintained (Jevas and Yan, 2001). Measures on simple reaction time improved with age up until the late 20s and then slowly decreased until the 50s and 60s. By the 70s, reaction time has considerably deteriorated (Jevas and Yan, 2001; Der and Deary, 2006). This is particularly noticeable when undertaking tasks that are viewed as complex reaction time tasks. The reason for this reduction due to age may be physiologically based, e.g. it could be a sign of Alzheimer's (Gorus, De Raedt, Lambert, Lemper and Mets, 2008), though it could be based on experience in processing as older people tend to be quicker at collating information (Myerson, Robertson and Hale, 2007) though more considered in their response (Botwinick, 1996). Older people prefer concentrating on one task at a time rather than multitasking as younger people often do (Redfern, Muller, Jennings and Furman, 2002). Therefore studies need to isolate age, as this may be a significant factor.

Gender testing and transgender criteria in sport

Following the World Athletics Championships of 2009, South African runner, Caster Semenya was administered a biological test to determine if she was entitled to compete as a woman. She was subjected to an international media frenzy and was banned from competition until June 2010. The International Olympic Committee (IOC) feels that there is an intricacy in categorizing athletes as either male or female because some competitors fall somewhere between these classifications due to genetic abnormalities. They feel that it is important to have parity among all competitors. When an athlete doesn't fit neatly into a male/female category they are concerned that either this athlete or other athletes may be either advantaged or disadvantaged.

If Caster hadn't been determined to be biologically female then she would have been banned from sport. More recently, Caitlyn Jenner (formerly Bruce Jenner), an Olympic decathlon gold medallist in 1976, has transitioned. This has resulted in an online petition by designated groups for her gold medal to be revoked. The IOC supports Jenner in keeping her medal.

The latest on transgender competitors in sport is that if competitors meet the following criteria then they are free to compete in their designated category (IOC regulations, 2012): they have had gender reassignment surgery; they have completed at least two years of hormone therapy; and they have legal recognition of their assigned gender in their home country.

IS SPORT HOMOPHOBIC?

In addition to gender issues, there is discrimination against sexual orientation in sport. In 2008, a review undertaken by Sport Scotland, UK Sport, Sport England and Sport Northern Ireland found there was limited research in this area. A more recent international study on homophobia in sport entitled, 'Out on the Fields' (2015), surveyed 9,500 lesbian, gay, bisexual and heterosexual participants. Results revealed that 80 per cent cited first-hand experience in witnessing homophobia while playing or watching sport. Of those surveyed, 75 per cent believe that an LGB person would not be *safe* as a sport spectator. Of those surveyed, 63 per cent of all participants and 70 per cent of LGB participants believed homophobia is more common in UK sports than in the rest of society.

Organizations, such as Stonewall, are working to combat discrimination and they have initiated campaigns such as Rainbow Laces (in partnership with Paddy Power) and reports, including 'Leagues Behind', in order to encourage a homophobia free sport. Kick It Out is another organization designed to tackle discrimination and racism in football where there needs to be a cultural shift.

In conclusion, there are a lot of similarities between participants in sport; however, there are also differences in the needs of athletes. Gender issues may be levelling out, but understanding what differences may exist in sport can only make you a better player, coach, psychologist, researcher or parent.

Questions to consider

1. What techniques can be applied in working specifically with women to improve their performance?
2. How could the growth of women's sport be developed internationally?
3. What can be done to combat discrimination in sport?

REFLECTIVE PRACTICE: OBSERVING GENDER DIFFERENCES

Watch video clips of two men's and two women's sports, e.g. football, rugby, hockey or tennis. These should be the same two sports at the same level of competition. Rather than compare the level of play, focus on the difference in the psychological approach to the sport in men to women. What have you learned from doing this?

Watch two sports when men and women compete side-by-side, e.g. equestrian sports, sailing and badminton. Once again, note what, if any, are the differences in the psychological approach to the sport between men and women. What have you learned from doing this?

Further Reading

Hargraves, J. and Anderson, E. (eds.) (2014). *Handbook on Sport Gender and Sexuality*. Oxford, Oxon: Routledge.

Pfister, G. and Sisjord, M. (2013). *Gender and Sport: Changes and challenges*. Münster, Germany: Waxmann Verlag.

Ryba, T. and Schinke, R. (eds.) (2010). *The Cultural Turn in Sport Psychology*. Morgantown, WV: Fitness Information Technology.

PART 6
INTO THE FUTURE

Figure skater Peggy Fleming

USING SOCIAL MEDIA TO IMPROVE AND
18 ENHANCE SPORT AND EXERCISE PSYCHOLOGY

'When I started competing you had to have your coach there. Now you can be coached from a home office, via Skype or video.'
Jackie Joyner-Kersee (multiple-gold medallist in heptathlon)

'I think social networks are really working for the (racing) drivers, because we're able to talk directly to fans and they get first-hand information. And I think it's great for the partners as well and the businesses that are involved in Formula One.'
Jenson Button (Formula 1 racing driver)

Objectives

1. Online social media in sport that can help you follow sport psychology
2. Devices to support training and fitness, e.g. watches, phones, apps and sportswear of the future

Sport psychology is part of a worldwide community that is connecting more and more every day. This chapter focuses on what you can do to tap into the ever-expanding sport psychology resources that are available online. If you travel for training or competitions, then there are always forums and communities where you can join others involved in your sport and reduce potential feelings of isolation; there are also interesting articles, videos, informative research as well as motivational stories.

HOW CAN YOU USE SOCIAL MEDIA TO FIND OUT MORE ABOUT SPORT AND EXERCISE PSYCHOLOGY?

Learning and Disseminating Sport Exercise Psychology

A social networking service is an online platform that allows people who share ideas and interests to connect. Social networking services can be used to obtain relevant information on specific topics or categories. If this book has stimulated your interest in this area, you should consider joining some sport psychology communities. The specifics, i.e. websites and apps, change all the time, so use this section to understand what is available now, and by doing so you will be able to keep up with the future development of these resources.

There are various sports related pages on Facebook, which boasts over 300 million users. You can create your own page and accept followers. You can join or 'like' other pages, which can be private individuals or businesses or organized teams, clubs and governing bodies.

Universities display their degree programmes for study. Organizations, such as the American Psychological Association (APA), the British Psychological Society (BPS) and the British Association of Sport and Exercise Sciences (BASES), provide lists of universities that have accredited professional programmes. There are some free online modules as well, offered by some of the most prestigious universities. These are called MOOCs, i.e. Massive Online Open Courses. Of course, there are also distance education programmes and short online courses run through professional bodies.

Universities also provide information on staff research. Sometimes there are links on staff expert pages, which give you free access. Sometimes these links will take you to a publisher who allows you to download articles for a fee, though you may be able to read some of the highlights (or the abstract) for free. Some free open access journals also exist, such as *Athletic Insight*, or some university research repositories. At the moment there are new open access sites where research is available to read for free. The author or researcher pays for the publication to be published online. Search engines, such as Google Scholar, are useful in scanning for authors or key terms and they will bring up relevant research.

Multimedia such as YouTube can provide you with instructional videos, talks by psychologists and coaches. Along these lines there is also a series of 'TED talks' (Technology, Entertainment, Design), which provide you with short clips on the latest developments in various academic fields. There are videos on various sports to provide you with insight. Some of these sites use 'Go Pro' cameras or drones, which photographically or through video help you feel like you are there and help you to gain insight into how it feels to participate in these sports.

Twitter is great for short chat, quick video or a text response. It updates quickly and there are many sport and exercise psychologists who tweet regularly with motivational sayings, links to articles, conferences, courses, research, etc. People who are interested in following get short updates, of 140 characters or less, transmitted within a few seconds. There are over 288 million active monthly users on Twitter (2014) and everyone can be a journalist. However, always remember that quality is not monitored! This medium has given me access to athletes, psychologists, sport professionals, fitness trainers, coaches, television and radio, as well as providing me with consultancy opportunities. People can send you replies or a message. You can share anything interesting: about competitive anxiety, the latest research, a newspaper article, conference details or a new fact that can then be sent around a whole network of people who wouldn't normally interact with you. You can get into more places if you use hash tags. Hashtags are words or phrases prefixed with the symbol #, so short messages may be tagged #sportpsychology or #extremesport. By adding a hash mark it makes it easier to find topics in a search. Then, a person can search for the string and this tagged word will appear in the timeline-trending, messages or search.

Blogs are like online diaries or magazines, which take you through people's journeys or life experiences or interests. More than 60 per cent of internet users will be reading blogs in 2016, suggesting their growing importance in the world of web communications (eMarketer, 2014). Blogs are also an important tool if you are trying to grow your business. By 2020, 85 per cent of people will manage their relationships without talking to a human being. Those who blog daily will acquire a new customer 82 per cent of the time using their blog, as opposed to those who blog monthly and acquire new customers 57 per cent of the time (HubSpot State of Inbound, 2013). LinkedIn boasts over 50 million professionals including sport psychologists or teams, groups or professional coaches. Once again, those who are active on LinkedIn can post articles, messages and sayings, which those who are connected can read and respond to if they are interested. There are also groups centred on sport psychology and other relevant areas.

There are ways to monitor your favourite psychologist, athletes or sports or topics through search engines such as Google Alert. There are also many websites that you can follow using RSS feeds or searches at any given time.

Supporting athletes through all of the above and through online talking means one can keep in touch with those who are travelling to and from training and competitions. There are also ways that online tests, surveys and forums can be used. Of course, podcasts and vodcasts are also useful for athletes, who can tune into short talks if they are feeling a certain way or use a podcast relaxation clip, for example.

Supporting Fitness and Training

There are various downloadable apps for your phone, fitness bands and watches, such as fitness and sports trackers (under various names), by which you can track and assess your progress in terms of speed, distance, elevation, calories and time. They may use GPS so you can track your location and map out your walk or run. They often provide route maps so you can visualise the area that you have covered. You can share your training online with family, friends, teammates or others in the 'global' community or even link it to Facebook and Twitter. You can compare your times with your friends or others you have placed in the settings. You can even set up a leader board and challenge others with achievements. These apps/devices can provide you with the number of steps you take, similar to a pedometer. For years some trainers have had the option of microchips linked in with your devices. You can also make use of an 'electronic' coach who updates you on your progress and may even motivate you to push harder. There is also the development of technological clothing such as athletic clothing which monitors heart rate and respiratory activity, socks that can collate information such as speed and weight distribution.

In conclusion, if you tap into what people are doing you can have access to millions of people around you who are interested in the same topic or event and you can all share information in a supportive and challenging way. You can have your own personal trainer in your 'pocket'. If you really desire autonomy and self-regulation electronically, then apps or watches are a great way to do this. What next? Perhaps, a personal fitness robot or drone that trains you and monitors your progress to make you go the distance.

Questions to consider

1. How do you know if the advice you are receiving on a blog or website is legitimate?
2. Could the use of online consultation in sport psychology ever replace a face-to-face session?

REFLECTIVE PRACTICE: JOINING SOCIAL MEDIA

Try something in social media that you haven't done before, for example:

- Join a Facebook page for your sport
- Set yourself up with a LinkedIn page and join sports clubs
- Set up an account that follows your favourite athletes
- Watch a TED talk on sport or psychology
- Download a new fitness or sports app

- Find your sport on YouTube and watch instructional as well as motivational videos
- Go on to Google Scholar and find a sport psychology research article on something you find interesting

Further Reading

Schaefer, M. W. (2014). *Social Media Explained: Untangling the world's most misunderstood business trend.* Knoxville, TN: Schaefer Marketing Solutions.

19 CONSIDERATIONS IN USING SPORT PSYCHOLOGY

'The fight is won or lost far away from witness-behind the lines, in the gym and out there on the road, long before I dance under the lights'
Mohammad Ali (World Boxing Champion)

Objectives

1. The essence of the athlete and sport psychologist relationship: communication, counselling, professionalism and sport specific
2. Typical structure within the athlete–psychologist relationship
3. Practising sport psychology under a regulatory body
4. Developing a psychological training programme

There are unique challenges in working psychologically with athletes in sport, mostly due to its integrative nature. There are many elements that need to come together for those working in sport, such as coaching, training, skills, physiotherapy, sport rehabilitation, relationships with teammates, parental influence, media involvement, sponsorship commitments, etc. Sport is also distinct in having a competitive element, though working with athletes is not necessarily different from dealing with musicians or actors, for example. This chapter is about the relationship between the athlete and the sports psychologist, in terms of importance and professionalism. Understanding this subject will be extremely helpful for anyone planning to work in this capacity, work with a psychologist, work with others or work on improving your own psychological well-being. Various organizations exist internationally, which take the lead on the development of professional and ethical principles within sport in their respective countries.

WHAT IS THE KEY ISSUE IN WORKING EFFECTIVELY WITH SPORT PSYCHOLOGY?

Working in sport psychology is all about the quality of the relationship between two people, e.g. psychologist and athlete (Andersen, 2005). It is this quality that sustains it and drives the relationship forward. Therefore though a quick fix (i.e. brief intervention) may be satisfactory in covering a 'small wound' in performance, sport psychology is about a relationship and should not be something done as a last-minute crisis intervention. The concern for your or the player's well-being and happiness is key to this relationship and co-exists with the focus on performance. It is important that athletes, coaches and parents clearly appreciate the relationship between sport psychologists and athletes.

The objective of a sport psychologist depends on the combination of areas that he/she integrates. Similar to others, I would classify where a sport psychologist works into four basic areas: education, research innovation, personal growth and performance enhancement. Those working in education would be engaged in formalised teaching at a school, college or university. They could be presenting information on sport psychology to parents, players and coaches at a club or an academy. Psychologists working in the research category are involved in the investigation of sport psychology and this focus may be applied or theoretical with implications for guiding practice. Performance psychology concentrates on mental techniques related to enhancing performance. Personal psychology works specifically on athletes, parents and coaches and could be one-to-one sport psychology as well as life coaching. Of course, these aspects can be in combination and may even overlap. Health, clinical, or counselling psychologists may also get involved with players, though they are not necessarily specialists in sport. In addition, sport psychologists may have different theoretical orientations, such as a CBT or humanistic approach, which will underpin their methods.

There is a range of suggested traits that psychologists require in order to meet the needs of athletes and coaches. These are based on research as well as practical experience. There are various skills grouped together (CCPS), which are important if you are working with a psychologist or if you are an athlete:

Communication skills: Being a good communicator is essential and this requires not only having well developed conversational skills with athletes but also effective interpersonal skills with others in and around teams (e.g. coaches, physiotherapists, sport rehabilitators, the media, etc.). Being a team player and able to provide feedback in a useful and appropriate way is important.

Counselling skills: There are several essential qualities according to Rogerian counselling theory, which make a good counsellor or psychologist. These are: empathy (understanding how others feel), being genuine (being real as opposed to putting on an act) and listening attentively.

Professional skills: This aspect requires having a sense of professionalism, which includes honesty, trustworthiness and a respect for boundaries. Being reflective is an essential part of the job. Professional bodies regulate these skills.

Sport specific skills: This starts with either knowledge and/or willingness to learn about the sport. It also includes understanding interventions and being effective in your role. Using the internet is a great way to find material on a particular sport though coaches and players may also be helpful in recommending focused reading. Of course, if you have also played the sport then this is an advantage. Psychologists should have an interest in finding out more about the sport they are working with.

Like a proficient athlete or coach, most people in sport demonstrate these types of qualities. If you have these then fitting in with a team will be that much smoother. On the other hand, ineffective sport psychologists have been identified as not being sport specific enough, having poor time management of intervention support and giving limited feedback (Yukelson, 1997; Anderson, Miles, Robinson and Mahoney, 2004).

Structuring the athlete–psychologist relationship

This is likely to include one or two initial sessions between athlete and psychologist to identify needs, i.e. strengths and weakness, in order to develop a focus for an ongoing programme. This would include watching the sport, probably together, and discussing what you see. The next step is the development of an action plan, which is usually based on some type of assessment of the current level of the athlete's skill. Psychological strategies are worked on and put into place for pre-routine and competition. Finally the athlete and psychologist will undertake evaluation and monitoring.

The relationship between athlete and coach is important, especially in elite sport, as there may be implications for a power imbalance (Kremer, et al., 2012). Psychologists need to consider that their focus as a professional is for the care of the athlete. A psychologist–player dyad is a dynamic relationship which develops and changes over time. Psychologists must consider what type of intervention will work within the sport and perhaps fit with the athlete or player's personality. Sometimes only a light touch may be required. In fact, if a player remains wary and only wants to hear suggested interventions from their coach, it may even be better to work discreetly through the coach. A few coaches have control issues themselves and worry about not maintaining complete control over their players. Referrals should be recommended if the relationship isn't working or if a different professional may be better suited (e.g. Hardy, Jones and Gould, 1996).

WHO REGULATES THE ETHICAL AND PROFESSIONAL ISSUES INVOLVED?

Sport psychologists follow the professional regulatory codes of practice, which although they vary internationally, remain quite similar in their objectives. There are several psychological governing bodies that regulate the protected title of 'Sport and Exercise Psychologist'. In the UK, there is a sport and exercise psychologist route, a sport scientist pathway or, if you have experience, you can join an independent psychology practitioners' group. The British Psychological

Society (BPS) stipulates a first degree in Psychology, which is BPS accredited. This then gives you Graduate Basis for Chartered membership (GBC). If you don't have this, then you can follow an approved BPS conversion year or if you are an independent practitioner then you can apply straight to the Health Care and Professions Council (HCPC).

The next step along the BPS route is to undertake an MSc in Sport Psychology, which meets stage 1 BPS requirements. Upon completion, you can then undertake a supervisory experience (stage 2) under a qualified supervisor who is on the register of Applied Psychology Practice Supervisors. After receiving your official registration as a Sport and Exercise Psychologist from the BPS, you then apply to the HCPC who regulate the title and oversee the standards of proficiency. UK psychologists or independent psychology practitioners (BPS special group) can also apply directly to HCPC. This is all on the BPS website (www.bps.org.uk). In the UK, psychologists can also achieve chartered status as a scientist (CSci) through BPS.

The British Association of Sport Exercise Scientists (BASES) is another accredited sport scientist route. There are MSc programmes offered by various universities in Sport and Exercise Science, some with a psychology focus. Post graduation, there is then a supervisory experience programme advertised on the BASES website (www.bases.org.uk) under BASES accredited supervisors. BASES has issued a number of expert statements for those working in sport science, which give clear guidance on the briefs for working with specific groups.

The Fédération Européenne de Psychologie des Sports et des Activités Corporelles (FEPSAC), aka the European Federation of Sport Psychology, issues ethical guidelines for sport and exercise psychology practitioners. These fall under the categories of professional and social responsibility, competence, consent, confidentiality and integrity. FEPSAC also advertises a European master's degree in Sport and Exercise Psychology, which is run by a consortium of 13 universities around Europe. In Ireland, the Psychological Society of Ireland (PSI) oversees the codes of conduct for practising psychologists.

In the USA, the APA is an accredited regulatory and professional body for all licensed psychologists practising under APA Ethical Principles. Many sport psychologists undertake a master's degree in counselling before continuing on with PhD training programmes in psychology. (APA) Division 47 is the representative section for those practising, teaching or researching in Exercise and Sport Psychology. Sport Psychologists are not regulated as a profession separately from other psychologists. However, according to the APA, members working as sport psychologists should be experienced, competent and knowledgeable in working with those in sport.

Regardless of which route you choose there are certain ethical principles that all those working in sport psychology share. These are the APA's five ethical principles, revised in 2010:

- Beneficence and non-maleficence – benefit and not harm anyone
- Fidelity and responsibility – trusting relationship

- Integrity – honest and truthful
- Justice – fair and equal
- Respect for people's rights and dignity

Working professionals using sport psychology but who are not licensed psychologists can join the APA as affiliates and work under the established code of ethics. These are not only what anyone would expect from a professional, but also fit into what athletes and coaches want with sport experts.

In 1965, The Association for Applied Sport Psychology (AASP), the Association for the Advancement of Applied Sport Psychology (AAASP), the North American Society for the Psychology of Sport and Physical Activity (NASPSPA) and the American Psychological Association (APA: division 47) jointly formed the International Society of Sport Psychology (ISSP), which focuses on research, application and the growth of sport psychology globally.

Partly through its good offices, the role of the sport psychologist is now recognised worldwide, though it is still a developing profession. It is progressing through the recognition that those practising are accountable for ethical principles and regulations as established by various professional organizations worldwide. Being regulated as a profession places more demands on those who work in the field. However, it is clear that this thrust forward has accelerated the demand for sport psychology input at various levels from youth teams to academies to professional clubs. In addition, professional organizations are encouraging, if not requiring as part of a qualification, that sport psychologists take a lead in research. This has also led to the increased number of professional academic journals in sport psychology as well as conferences. Continued Professional Development (CPD) is either required or becoming the norm. Workshops and seminars are offered in many areas, such as CBT, counselling and high performance interventions. Exercise psychology and psychology of injuries is often part of the remit of a sport psychologist. Sport psychology as a career is exciting and it is growing.

HOW CAN I DEVELOP A PSYCHOLOGICAL TRAINING PROGRAMME?

The following psychological skills training programme may be helpful when you are working with athletes though it is absolutely paramount that sport psychologists, like athletes, need to be reflective.

This seven-phase model was developed by Morris and Thomas (2003). Ensuring there is a firm commitment is important right from the start. Phase 1 is an *orientation* where the objectives are identified and the purpose is determined. Phase 2 is an *analysis* by the psychologists or coach, which should include more than sport psychology (e.g. physiology and biomechanics) so that the athlete's experience is understood on different levels. Phase 3 is the *needs assessment* stage, which includes psychometric testing as well as structured interviewing and observation. This is also often where performance profiling is useful. Phase 4 is the *conceptual* phase where the profile is analysed and the athlete's education programme is developed. Phase 5 is the psychological skills training or *skills development* phase (e.g. self-confidence training, anxiety management training and so on). Phase 6 is *implementation or practising*, which is developing a routine and practising. Phase 7 is the *evaluation*. The evaluation then feeds back into the first phase.

There are some important items to note in using this type of framework. The first is that the nature of sport is interdisciplinary, so the coach, sport scientist, medical team, parents, and school or university, are also important to the overall health of the athlete. Sport psychology training usually involves other people. In addition, the phases do not have to be adhered to in a strict order especially if a relationship continues over a substantial period of time. Regular one-to-one 'check-up' sessions are often useful at various points but could be more useful later on in a relationship or at certain specific times during a relationship.

Questions to consider

1. When should a sport psychologist consider a referral to another professional or specialist?
2. What problems of confidentiality do those working in sport psychology face?
3. As an athlete how can you work most effectively with a sport psychologist?

REFLECTIVE PRACTICE: IS A CAREER IN SPORT PSYCHOLOGY RIGHT FOR YOU?

Answering the questions below can help you decide whether a career as a psychologist is right for you? However, they will also help you as an athlete deciding what you may need to work on in developing an effective relationship with a sport psychologist. Write your answers to the following questions and be honest:

1. Do you have special talents for listening, being empathetic, helping others to solve problems?
2. Do you believe in change?
3. Are you concerned with athlete welfare on many levels so that you can support your athlete - such as educational support, settling into a new country, working with the media, challenges in working with disadvantages or vulnerable groups in the community, recovering from injury ...)?

4. Are you aware enough of your own thoughts and behaviours enough to understand others thoughts and behaviours?

5. Are you good at identifying an objective, knowing what action to take and understanding the resultant outcome?

6. What are the reasons why you may find it difficult to work with some people? What are the reasons why certain people find it difficult to work with you?

7. Consider the qualities and skills of a psychologist. Then place them in order of your strengths and reflect on how these relate to the role of an effective psychologist: e.g. listening skills.

8. Based on the question above, what do you still need to develop this as a career and how do you plan on enhancing these qualities and skills ?

9. Do you understand the different roles of those in an interdisciplinary team e.g. coaches, physiotherapists, nutritionalist ...?

10. Do you mind working for free while you build your career, keeping up to date by studying and reading, and perhaps researching?

Further Reading

careersinpsychology.org/becoming-a-sports-psychologist/

Dosil, J. (ed.) (2006). *The Sport Psychologist's Handbook: A guide for sport specific performance enhancement.* Chichester, West Sussex: John Wiley & Sons.

Olympic athlete Jesse Owens

GLOSSARY

Anxiety (state) is a transient and less permanent condition of anxiety related to a situation. Playing sport in a high level elite competition or perhaps against a specific opponent can evoke feelings of worry and apprehension in players. This may be a temporary situation, which can easily change during the course of a match.

Anxiety (trait) is a predisposed personality trait to feel nervous and apprehensive. It is a relatively stable trait so it is a general disposition to feel anxiety and is induced by situations that are perceived as threatening or anxiety provoking

Arousal is a response to a real threat. It is a bodily energy, which prepares you for action through the sympathetic nervous system.

Attention is alertness and selectivity of information. It is a mental effort, which is multidimensional and comprised of various components. It is deliberate, selective and allows you to multitask.

Boredom susceptibility is part of the sensation-seeking trait caused by boredom or the monotony of everyday life, which pushes you to do something more exciting.

Cognitive Behaviour Therapy is a way of working on improving your behaviour by examining the relationship between your thoughts and actions.

Concentration means that you choose to attend to something you consider to be important. For example, in football, the team discusses the game plan before the match and everyone must concentrate on overall strategy.

Confidence is the belief that you can accomplish something successfully and that you have the resources to do it. Confidence is an overall global concept.

Coping strategies: emotional coping and problem coping is dealing with life by focusing either on how to manage your emotions or by dealing directing with solutions to solve the problem, e.g. emotion focus – deep breathing techniques to lessen anxiety; problem focus – getting someone to collect you and take you to practice due to an injury.

Disinhibition is part of the sensation-seeking trait where you seek sensations because you like to go against the normal and against society, e.g. through drugs or doing things that are illegal.

Ego orientation is linking your achievement into your own persona or ego – 'I am going to be the best'.

Extraverts seek excitement often via the company of others. They are recognised as friendly and assertive. Introverts on the other hand, are less outgoing, more self-reserved and less sociable, requiring less stimulation from others, though this may be because they are content with their own thoughts.

Extreme sport is a 'competitive (comparison or self-evaluative) activity within which the participant is subjected to natural or unusual physical and mental challenges such as speed, height, depth or natural forces and where fast and accurate cognitive perceptual processing may be required for a successful outcome. An unsuccessful outcome is more likely to result in the injury or even the fatality of the participant than in a non-extreme sport' (Cohen, 2012).

Extrinsic motivation is when you are driven to accomplish things because others encourage you or because you receive something for your efforts (e.g. money, medals or other awards).

Fear of failure is being stricken with a belief and worry that you won't be successful.

Flow is a state of consciousness and focus where you are totally absorbed in what you are doing. It is the effortless collaboration of mind and body.

Focus is where you direct your attention. Selective attention means being able to direct your energy at what is relevant rather that what is irrelevant, e.g. concentrating on the ball when receiving a serve in tennis. You are then selective in picking out specific cues to direct your attention.

Gender is how we identify ourselves, e.g. male or female.

Goal setting requires you to set targets as a means of motivation and a way of achieving your objectives. The SMART(ER) guidelines are often used.

Imagery is the process of visualizing images, which can be instructional or motivational. This is a sensory experience.

Intrinsic motivation is an internal motivation where you are driven to accomplish things because you want to and not because others want you to.

Mental toughness is having a psychological edge that empowers you to cope more efficiently with the environment and its physical demands. This can be a package of traits, qualities and/or skills.

Mindfulness is being aware and staying in the moment.

Motor learning is the process by which you acquire motor skills through practice and experience. This type of learning is affected by anxiety and self-confidence, which can impact on your response time.

Motor performance is when you can see someone attempt a voluntary movement. This observable behaviour is affected by factors such as your motivation, anxiety or fatigue.

Motor skills are specific, physical as well as purposeful movements, such as kicking a football or swinging a golf club.

Neuroticism is a trait in Eysenck's personality theory, concerned with the tendency to experience negative emotional states.

Neuro Linguistic Programming (NLP) stands for *Neuro* – the nervous system through which experience is received and processed through the five senses; *Linguistic* – language and nonverbal communication systems through which neural representations are coded, ordered and given meaning; *Programming* – the ability to organise our communication and neurological systems to achieve specific desired goals and results.

OLA (Optimal Level of Arousal) is being at the best physical and cognitive state so that you are balanced and your needs are met. If your arousal is too high you worry and get apprehensive.

OLS (Optimal Level of Stimulation) is being at the best physical and cognitive state of having as much input as you need. If your OLS is low enough then you may desire to go out and do something exciting in order to raise it.

Overtraining syndrome is being so stressed from overdoing training and sport that you become physically and often psychologically ill. Performance may plateau or decline. It becomes a syndrome if there are several symptoms.

Personality is the relatively stable way in which we behave and by which others recognise us. This is made up of a genetic core as well as the way we respond to our environment.

Reaction time is defined as 'the interval between the commencement of a sudden signal or sign, such as a starting gun, to the initiation of the response, such as moving off the blocks'.

Self-Determination Theory (SDT) is a theory that looks at motivation according to autonomy, competency and relatedness.

Self-efficacy is a belief that you can manage and carry out actions needed toward the achievement of specific goals. It is a conviction to achieve your objectives, which drives your behaviour.

Self-talk is any self-statement or thought about yourself that is useful in helping you focus on the present and keep your mind from being distracted.

Sensation seeking is described as a 'trait defined by the seeking of varied, novel, complex and intense sensations and experiences and the willingness to take physical, social, legal and financial risks for the sake of such experiences' (Zuckerman, 1994).

Sex is biological and chromosomal.

Stress is when the environmental demands exceed your perceived abilities to cope. You are in a state of flux as you consider whether your resources are enough to handle the situation or whether you are in danger.

Task orientation is a motivation to work towards the completion of the task, e.g. 'I am going to knock 10 seconds off my time'.

Thrill and adventure seeking is a part of the sensation-seeking trait where you look for thrills and exciting opportunities.

Zone is the optimal place for you to function at your best.

Skiier Lindsey Vonn

BIBLIOGRAPHY AND OTHER RESOURCES

Abbott, A., Collins, D., Martindale, R. and Sowerby, K. (2002). 'Talent Identification and Development: An academic review'. A report for sportscotland by the University of Edinburgh. Edinburgh: sportscotland.

Abbott, A. & Collins, D. (2004). Eliminating the dichotomy between theory and practice in talent identification and development: considering the role of psychology. *Journal of Sports Sciences*, 22(5) 395–408.

Abbott, A., Collins, D., Sowerby, K. and Martindale, R. (2007). 'Developing the Potential of Young People in Sport'. A report for sportscotland by the University of Edinburgh. Edinburgh: sportscotland.

Abernethy, B. (1987). 'Review: Selective attention in fast ball sports. II: expert–novice differences'. *Australian Journal of Science and Medicine in Sport*, 19, 7–16.

Aidman, E. V. (2007). 'Attribute-based Selection for Success: The role of personality attributes in long-term predictions of achievement in sport'. *The Journal of the American Board of Sport Psychology*, 1, 3, 1–18.

Ajzen, I. (2005). *Attitudes, Personality and Behaviour* (2nd ed.). Milton Keynes, Bucks: Open University Press.

Ajzen I. and Fishbein, M. (1974). 'Factors influencing intentions and the intention-behaviour relation'. *Human Relations*, 27, 1, 1–15.

Allard, F. and Starkes, J. L. (1980). 'Perception in sport: Volleyball'. *Journal of Sport Psychology*, 2, 22–33.

Andersen, M. B. (ed.) (2005). *Sport Psychology in Practice*. Champaign, IL: Human Kinetics.

Andersen, M. B. and Williams, J. M. (1988). 'A model of stress and athletic injury: Prediction and prevention'. *Journal of Sport and Exercise Psychology*, 10 (3), 294–306.

Anderson, A., Miles, A., Robinson, P. and Mahoney, C. (2004). 'Evaluating the athlete's perception of the sport psychologist's effectiveness: What should we be assessing?' *Psychology of Sport and Exercise*, 55, 255–277.

Annesi, J. J. (2005). 'Changes in depressed mood associated with 10 weeks of moderate cardiovascular exercise in formerly sedentary adults'. *Psychological Reports*, 96, 855–862.

Anshel, M. (2005). *Applied Exercise Psychology: A Practitioner's Guide to Improving Client Health and Fitness*. New York, NY: Springer Publishing Company.

Apter, M. J. (ed.) (2001). *Motivational styles in everyday life: A guide to reversal theory*. Washington, DC: American Psychological Association.

Apter, M. J. (2007). *Danger: Our Quest for Excitement*. Oxford, Oxon: Oneworld Publications.

Arent, S. M., Alderman, B. I., Short E. J. and Landers, D. M. (2007). 'The impact of the testing environment of affective changes following acute resistance exercise'. *Journal of Applied Sport Psychology*, 19, 436–444.

Arnett, J. (1994). 'Sensation seeking: A new conceptualization and a new scale'. *Personality and Individual Differences*, 16 (2), 289–296.

Auweele, Y. A., Rzewnicki, R. and Van Mele, V. (1997). 'Reasons for not exercising and exercise intentions: A study of middle-aged sedentary adults'. *Journal of Sport Sciences*, 15, 151–165.

Baltzell, A. and Ashtar, V. L. (2012). 'Mindfulness Meditation Training for Sport (MMTS) Intervention: Impact of MMTS with Division I female athletes'. In A. Le, C., Ngnoumen and E. Langer (eds.) (2014). *Handbook of Mindfulness*. Oxford, Oxon: Wiley-Blackwell.

Bandura, A. (1977). 'Self-efficacy: Toward a unifying theory of behavioural change'. *Psychological Review*, 84, 191–215.

Bandura, A. (1997). *Self-Efficacy: The Exercise of Control.*, New York, NY: W. H. Freeman

Beattie, S., Hardy, L., Savage, J., Woodman, T., and Callow, N. (2011). 'Development and validation of a trait measure of self-confidence'. *Psychology of Sport and Exercise*, 12, 184–191.

Becker, M. H. (ed.) (1974). 'The health belief model and personal health behaviour'. *Health Education Monographs*, 2, 324–508.

Bedon, B. G. and Howard, D. E. (1992). 'Memory for the frequency of occurrence of karate techniques: A comparison of experts and novices'. *Bulletin of the Psychonomic Society*, 30, 117–119.

Beneca, A., Maliou, P., Theodorakis, Y. and Godolias, G. (2000). 'The effect of self-talk and goal setting in muscular performance of knee injured athletes during the rehabilitation period'. *Nauka, Bezbednost, Policja*, 5 (1), 109–122.

Berger, B. G. and Motl, R. W. (2000). 'Exercise and Mood: A selective review and synthesis of research employing the profile of mood states'. *Journal of Sport Psychology*, 12, 69–92.

Berger, B. G., Pargman, D. and Weinberg, R. S. (2002). *Foundation of Exercise Psychology*. Morgantown, WV: Fitness Information Technology.

Bianco, T. (2001). 'Social support and recovery from sport injury: Elite skiers share their experiences'. *Research Quarterly for Exercise and Sport*, 72, 376–388.

Bianco, T. and Eklund, R. C. (2001). 'Conceptual consideration for social support research in sport and exercise settings: The case of sport injury'. *Journal of Sport & Exercise Psychology*, 23, 85–107

Biddis, E. and Irwin, J. (2010). Active video games to promote physical activity in children and youth: a systematic review. *Archive of Pediatric Adolescent Medicine*, 164, 664–672.

Biddle, S. J. H. and Mutrie, N. (2008). *Psychology of Physical Activity: Determinants, well-being and interventions* (2nd ed.). London: Routledge.

Biddle, S. J. H. and Nigg, C. R. (2000). 'Theories of Exercise Behaviour'. *International Journal of Sport Psychology*, 31, 290–304.

Bloom, B. S. (1985). *Developing Talent in Young People*. New York, NY: Ballantine.

Breivik, G. (ed.) (1999). *Personality, Sensation Seeking and Arousal in High Risk Sports*. Oslo: Norwegian University of Sport and Physical Education.

Brewer, B. W. (1994). 'Review and critique of models of psychological adjustment to athletic injury'. *Journal of Applied Sport Psychology*, 1041–3200, 6 (1), 87.

Brewer, B. W. (2001). 'Psychology of Sport Rehabilitation'. In R. N. Singer, H. A. Hausenblau and C. M. Janelle (eds.), *Handbook of Sport Psychology*, 787–809. New York, NY: Wiley.

Brewer, B. W. (2009). 'Injury prevention and rehabilitation'. In B. W. Brewer (ed.), *Handbook of Sports Medicine and Science, Sport Psychology*, 75–86. Chichester, Sussex: Wiley-Blackwell.

Brewer, B. W., Andersen, M. B. and Van Raalte, J. L. (2002). 'Psychological aspects of sport rehabilitation: Towards a biopsychosocial approach'. In D. L. Mostofsky and L. D. Zaichkowsky (eds.), *Medical and Psychological Aspects of Sport and Exercise*, 41–54. Morgantown, WV: Fitness Information Technology.

Brewer, B. W., Jeffers, K. E., Petitpas, A. J. and Van Raalte, J. L. (1994). 'Perceptions of psychological interventions in the context of sport injury rehabilitation'. *The Sport Psychologist*, 8, 176–188.

Brink, M. S. (2010). 'Monitoring Stress and Recovery: New insights for the prevention of injuries and illness in elite youth soccer players'. *British Journal of Sports Medicine*, 44, 809–815.

Brymer, E. (2009). 'Extreme sports as a facilitator of egocentricity and positive life changes'. *World Leisure Journal*. 51, 1, 47–53.

Buckworth, J. and Dishman, R. K. (2007). 'Exercise adherence'. In G. Tenenbaum and R. C. Eklund (eds.), *Handbook for Sport Psychology* (3rd ed.), 509–536. New York, NY: Wiley.

Burton, D. and Weiss, C. L. (2008). 'The fundamental goal concept: the path to process and performance success'. In T. Horn (ed.), *Advances in Sport Psychology* (3rd ed.), 339–375. Champaign, IL: Human Kinetics.

Butler, R. (ed.) (2000). *Sports Psychology in Performance*. London: Arnold.

Campbell, D. and Johnson, E. (2005). 'If it can't kill you, it just isn't sporting'. *The Observer*, 27 March 2005, page 6.

Carson, F. and Polman, R. (2008). 'ACL injury rehabilitation: A psychological case study of a professional rugby union player'. *Journal of Clinical Sport Psychology*, 2 (2), 71–90.

Carver, C. S. and Scheier, M. F. (1998). *On the Self-regulation of Behaviour*. Cambridge, Cambs: Cambridge University Press.

Carver, C. S. and Scheier, M. F. (2011). 'Self-regulation of action and affect'. In K. K. Vohs and R. F. Baumeister (eds.), *Handbook of Self-regulation Research, Theory and Applications* (2nd ed.), 3–21. New York, NY: Guilford Press.

Chase, M., Magyar, M., & Drake, B. (2005). Fear of Injury n Gymnastics : Self efficacy and psychological strategies to keep tumbling, *Journal of sport scinces*, 23 (5), 465–475.

Chesney, M. A., Neilands, T. B., Chambers, D. B., Taylor, J. M. and Folkman, S. (2006). 'Validity and reliability study of the coping self-efficacy scale'. *British Journal of Health Psychology*, 11, 421–437.

Christakou, A. and Zervas, Y. (2007). 'The effectiveness of imagery on pain, edema and range of motion in athletes with a grade II ankle sprain'. *Physical Therapy in Sport*, 8 (3), 130–140.

Clement, D., Shannon, V. R. and Cannole, I. J. (2011). 'Performance enhancement groups for injured athletes'. *International Journal of Athletic Therapy and Training*, 16, 34–36.

Clough, P., Earle, K. and Sewell, D. (2002). 'Mental toughness: The concept and its measurement'. In I. Cockerill (ed.), *Solutions in Sport Psychology*, 32–45. London: Thomson.

Cohen, R. (1995). Video interviews: 'Hooked on Exercise'. In J. Annett, B. Crisps, B. and H. Steinberg (eds.), *Exercise Addiction*. Sport and Exercise Psychology Section of BPS. Leicester. BPS Conference, Warwick University.

Cohen, R. (2012). 'The relationship between personality, sensation seeking, reaction time and sport participation: Evidence from drag racers, sport science and archers'. PhD 2012. Middlesex University Research Repository.

Cohen, R., Nordin, S. and Abrahamson, E. (2010). 'Psychology and sports rehabilitation'. In P. Comfort and E. Abrahamson (eds.), *Sports Rehabilitation and Injury Prevention*. London: Wiley-Blackwell.

Coleman, J. and Brooks, F. (2009). *Key Data on Adolescence* (7th ed.). Brighton, East Sussex: Young People in Focus.

Colley, A., Roberts, N. & Chipps, A. (1985). 'Sex Role Identify, personality and participation in team and individual sports by males and females'. *International Journal of Sport Psychology*. 16, 103–112.

Colvin, G. (2008). *Talent is Overrated: What really separates world-class performers from everyone else.* London: Nicholas Brealey Publishing Ltd.

Convoy, D. E., Willow, J. P. and Meltzer, J. N. (2002). 'Multidimensional fear of failure measurement: The performance failure appraisal inventory'. *Journal of Applied Sport Psychology*, 14, 76–90.

Cooky, C., Messner, M. A., and Hextrum, R. (2013). 'Women play sports, but not on TV: a Longitudinal study of televised news'. *Communication & Sport*, 1, 203–231.

Cratty, B. J. (1983). *Psychology in Contemporary Sport.* Englewood Cliff, NJ: Prentice-Hall.

Csikszentmihalyi, M. (1990). *Flow: The Psychology of Optimal Experience.* New York, NY: Harper & Row.

Culver, D. M., Gilbert, W. D. and Trudel, P. (2003). 'A decade of qualitative research in sport psychology journals: 1990–1999'. *The Sport Psychologist*, 17, 1–15.

Cupal, D. D. (1998). 'Psychological intervention in sport injury prevention and rehabilitation'. *Journal of Applied Sport Psychology*, 103–123.

Cupal, D. D. and Brewer, B. W. (2001). 'Effects of relaxation and guided imagery on knee strength, re-injury anxiety and pain following anterior cruciate ligament reconstruction'. *Rehabilitation Psychology*, 46, 28–43.

Dale, G. A. (2000). 'Distraction and coping strategies of elite decathletes during their most memorable performances'. *The Sport Psychologist*. 14, 17–41.

Davis, J. O. (1991). 'Sport injuries and stress management: An opportunity for research'. *The Sport Psychologist*, 5, 175–182.

De Moor, M. H. M., Beem, A. L., Stubbe, J. H., Boomsma, D. I. and De Geus, E. J. C. (2006). 'Regular exercise, anxiety, depression and personality: A population based study'. *Preventive Medicine*, 42, 273–279.

Deaner, H. and Silva, J. M. (2002). 'Personality and sport performance'. In J. M. Silva and D. E. Stevens (eds.), *Psychological Foundations of Sport*, 48–65. Boston, MA: Allyn & Bacon.

Deci, E. L. and Ryan, R. M. (1985). *Intrinsic Motivation and Self-Determination in Human Behaviour*. New York, NY: Plenum Press.

Deci, E. L. and Ryan, R. M. (2000). 'Self-determination theory and the facilitation of intrinsic motivation, social development and well-being'. *American Psychologist*, 55, 68–78.

Deci, E. L. and Ryan, R. M. (2008). 'Facilitating optimal motivation and psychological well being across life's domains'. *Canadian Psychology*, 49, 14–23.

Deci, E. L., Ryan, R. M., Schultz, P. P. and Niemiec, C. P. (2015). 'Being aware and functioning fully: Mindfulness and interest taking within self-determination theory'. In K. W. Brown, J. D. Creswell and R. M. Ryan, *Handbook of Mindfulness: Theory, Research and Practice*. New York, NY: Guilford Press.

Deeley, L. and Tod, D. (2008). 'Debate: Is there any evidence that NLP (Neuro Linguistic Programming) can help athletes?' *Sport & Exercise Psychology Review*, 4, 2, August 2008.

Deroche, T., Stephan, Y., Brewer B. W. and Le Scanff, C. (2007). 'Predictors of perceived susceptibility to sport-related injury'. *Personality and Individual Differences*, 43, 2218–2228.

DiBartolo, P. M., Lin, L., Montoya, S., Neal, H. and Shaffer, C. (2007). 'Are there healthy and unhealthy reasons for exercise? Examining individual differences in exercise motivations using the Function of Exercise scale'. *Journal of Clinical Sport Psychology*, 1, 93–120.

Dosil, J. (ed.) (2006) *The Sport Psychologist's Handbook: A guide for sport specific performance enhancement*. Chichester, West Sussex: John Wiley & Sons.

Driediger, M., Hall, C. and Callow, N. (2006). 'Imagery use by injured athletes: A qualitative analysis'. *Journal of Sport Sciences*, 24, 261–272.

Dryden, W. (2011). *Dealing with Emotional Problems Using Rational-Emotive Cognitive Behaviour Therapy*. London: Routledge.

Duda, J. L. (1989). 'The relationship between task and ego orientation and the perceived purpose of sport among male and female high school athletes'. *Journal of Sport and Exercise Psychology*, 11, 318–335.

Duda, J. L. and Nicholls, J. G. (1992). 'Dimensions of achievement motivation in schoolwork and sport'. *Journal of Educational Psychology*, 84, 290–299.

Duffy, L. J, Baluch, B. and Ericsson, K. A. (2004). 'Dart Performance as a function of facets of practice amongst professional and amateur men and women players'. *International Journal of Sport Psychology*, 35, 232–245.

Dunn, D. L., Madhukar, H., Trivedi, M. D., Kampert, J. B., Clark, C. B. and Chambliss, H. O. (2005). 'Exercise treatment for depression – efficacy and dose response'. *American Journal of Preventive Medicine*, 28, 1–8.

Dunn, J. G. H. and Syrotuik, D. G. (2003). 'An investigation of multidimensional worry dispositions in a high contact sport'. *Psychology of Sport and Exercise*, 4, 265–282.

Easterbrook, J. A. (1959). 'The effect of emotion on cue utilization and the organization of behaviour'. *Psychological Review*, 66, 183–201.

Edmunds, J., Ntoumanis, N. and Duda, J. (2006). 'A test of self-determination theory in the exercise domain'. *Journal of Applied Social Psychology*. 36, 9, 2240–2265.

Ericsson, K. A. (2006). 'Protocol analysis and expert thought: Concurrent verbalizations of thinking during experts' performance on representative tasks. In K. A. Ericsson, N. Charness, O. J. Feltovich and R. R. Hoffman (eds.), *The Cambridge Handbook of Expertise and Expert Performance*, 223–241. New York, NY: Cambridge University Press.

Evans, L., Hare, R. and Mullen, R. (2006). 'Imagery use during rehabilitation from injury'. *Journal of Imagery Research in Sport and Physical Activity*, 1, 1, 1–21.

Eysenck, M. W., Derakshan, N., Sanots, R. and Calvo, M. G. (2007). 'Anxiety and cognitive performance: Attentional control theory'. *Emotion*, 7, 336–353.

Eysenck, H. J. and Eysenck, M. W. (1985). *Personality and Individual Differences.* New York, NY: Plenum Press.

Fawkner, H. J., McMurray, N. and Summer, J. J. (1999). 'Athletic injury and minor life events: A prospective study'. *Journal of Science and Medicine in Sport*, 2, 117–124.

Fontani, G., Lodi, L., Felicia, A., Migliorini, S. and Corradeschi, F. (2006). 'Attention in athletes of high and low experience engaged in different open skill sports'. *Perceptual and Motor Skills*, 102, 3, 791–816.

Freeman, P., Coffee, P. and Rees, T. (2011). 'The PASS-Q: The Perceived Available Support in Sport questionnaire. *Journal of Sport and Exercise Psychology*, 33, 54–74.

Fuller, R. (1984). 'A conceptualization of drinking behaviour as a threat avoidance'. *Ergonomics*, 27, 1139–1155.

Galambos, S., Terry, P., Moyle, G., Locke, S. and Lane, A. (2005). 'Psychological predictors of injury among elite athletes'. *British Journal of Sports Medicine*, 39 (6), 351–354.

Gallagher, B. and Gardner, F. (2007). 'An examination of the relationship between early maladaptive schemas, coping and emotional response to athletic injury'. *Journal of Science and Medicine in Sport*, 3 (1), 17–29.

Gallucci, N. (2014). *Sport Psychology: Performance enhancement, performance inhibition, individuals and teams* (2nd ed.). New York, NY: Psychology Press.

Gay, J. L., Saunders, R. P. and Dowda, M. (2011). 'The relationship of physical activity and the built environment within the context of self-determination theory'. *Annuals of Behavioural Medicine*, 42, 188–196.

Gee, C. J. (2010). 'How does sport psychology actually improve athletic performance? A framework to facilitate athletes' and coaches' understanding'. *Behaviour Modification*, 34, 386–402.

Gee, C. J., Marshall, J. and King, J. (2010). 'Should coaches use personality assessments in the talent identification process? A 15-year study on professional hockey players'. *International Journal of Coaching Science*, 4, 1, 1–10.

Gilbourne, D. and Taylor, A. H. (1998). 'From theory to practice: The integration of goal perspective theory and life development approaches within an injury specific goal setting program'. *Journal of Applied Sport Psychology*, 10, 124–139.

Gill, D. L. and Deeter, T. E. (1998). 'Development of the Sport Orientation questionnaire'. *Research Quarterly for Exercise and Sport*, 59, 191–202.

Gill, S., Kolt, G. S. and Keating, J. (2004). 'Examining the multi-process theory: an investigation of the effects of two relaxation techniques on state anxiety'. *Journal of Bodywork and Movement Therapies*, 8, 288–296.

Goma-i-Freixanet, M. (1991). 'Personality profile of subjects engaged in high physical risk sports'. *Personal and Individual Differences*, 12, 10, 1087–1093.

Goodwin, R. C. (2003). 'Association between physical activity and mental disorders among adults in the United States'. *Preventative Medicine*, 36, 698–703.

Gould, D., Dieffenbach, K. and Moffett, A. (2002). 'Psychological characteristics and their development in Olympic champions'. *Journal of Applied Sport Psychology*, 14, 172–204.

Gould, D., Greenleaf, C., and Krane, V. (2002) 'Arousal-anxiety and sport'. In T. S. Horn (ed.) *Advances in Sport Psychology* (2nd ed.), 207–241. Champaign, IL: Human Kinetics.

Granito,V. J., Jr. (2002) Psychological Responses to Injury: Gender Differences. *Journal of Sport Behaviour*, 25, 243–259.

Grant, T. (2000). 'Physical activity and mental health: National consensus statements and guidelines for practice'. London: Health Education Authority.

Green, L. B. (1992). 'The use of imagery in the rehabilitation of injured athletes'. In D. Pargman (ed.) *Psychological Bases of Sport Injury* (2nd ed.). Morgantown, WV: Fitness Information Technology, 235–251.

Greenberger, D. and Padesky, C. (2015). *Mind Over Mood: Change How You Feel by Changing the Way You Think.* (2nd ed.) New York, NY: Guilford Press.

Gregg, M., Hall, C. and Butler, A. (2010). 'The MIQ-RS: a suitable option for examining movement imagery ability'. *Evidence-Based Complementary and Alternative Medicine*, 7, 2, 249–257.

Grinder, J. and Bandler, R. (1981). *Frogs into Princes: Neurolinguistic Programming.* Moab, UT: Real People Press.

Gucciardi, D. F. and Gordon, S. (2009). 'Revisiting the Performance Profile Technique: Theoretical underpinnings and application'. *The Sport Psychologist*, 23, 93–117.

Gucciardi, D. F. and Gordon, S. (2012). *Mental Toughness in Sport: Developments in Theory and Research.* New York, NY: Taylor & Francis.

Gucciardi, D., Hanton, S., Gordon, S., Mallett, C. and Temby, P. (2015). 'The concept of mental toughness: Tests of dimensionality, nomological network and traitness, *Journal of Personality*. 83, 1, 26–44

Guttmann, A. (1991). Women's sports: A history. New York: Columbia University Press.

Hale, B. and Crisfield, P. (2005). *Imagery Training: Guide for Sports Coaches and Performers*. Leeds: Sports Coach UK.

Hall, H. K., Hill, A. P., Appleton, P. R. and Kozub, S. A. (2009). 'The mediating influence of unconditional self-acceptance on the relationship between perfectionism, labile self-esteem and exercise dependence'. *Psychology of Sport and Exercise*, 10, 35–44.

Hall, C. R., and Martin, K. A. (1997). 'Measuring movement imagery abilities: A revision of the Movement Imagery questionnaire'. *Journal of Mental Imagery*, 21, 143–154.

Hall, C. R., Stevens, D. E. and Paivio. A. (2005). 'Sport Imagery Questionnaire: test manual. *Fitness Information Technology*.

Hanin, Y. L. (1995). 'Individual zones of optimal functioning (IZOF) model: An idiographic approach to performance anxiety'. In K. Henschen and W. Straub (eds.), *Sport Psychology: An analysis of athlete behaviour*, 103–119. Longmeadow, MA: Movement Publications.

Hanin, Y. L. (2007). 'Emotions in sport: current issues and perspectives'. In G. Tenenbaum and R. C. Eklund (eds.), *Handbook for Sport Psychology* (3rd ed.), 31–58. New York, N.Y: Wiley.

Hanson, S., McCullagh, P., and Tonymon, P. (1992). 'The relationship of personality characteristics, life stress and coping resources to athletic injury'. *Journal of Sport and Exercise Psychology*, 14 (3), 262–272.

Hardy, J. (2006). 'Speaking clearly: A critical review of the self-talk literature'. *Psychology of Sport and Exercise*, 7, (1), 81–97.

Hardy, L., Jones, G. and Gould, D. (1996). *Understanding Psychological Preparation for Sport*. Chichester, West Sussex: Wiley.

Hardy, L., Beattie, S. and Woodman, T. (2007). 'Anxiety induced performance catastrophes: Investigating effort required as an asymmetry factor'. *British Journal of Psychology*, 98, 1, 15–31.

Hardy, L. and Parfitt, G. (1991). 'A catastrophe model of anxiety and performance'. *British Journal of Psychology*, 82, 163–178.

Hardy, J., Richman, J. and Rosenfeld, L. (1991). 'The role of social support in the life stress/injury relationship'. *The Sport Psychologist*, 5 (2), 128–139.

Hargraves, J. and Anderson, E. (eds.) (2014). *Handbook on Sport Gender and Sexuality*. Oxford, Oxon: Routledge.

Hathaway, C. and Eiring, K. (2012). *Mindfulness and Sports Psychology for Athletes: Consider awareness your most important mental tool*. Madison, WI: Lulu Press.

Hausenblas, H. A. and Giacobbi, P. R. Jr. (2004). 'Relationship between exercise dependence symptoms and personality'. *Personality and Individual Differences*, 36, 1265–1273.

Heil, J. (1993). *Psychology of Sport Injury*. Champaign, IL: Human Kinetics.

Hill, K. (2001). *Frameworks for Sport Psychologists*. Champaign, IL: Human Kinetics.

Holmes, P., & Collins, D. (2002). 'Functional equivalence solutions for problems with motor imagery'. In I. Cockerill (ed.), *Solutions in Sport Psychology*, 120–140. London: Thompson.

Holstein, J. and Gubrium, J. (1997). *Active interviewing in D. Silverman Qualitative Research*, 113–129. Thousand Oaks, CA: Sage Publications.

Hull, C. L. (1943). *Principles of Behaviour*. New York, NY: Appleton Century Crofts.

Humphreys, M. S. and Revelle, W. (1984). 'Personality, motivation and performance: A theory of the relationship between individual differences and information processing'. *Psychological Review*, 91, 153–184.

Ievleva, L. and Orlick, T. (1991). 'Mental links to enhance healing'. *The Sport Psychologist*, 5 (1) 25–40.

Jackson, S. A. and Csikszentmihalyi, M. (1999). *Flow in Sports: The keys to optimal experiences and performances*. Leeds, Yorks: Human Kinetics.

Jackson, S. A. and Eklund, R. C. (2002). 'Assessing flow in physical activity: The flow state scale-2 and dispositional flow scale-2'. *Journal of Sport and Exercise Psychology*, 24, 133–150.

Jackson, S. A. and Marsh, H. W. (1996). 'Development and validation of a scale to measure optimal experience: The flow state scale'. *Journal of Sport and Exercise Psychology*, 18, 17–35.

Jackson, R. C. and Morgan, P. (2007). 'Advance visual information, awareness and anticipation skill'. *Journal of Motor Behaviour*, 39, 341–351.

Jackson, S. A., Thomas, P. R., Marsh, H. W. and Smethurst, C. J. (2001). 'Relationships between flow, self-concept, psychological skills and performance'. *Journal of Applied Sport Psychology*, 13, 129–153.

Jacobson, E. (1938). *Progressive Relaxation*. Chicago, IL: University of Chicago Press.

Jevas, S. & Yan, J. H. (2001). 'The effect of aging on cognitive function: a preliminary quantitative review'. *Research Quarterly for Exercise and Sport*. 72, 1–49.

Johnson, U. (2007). 'Psychosocial antecedents of sport injury, prevention and intervention: An overview of theoretical approaches and empirical findings'. *International Journal of Sport and Exercise Psychology*, 5, 352–369.

Johnson, U., Ekengren, J, and Andersen, M. B. (2005). 'Injury prevention in Sweden: Helping soccer players at risk'. *Journal of Sport and Exercise Psychology*, 27, 11.

Jones, J. G., Hanton, S., & Connaughton, D. (2002). What is this thing called mental toughness? An investigation of elite sport performers. *Journal of Applied Sport Psychology*, 14, 205-218.

Jones, G., Hanton, S. and Connaughton, D. (2002). 'What is this thing called mental toughness? An investigation of elite top performers'. *Journal of Applied Sport Psychology*, 14 (3), 205–218.

Jones, G., Hanton, S. and Connaughton, D. (2007). 'A framework for mental toughness in the world's best performers'. *The Sport Psychologist*, 21, 243–264.

Jones, G. and Moorhouse, A. (2007). *Developing mental toughness: Gold medal strategies for transforming your business performance*. Oxford, Oxon: Spring Hill.

Jones, J. G. and Swain, A. (1995). 'Predispositions to experience debilitative and facilitative anxiety in elite and non-elite performers'. *The Sport Psychologist*, 9, 201–211.

Jones, J. G., Swain, A. and Cale, A. (1991). 'Gender differences in pre-competition temporal patterning and antecedents of anxiety and self-confidence'. *Journal of Sport and Exercise Psychology*, 13, 1–15.

Judge, T. A., Bono, J. E., Ilies, R. and Gerhardt, M. W. (2002). 'Personality and leadership: A qualitative and quantitative review'. *Journal of Applied Psychology*, 87, 4, 765–780.

Judge, T. A., & Ilies, R. (2002). 'Relationship of personality to performance motivation: A meta-analytic review'. Journal of Applied Psychology. 87, (4), 797-807.

Kabat-Zinn, J. (2011). *Mindfulness for Beginners*. Louisville, CO: Sounds True.

Kabat-Zinn, J., Beall, B. and Rippe, J. (1985). 'A systematic mental training program based on mindfulness meditation to optimize performance in collegiate rowers'. In Kabat-Zinn, J. (1986). *The Sports Performance Factors*. New York, NY: Putman.

Karageorghis, C. I. (2008). 'The scientific application of music in sport and exercise'. In A. M. Lane (ed.), *Sport and Exercise Psychology: Topics in applied psychology*, 109–137. London: Hodder Education.

Kaufman, K. A., Glass, C. R. and Arnkoff, D. B. (2009). 'Evaluation of mindful sport performance enhancement (MSPE): A new approach to promote flow in athletes'. *Journal of Clinical Sport Psychology*, 4, 334, 356.

Kelly, G. A. (1945). *The Psychology of Personal Constructs. Vol. 1*. New York, N.Y: Norton.

Kerr, G. and Goss, J. (1996). 'The effects of a stress management program on injuries and stress levels'. *Journal of Applied Sport Psychology*, 12, 115–133.

Kingston, K., Lane, A. and Thomas, O (2010). 'A temporal examination of elite performers sources of sport confidence'. *The Sport Psychologist*, 18, 313–332.

Kioumourtzoglou, E., Kourtessis, T., Michalopoulou, M. and Derri, V. (1998). 'Differences in several perceptual abilities between experts and novices in basketball, volleyball and water-polo'. *Perceptual and Motor Skills*, 86, 899–912.

Knubben, K., Reischies, F. M., Adli, M., Schlattmann, P., Bauer, M. and Dimeo, F. A. (2007). 'A randomized controlled study on the effects of a short term endurance training programme in patients with major depression'. *British Journal of Sports Medicine*, 41, 29–33.

Kobasa, S. C. (1979). 'Stressful life events, personality and health: An inquiry into hardiness'. *Journal of Personality and Social Psychology*, 37, 1–11.

Koivula, N. (2001). 'Perceived characteristics of sport characterized as gender neutral feminine and masculine. *Journal of Sport Behaviour*, 24, 377–393.

Kolt, G. S., Hume, P., Smith, P. and Williams, M. M. (2004). 'Effects of a stress-management program on injury and stress of competitive gymnasts'. *Perceptual and Motor Skills*: Vol. 99, 195–207.

Kolt, G. S. and Kirkby, R. (1996). 'Injury in Australian female competitive gymnasts: a prospective study'. *Australian Physiotherapy*, 42, 121–126.

Kolt, G. S. and Roberts, P. D. (1998). 'Self-esteem and injury in competitive field hockey players'. *Perceptual Motor Skills*, 87 (1), 353–354.

Korn, E. R. (1983). 'The use of altered states of consciousness and imagery in physical and pain rehabilitation'. *Journal of Mental Imagery*, 7, 24–34.

Kremer, J., Moran, A., Walker, G. and Craig, C. (2012). *Key Concepts in Sport Psychology*. London: Sage.

Kontos, A. P. (2004). 'Perceived Risk, risk taking, estimation of ability and injury among adolescent sport participants'. *Journal of Pediatric Psychology*, 29, 447–455.

Kübler-Ross, E. (1969). *On Death and Dying*. London: Macmillan.

Landers, D. M. and Arent, S. M. (2007) 'Physical activity and mental health'. In G. Tenenbaum & R. C. Eklund (eds.), *Handbook for Sport Psychology* (6th ed.), 221–246. New York, NY: Wiley.

Landers, D. M. and Arent, S. M. (2010). 'Arousal-performance relationships'. In J. M. Williams (ed.). *Applied Sport Psychology: personal growth to peak performance* (6th ed.), 221–246, New York: NY: McGraw-Hill.

Law, B., Driediger, M., Hall, C. and Forwell, L. (2006). 'Imagery use, perceived pain, limb functioning and satisfaction in athletic injury rehabilitation'. *New Zealand Journal of Physiotherapy*, 34 (1), 10–16.

Lazarus, J. (2014). *Ahead of the Game: How to use your mind to win in sport*. Penrith, Devon: Ecademy Press.

Lazarus, R. S. (1991). 'Progress on a cognitive-motivational-relational theory of emotion'. *American Psychologist*, 46 (8), 819.

Lazarus, R. S. and Folkman, S. (1984). *Stress, Appraisal and Coping*. New York, NY: Springer Publishing Company.

Levy, A. R., Polman, R. C. J. and Clough, P. J. (2008). 'Adherence to sport injury rehabilitation programs: an integrated psychosocial approach'. *Scandinavian Journal of Medicine and Science in Sports*, 18, 798–809.

Linder-Pelz, S. and Hall, L. M. (2007) 'The theoretical roots of NLP-based coaching'. *The Coaching Psychologist*, 3 (1), 12–17.

Linder-Pelz, S. and Hall, L. M. (2008) 'Meta-coaching: a methodology grounded in psychological theory'. *International Journal of Evidence Based Coaching and Mentoring*, Vol. 6, No. 1, 43.

Linke, S. E, Gallo, L. and Norman, G. (2011). 'Attrition and adherence rates of sustained vs. intermittent exercise interventions'. *Annals of Behavioral Medicine*, 42(2), 197–209.

Locke, E. A. (1996). 'Motivation through conscious goal setting'. *Applied and Preventive Psychology*, 5, 117–124.

Locke, E. and Latham, G. (2012). *New Developments in Goal Setting and Task Performance*. London: Routledge.

Loehr, J. (1995). *The New Toughness Training for Sport*. New York, NY: Plume.

MacDonald, D. J., Cheung, M., Cote, J. and Abernethy, B. (2009). 'Place but not date of birth influences the development and emergence of athletic talent in American football'. *Journal of Applied Sport Psychology*, 21, 1, 80–90.

MacNamara, A. and Collins, J. (2011). 'Development and initial validation of the psychological characteristics of developing excellence questionnaire'. *Journal of Sports Sciences*, 29, 12, 1273–1286.

Maddison, R. and Prapavessis, H. (2005). 'A psychological approach to the prediction and prevention of injury'. *Journal of Sport and Exercise Psychology*, 27 (3), 289–310.

Markland, D. and Hardy, L. (1993). 'The exercise motivation inventory: preliminary development and validation of a measure of individuals' reasons for participation in regular activity'. *Personality and Individual Differences*, 15, 3, 289–296.

Markland, D. and Ingledew, D. K. (1997). 'The measurement of exercise motives: factorial validity and invariance across gender of a revised exercise motivation inventory'. *British Journal of Health Psychology*, 2, 361–376.

Martin, A. J. and Jackson, S. A. (2008). 'Brief approaches to assessing task absorption and enhanced subjective experience: Examining "short" and "core" flow in diverse performance domains'. *Motivation and Emotion*, 32, 141–157.

Martindale, R., Collins, D., and Abraham, A. (2007). 'Effective Talent Development: The elite coach perspective in UK sport'. *Applied Sport Psychology*, 19:2, 187–206.

Martindale, R., Collins, D., Douglas, C. and Whike, A. (2013). 'Examining the ecological validity of the Talent Development Environment Questionnaire for sport. *Journal of Sports Science*, 31(1), 41–47.

Martindale, R., Collins, D., Wang, C. K. J., McNeil, M., Lee, K. S., Sproule, J. and Westbury, T. (2010). 'Development of the Talent Development Environment Questionnaire (TDEQ)'. *Journal of Sports Science*, 28, 1209–1221.

Martinsen, E. and Raglin, J. (2007). 'Themed Review: anxiety/depression'. *American Journal of Lifestyle Medicine*, 1, 159–166.

Masters, R. S. W. (1992). 'Knowledge, nerve and know-how: The role of explicit versus implicit knowledge in the breakdown of a complex motor skill under pressure'. *British Journal of Psychology*, 83, 343–358.

Masters, R. S. W. and Maxwell, J. P. (2008). 'The theory of reinvestment'. *International Review of Sport and Exercise Psychology*, 2, 160–183.

Masters, R. S. W., Polman, R. C. J. and Hammond, N. V. (1993). 'Reinvestment: A dimension of personality implicit in skill breakdown under pressure', *Personality and Individual Differences*, 14, 655–666.

May, J. R. and Brown, L. (1989). 'Delivery of psychological service to the US Alpine Ski team prior to and during the Olympics in Calgary'. *The Sport Psychologist*, 3, 320–329.

McClelland, D. C. (1985). *Human Motivation*. Glenview, IL: Scott, Foresman and Co.

McClymont, D. D. (1999). 'A proposed model for the identification and development of sporting talent in New Zealand'. *Journal of Physical Education New Zealand*, 29, 4, 14–18.

McNair, D., Lorr, M. and Droppleman, L. (1992). *POMS Manual*, San Diego, CA: Educational and Industrial Testing Services.

McNamara, J. and McCabe, M. P. (2012). 'Striving for success or addiction: Exercise dependence among elite Australian athletes'. *Journal of Sport Sciences*, 30, 755–766.

Meichenbaum, D. (1997). *Treating Post-Traumatic Stress Disorder. A handbook and practice manual for therapy*. Chichester, West Sussex: John Wiley & Sons.

Meyer, C. and Taranis, L. (2011). 'Exercise in the eating disorders: Terms and definitions'. *European Eating Disorders Review*, 19, 169–173.

Middleton, S., Marsh, H., Martin, A., Richards, J. and Perry, Jr, C. (2005). 'Making the leap from good to great: Comparisons between sub elite and elite athletes on mental toughness'. In Peter L. Jeffery (ed.) 'Proceedings of the Australian Association for Research in Education Conference'. Parramatta, Australia.

Moran, A. (2012). *Sport and Exercise Psychology: A Critical Introduction* (2nd ed.). London: Routledge.

Morris, T. and Thomas, P. (2003). Approaches to applied sport psychology. In Morris, T. and Summers, J. (eds) Sport Psychology: Theory, Applications and Issues. 2nd ed. Brisbane: Jacaranda Wiley. pp. 215–252.

Morris, T., Spittle, M. and Watt, A. (2005). *Imagery in Sport*. Champaign, IL: Human Kinetics.

Muller, S., Abernethy, B. and Farrow, D. (2006). 'How do world-class cricket batsmen anticipate a bowler's intention?' *Quarterly Journal of Experimental Psychology*, 59, 2162–2186.

Murgatroyd, D. L., Rushton, C., Apter, M. J. and Ray, C. (1978). 'The development of the telic dominance scale'. *Journal of Personality Assessment*, 42, 519–528.

Murphy, S. (2005). *The Sport Psych Handbook*. Champaign, IL: Human Kinetics.

Napier, V., Findley, C. and Self, D. (2007). 'Risk homeostatis: A case of the adoption of a safety innovation on the level of perceived risk'. Paper presented at the 14th Annual Meeting of the American Society of Business and Behavioral Sciences.

Nicholls, A. R., Polman, R. and Levy, A. R. (2010). 'Coping self-efficacy, pre-competitive anxiety and subjective performance among athletes'. *European Journal of Sport Science*, 10, 97–102.

Nicholls, J. G. (1984). 'Achievement motivation: Conceptions of ability, subjective experience, task choice and experience'. *Psychological Review*, 91, 328–346.

Nideffer, R. M. (1976). 'Test of attentional and interpersonal style'. *Journal of Personality and Social Psychology*, 34, 394–404.

Nideffer, R. M. and Sagal, M. S. (2001). *Assessment in Sport Psychology*. Morgantown, MW: Fitness Information Technology.

Noh, Y. E., Morris, T. and Andersen, M. B. (2005). 'Psychosocial factors and ballet injuries'. *International Journal of Sport and Exercise Psychology*, 1, 79–90.

Ogden, J., Veale, D. and Summers, Z. (1997). 'The development and validation of the Exercise Dependence Questionnaire. *Addiction Research*, 5, 343–353.

Osborn, Z. H., Blanton, P. D. and Schwebel, D. C. (2009). 'Personality and injury risk among professional hockey players'. *Journal of Injury and Violence Research*, 1, 15–19.

Pankhurst, A., Collins, D., and MacNamara, A. (2013). 'Talent development: Linking the stakeholders to the process'. *Journal of Sport Science*, 31(4); 370–380.

Pargman, D. (2013). *Managing Performance Stress: Models and Method*. London: Routledge.

Pargman, D., & Lunt, S. D. (1989). 'The relationship of self-concept and locus of control to the severity of injury in freshman collegiate football players'. *Sports Medicine, Training and Rehabilitation*, 1, 201–208.

Parnabas, V., Parnabas, J. and Parnabas, M. (2015). 'The level of cognitive anxiety and sport performances among handball players'. *The International Journal of Indian Psychology*, Vol. 2, special issue.

Pelletier, L. G., Fortier, M. S., Vallerand, R. J., Tuson, K. M. and Brière, N. M., (1995). 'The Sport Motivation Scale (SMS-28)'. *Journal of Sport and Exercise Psychology*, 17, 35–53.

Pellizzari, M., Bertollo, M. and Robazza, C. (2011). 'Pre and post-performance emotions in gymnastics competitions'. *International Journal of Sport Psychology* 42, 378–402.

Perna, F. M., Antoni, A. H., Baum, M., Gordon, P. and Schneiderman, N. (2003). 'Cognitive behavioural stress management effects on injury and illness among competitive athletes: A randomized clinical trail'. *Annals of Behavioural Medicine*, 25, 66–73.

Petrie, T. A. and Falkstein, D. L. (1998). 'Methodological, measurement and statistical issues in research on sport injury prediction'. *Journal of Applied Sport Psychology*, 10, 26–45.

Pfister, G and Sisjord, M. (2013). *Gender and Sport: Changes and Challenges*. Münster, Germany: Waxmann Verlag.

Podlog, L. and Eklund, R. C. (2007). 'Professional coaches' perspectives on the return to sport following serious injury'. *Journal of Applied Sport Psychology*, 19, 207–225.

Podlog, L., Kleinert, J., Dimmock, J., Miller, J. and Shipherd, A. M. (2012). 'A parental perspective on adolescent injury rehabilitation and return to sport experience'. *Journal of Applied Sport Psychology*, 24, 175–190.

Prapavessis, H., Gaston, A. and DeJesus, S. (2015). 'The Theory of Planned Behavior as a model for understanding sedentary behavior'. *Psychology of Sport and Exercise*. 19, 23–32.

Prochaska, J. O. and DiClemente, C. C. (1982). 'Transtheoretical therapy: Towards a more integrative model of change'. *Psychotherapy: Theory, research and practice*, 20, 161–173.

Prochaska, J. O. and Marcus, B. H. (1994) 'The Transtheoretical Model: Applications to exercise'. In R. K. Dishman (ed.), *Advances to Exercise Adherence*. Champaign, IL: Human Kinetics.

Raglin, J. S. (2001). 'Psychological factors in sport performance: The mental health model revisited'. *Sports Medicine*, 31, 12875–12890.

Rees, T. and Hardy, L. (2004). 'Matching social support with stressors: Effects on factors underlying performance in tennis'. *Psychology of Sport and Exercise*, 5, 319–337.

Rethorst, C. D., Wipfli, B. M. and Landers, D. M. (2009). 'The antidepressive effects of exercise. A meta-analysis of randomised trials'. *Sports Medicine*, 39, 491–511.

Roberts, G. C., Treasure, D. C. and Balague, G. (1998). 'Achievement goals in sport: The development and validation of the Perception of Success Questionnaire. *Journal of Sport Sciences*, 16, 337–347.

Roberts, R., Callow, N., Hardy, L., Markland, D. and Bringer, J. (2008). 'Movement imagery ability: Development and assessment of a revised version of the vividness of movement imagery questionnaire'. *Journal of Sport and Exercise Psychology*, 30, 200–221.

Rogers, C. (1954), *Becoming A Person*. Oberln, OH: Oberlin College.

Rogers, T. J. and Landers, D. M. (2005). 'Mediating effects of peripheral vision in the life event stress/athletic injury relationship'. *Journal of Sport and Exercise Psychology*, 27, 271–288.

Rossi, B. and Cereatti, L. (1993). 'The sensation in mountain athletes as assessed by Zuckerman's Sensation Seeking Scale'. *International Journal of Sport Psychology*, 24, 417–431.

Roth, M. & Hammelstein, P. (2012). The Need Inventory of Sensation Seeking (NISS). *European Journal of Psychological Assessment*, 28, 11–18.

Roth, M. and Herzberg, P. (2004). 'A validation and psychometric examination of the Arnett Inventory of Sensation Seeking (AISS) in German adolescents'. *European Journal of Psychological Assessment*, 20, 3, 205–214.

Rumbold, J., Fletcher, D. and Daniels, K. (2012). 'A systematic review of stress management interventions with sport performers'. *Sport, Exercise and Performance Psychology*, 1 (3), 173–193.

Ryan, R. and Deci, E. (2007). 'Active human nature self-determination theory and the promotion and maintenance of sport exercise and health'. In M. S. Haggar and N. L. D. Chatzisarantis (eds.), *Intrinsic Motivation and Self-Determination in Exercise and Sport*, 1–19. Champaign, IL. Human Kinetics.

Ryan, R., Williams, G., Patrick, H. and Deci, E. (2009). 'Self-determination theory and physical activity: The dynamics of motivation in development and well-ness'. *Hellenic Journal of Psychology*, 6, 107–124.

Ryba, T. and Schinke, R. (eds.). (2010). *The Cultural Turn in Sport Psychology*. Morgantown, WV: Fitness Information Technology.

Sanchez, X., Boschker, M. S. J. and Llewellyn, D. J. (2010). 'Pre-performance psychological states and performance in an elite climbing competition'. *Scandinavian Journal of Medicine and Science in Sports*, 20, 356–363.

Scanlan, T., Ravizza, K. and Stein, G. (1989). 'An in-depth study of former elite figure skaters: I. Introduction to the project'. *Journal of Sport and Exercise Psychology*, 11, 54–64.

Scanlan, T., Ravizza, K. and Stein, G. (1991). 'An in-depth study of former elite figure skaters: III. Sources of Stress'. *Journal of Sport and Exercise Psychology* 13,103–120.

Scanlan, T., Stein, G. and Ravizza, K. (1989). 'An in-depth study of former elite figure skaters: II. Sources of Enjoyment'. *Journal of Sport and Exercise Psychology*, 11, 65–83.

Schaefer, M. W. (2014). *Social Media Explained: Untangling the world's most misunderstood business trend*. Knoxville, TN: Schaefer Marketing Solutions.

Scherzer, C. B., Brewer, B. W., Cornelius, A. E., Van Raalte, J. L., Petitpas, A. J., Sklar, J. H., Pohlman, M. H., Krushell, R. J. and Ditmar, T. D. (2001). 'Psychological skills and adherence to rehabilitation after reconstruction of the anterior cruciate ligament'. *Journal of Sport Rehabilitation*, 10, 165–172.

Schmidt, R. and Lee, T. (2014). *Motor Learning and Performance: From principles to application* (5th edn.). Champaign, IL: Human Kinetics.

Schomer, H. H. (1990). 'A cognitive strategy training program for marathon runners: Ten case studies'. *South African Journal of Research in Sport, Physical Education and Recreation*, 13, 47–78.

Seward, B. (2011). *Managing Stress: Principles and strategies for health and well-being*. Burlington, MA: Jones & Bartlett Learning.

Singh, N. A., Stavrinos, T. M., Scarbek, Y., Galambos, G., Liber, C. and Singh, M. A. F. (2005). 'A randomized control trial of high versus low intensity weight training versus general practitioner care for clinical depression in older adults'. *Journal of Gerontology: Medical Sciences*, 60, 768–776.

Slanger, E. and Rudestam, K. E. (1997). 'Motivation and disinhibition in high-risk sports: Sensation seeking and self-efficacy'. *Journal of Research in Personality*, 31, 355–373.

Smith, A. M., Scott, S. G. and Wiese, D. M. (1990). 'The psychological effects of athletic injury: Coping'. *Sports Medicine*, 9 (6), 352–369.

Smith, R. E. (2006). 'Understanding sport behaviour: A cognitive affective processing systems approach'. *Journal of Applied Sport Psychology*, 18, 1–27.

Smith, R. E., Smoll, F. and Ptacek, R. (1990). 'Conjunctive moderator variables in vulnerability and resiliency research: Life stress, social support and coping skills, and adolescent sport injuries'. *Journal of Personality Social Psychology*, 58 (2), 60–70.

Sordoni, C., Hall, C. and Forwell, L. (2002). 'The use of imagery in athletic injury rehabilitation and its relationship to self-efficacy'. *Physiotherapy Canada*, (Summer), 177–185.

Spielberger, C. S. (1966). 'Theory and research on anxiety'. In C. S. Spielberger (ed.) *Anxiety and Behaviour*, 3–20. New York, NY: Academic Press.

Stadler, M. (2008). *The Psychology of Baseball: Inside the mind of the Major League player*. New York, NY: Penguin.

Starkes, J. and Ericsson, K. A. (2003). *Expert Performance in Sports: Advances in research on sport expertise*. Champaign, IL: Human Kinetics.

Steffen, K., Pensgaard, A. M. and Bahr, R. (2008). 'Self-reported psychological characteristics as risk factors for injuries in female youth football'. *Scandinavian Journal of Medicine and Science in Sports*, 18, 1–10.

Stephan, Y., Deroche, T., Brewer, B. W., Caudroit, J. and Le Scanff, C. (2009). 'Predictions of perceived susceptibility to sport related injury among competitive runners: The role of previous experience, neuroticism and passion for running'. *Applied Psychology: An International Review*, 58, 672–687.

Syed, M. (2010). *Bounce: The myth of talent and the power of practice*. London: Fourth Estate.

Symons Downs, D., Hausenblas, H. A. and Nigg, C. R. (2004). 'Factor validity and psychometric examination of the Exercise Dependence Scale – revised'. *Measurement in Physical Education and Exercise Science*, 8, 183–201.

Talbot-Honeck, C. and Orlick, T. (1998). 'The essence of excellence: Mental skills of top classical musicians'. *The Journal of Excellence*, 1, 1, 66-81.

Tebbenham, D. (1998). 'The nature of talent development and importance of athletic transition in UK sport'. Unpublished Master's, Crewe & Alsager Faculty,

Manchester Metropolitan University, as in the *Daily Telegraph*, 22 January 2014. www.telegraph.co.uk/men/active/10568898/Sports-visualisation-how-to-imagine-your-way-to-success.html

Terry, P. C., Lane, A. M, and Fogarty, G. J. (2003). 'Construct validity of the Profile of Mood States – Adolescents for use with adults'. *Psychology of Sport and Exercise*, 4 (2), 125–139.

Theodorakis, Y., Beneca, A., Malliou, P. and Goudas, M. (1997). 'Examining psychological factors during injury rehabilitation'. *Journal of Sport Rehabilitation*, 6, 355–363.

Theodorakis, Y., Malliou, P., Papaioannou, A., Beneca, A. and Filactakidou, A. (1996). 'The effect of personal goals, self-efficacy, and self-satisfaction on injury rehabilitation'. *Journal of Sport Rehabilitation*, 5, 214–223.

Thomas, O., Hanton, S. and Maynard, I. (2007). 'Anxiety responses and psychological skill use during the time leading up to competition: Theory to practice I'. *Journal of Applied Sport Psychology*, 19, 379–397.

Thomas, P., Murphy, S., and Hardy, L. (1999). 'The test of performance strategies: development and preliminary validation of a comprehensive measure of athlete psychological skills'. *Journal of Sport Science*, 17, 697–711.

Thompson, K., Watt, A. and Liukkonen, J. (2009). 'Differences in ball sport athletes speed discrimination before and after exercise-induced fatigue'. *Journal of Sports Science and Medicine*, 8, 259–264.

Thompson, R. W., Kaufman, K. A., De Petrillo, L. A., Glass, C. R., & Arnkoff, D. B. (2011). One year follow-up of Mindful Sport Performance Enhancement (MSPE) for archers, golfers, and long-distance runners. *Journal of Clinical Sport Psychology*, 5, 99–116.

Tosey, P., Mathison, J. and Michelli, D. (2005). 'Mapping transformative learning: The potential of Neuro-Linguistic Programming'. *Journal of Transformative Education*, 3: (2), 140–167.

Tracey, J. (2003). 'The emotional response to injury and rehabilitation process'. *Journal of Applied Psychology*, 15 (4), 279–293.

Turman, P. D. (2003). 'Coaches and Cohesion: The impact of coaching techniques on team cohesion in the small group sport setting'. *Journal of Sport Behaviour*, 26, 86–104.

Urdy, E. (1999). 'The paradox of injuries: unexpected positive consequences'. In D. Pargman (ed.), *Psychological bases of sport injuries*, 79–88. Morgantown, WV: Fitness Information Technology.

Vallerand, R. J. (2007). 'Intrinsic and extrinsic motivation in sport and physical activity'. In G. Tenenbaum and R. C. Eklund (eds.), *Handbook for Sport Psychology* (3rd ed.), 59–83. New York, NY: Wiley.

Vealey, R. S. (1986). 'Conceptualization of sport confidence and competitive orientation: preliminary investigation and instrumental development'. *Journal of Sport Psychology*, 8, 221–246.

Vealey, R. S. (2001). 'Understanding and enhancing self-confidence in athletes'. In R. N. Singer, H. A. Hausenblau and C. M. Janelle (eds.), *Handbook of Sport Psychology*, 550–565. New York, NY: Wiley.

Vealey, R. S. (2007). 'Mental skills training in sport'. In G. Tenenbaum and R. C. Eklund (eds.), *Handbook for Sport Psychology* (3rd ed.), 287–309, New York, NY: Wiley.

Vealey, R. S. (2009). 'Confidence in Sport: Management of competitive stress in elite sport'. In B. W. Brewer (ed.), *Handbook of Sports Medicine and Science, Sport Psychology*, 43–52. Chichester, West Sussex: Wiley-Blackwell.

Vickers, J. (2007). *Perception, Cognition and Decision Training: The quiet eye in action*. Champaign, IL: Human Kinetics.

Visser, I., Raijmakers, M. E. J. and Molenaar, P. C. M. (2007). 'Characterizing sequence knowledge using online measures and hidden Markov models'. *Memory and Cognition*, 25, 6, 1502–15–18.

Waldron, M. and Worsfold, P. (2010). 'Differences in the game specific skills of elite and sub-elite youth football players: Implications for talent identification. *International Journal of Performance Analysis in Sport*, 10, 1.

Walker, N., Thatcher, J. and Lavallee, D. (2007). 'Psychological responses to injury in competitive sport: A critical review'. *Journal of the Royal Society for the Promotion of Health*, 127, 174–180.

Wiese-Bjornstal, D. M., Smith, A. M., Shaffer, S. M. and Morrey, M. (1998). 'An integrated model of response to sport injury: Psychological and sociological dynamics'. *Journal of Applied Sport Psychology*, 10, 1, 46–69.

Wilde, G. J. S. (1982). 'The theory of risk homeostasis: Implications for safety and health'. *Risk Analysis*, 2, 209–225.

Williams, A. M. (2002). 'Visual search behaviour in sport' (editorial). *Journal of Sports Sciences*, 20, 3, 169–170.

Williams, A. M., Ward, P., Knowles, J. M. and Smeeton, H. J. (2002). 'Perceptual skill in a real world task control across the life span'. *Developmental Psychology*, 35, 205–213.

Williams, J. M. (2001). 'Psychology of injury risk and prevention'. In R. N. Singer, H. A., Hausenblau and C. M. Janelle (eds.), *Handbook of Sport Psychology*, 766–786. New York, NY: Wiley.

Williams, J. M. and Andersen, M. B. (1998). 'A model of stress and athletic injury: prediction and prevention'. *Journal of Sport and Exercise Psychology*, 10 (3).

Williams, J. M. and Andersen, M. B. (2007). 'Psychosocial antecedents of sport injury and interventions for risk reduction'. In G. Tenenbaum and R. C. Eklund (eds.), *Handbook for Sport Psychology* (3rd ed.), 379–403. New York, NY: Wiley.

Williams, M., Davids, K., Burwitz, L., and Williams, J. G. (1994). 'Visual search strategies in experienced and inexperienced soccer players'. *Research Quarterly for Exercise and Sport*, 65, 2, 127–135.

Williams, J. M., Hogan, T. D. and Andersen, M. B. (1993). 'Positive states of mind and athletic injury risk'. *Psychosomatic Medicine*, 55, (5), 468–472.

Williams, J. M. and Scherzer, C. B. (2010). 'Injury Risk and rehabilitation: Psychological considerations'. In J. M. Williams (ed.), *Applied Sport Psychology: personal growth to peak performance* (6th ed.), 512–541. New York, NY: McGraw-Hill.

Williams, J. M., Tonymon, E. and Wadsworth, W. A. (1986). 'Relationship of stress to injury in intercollegiate volleyball'. *Journal of Human Stress*, 12 (11), 38–43.

Willig, C. (2008). 'A phenomenological investigation of the experience of taking part in extreme sports'. *Journal of Health Psychology*, 13, 5, 690–702.

Woll, S. (2002). *Everyday Thinking: Memory and Judgement in the Real World*. Hillsdale, NJ: Lawrence Erlbaum Associates.

Wolstencroft, E. (ed.) (2002). 'Talent identification and development: An academic review'. A report for sportscotland by the University of Edinburgh. Edinburgh: sportscotland.

Wood, G. and Wilson, M. R. (2008). 'Gaze behaviour and shooting strategies in football penalty kicks: Implications of a "keeper-dependent" approach'. *International Journal of Sport Psychology*, 39, 1–18.

Woodman, T., Hardy, L., Barlow, M. and Le Scanff. (2010). 'Motives for participation in prolonged engagement high-risk sports: An agentic emotion regulation perspective'. *Psychology of Sport and Exercise*, 11, 5, 345–352.

Woods, C., Hawkins, R., Hulse, M. and Hodson, A. (2002). 'The Football Association Medical Research Programme: An audit of injuries in professional football – analysis of pre-season injuries'. *British Journal of Sports Medicine*, 36, 436–444.

Wraga, M. and Kosslyn, S. (2002). 'Imagery'. In L. Nadel (ed.), *Encyclopaedia of Cognitive Science*, 2, 466–470. London: Nature Group.

Yang, J., Peek-Asa, C., Lowe, J. B., Heiden, D. and Foster, E. T. (2010). 'Social support patterns of elite athletes before and after injury'. *Journal of Athletic Training*, 45, 372–379.

Yerkes, R. M. and Dodson, J. D. (1908). 'The relationship of strength of stimulus to rapidity of habit formation'. *Journal of Comparative Neurology of Psychology*, 18, 459–482.

Zuckerman M. (1994). Behavioral expressions and biosocial bases of sensation seeking. New York: Cambridge University Press.

Yukelson, D. (1997). 'Principles of effective team building in sport: A direct services approach at Penn State University'. *Journal of Applied Sport Psychology*, 9, 73–96.

Zuckerman, M. (2005). *Psychobiology of Personality*, (2nd ed.). Cambridge, Cambs: Cambridge University Press.

Zuckerman, M. (2007). *Sensation Seeking and Risky Behaviour*. Washington DC: American Psychological Association.

Zuckerman, M., Kolin, E., Price, L. and Zoob, I. (1964). 'Development of a sensation seeking scale'. *Journal of Consulting Psychology*, 28, 477–482.

INDEX

Wimbledon Champion 2013, Andy Murray

Olympic swimmer Michael Phelps

Record-breaking sprinter Usain Bolt